# The Church

*Christ in the World Today*

## TEACHER GUIDE

*Living in Christ*

Anne T. Herrick, EdD; Rick Keller-Scholz;
and Ann Marie Lustig, OP

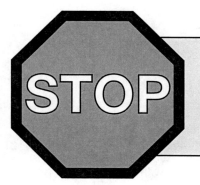

To access the ancillary teaching
resources for this course, go to
http://www.smp.org/resourcecenter/books/

saint mary's press

The publishing team included Gloria Shahin, editorial director; Steven McGlaun, project coordinator; prepress and manufacturing coordinated by the production departments of Saint Mary's Press

Cover Image: © The Crosiers / Gene Plaisted, OSC.

Printed in the United States of America

1249

ISBN 978-1-59982-061-3, Print
ISBN 978-1-59982-453-6, Kno
ISBN 978-1-59982-107-8, Saint Mary's Press Online Learning Environment

# Contents

# Introducing the Living in Christ Series

*The Church: Christ in the World Today* is the second-semester tenth-grade course in the Living in Christ series.

Saint Mary's Press developed the Living in Christ series in response to the needs of important stakeholders in the catechesis process. The courses follow the sequence and contain the material from the USCCB's Curriculum Framework. Each course also contains other material in the student book and teacher guide that students should know, understand, and be able to carry out. Each course responds to the varied needs that teachers have expressed, especially about limited time and the range of catechizing the young people in a high school religion class have had, offering wisdom from "secular" educational methods that can address both time limits and diversity in the classroom.

With the Living in Christ series, Catholic high school students will understand foundational concepts about the Bible, Jesus Christ as a member of the Trinity, the Paschal Mystery, the Church, the Sacraments, and morality. They will also have skills to learn more about their faith by studying the Scriptures, reading primary theological sources, consulting the Catholic faith community, doing self-reflection, and having conversations with their peers. With your guidance your graduates will possess a lived faith as they move into their future.

## The Living in Christ Series

The Living in Christ series has a different look and feel from traditional high school theology textbooks and teaching manuals.

- **The teacher guide, rather than the student book, provides the scope and sequence for the course.** Teaching with the student book is more like teaching with *The Catholic Faith Handbook for Youth* (Saint Mary's Press, 2008) than a textbook. The sequence of a textbook is important because the content builds on what has come before. A handbook provides material in a sensible order, but because the content does not rely on what has come before in quite the same way, the material can be presented in several different sequences.

- **The teacher guide provides you with ideas about how to teach not only with the student book but also with the Bible, resources on the Saint Mary's Press Web site *(smp.org/LivinginChrist)*, and other resources found on the Internet.** The teacher guide works as a command center for the course, providing ways for you to teach key concepts to the students by bringing in a wide variety of resources.

- **The Living in Christ series invites you as teacher to develop your abilities to facilitate learning.** This series asks you to become an expert about your own students, discern how they learn best, and then lead them to understand main concepts in a way that speaks to their lived experiences and the issues of the day.

- **The Living in Christ series invites the students to be more engaged in their own learning.** This series asks the students to take charge of their learning process and to practice what it will mean to be adult Catholics who must translate scriptural and Church teaching into their real world.

These changes will enable the students to consider the most important concepts in the course at a deeper level.

## The Series Web Site: *smp.org/LivinginChrist*

In addition to the teacher guide and student book, the Living in Christ series provides an extensive collection of digital resources for each course to assist you in guiding the learning of your students. The digital resources are sorted on the Web site by course and unit. For each unit in a course, you will find the following resources at *smp.org/LivinginChrist:*

- **Handouts** All handouts for a unit are provided in multiple digital formats, including Word and rich text formats that you can revise.
- **Method articles** Method articles explain teaching methods introduced in a unit that might be unfamiliar to some teachers.
- **Theology articles** Theology articles provide an in-depth exploration of key theological concepts presented in a unit to assist you in explaining the concept and responding to student questions.
- **PowerPoint presentations** Student learning in each unit is enhanced with PowerPoint presentations. Beyond simply repeating student book content, these PowerPoint presentations engage students through reflection and discussion. All of the Living in Christ PowerPoint presentations are in a format that allows you to revise them.
- **Useful links** Links to other resources are provided so you can enhance your students' learning with additional resources. The links direct your students to Web sites you can trust, and are continually checked for appropriateness and to ensure that they are active.
- **Student vocabulary quiz** For each unit there is an interactive vocabulary quiz for students. The quiz provides questions to assess students' knowledge of the vocabulary for a unit. Additionally, as the students respond to each vocabulary question, they are provided with the full definition along with a reference to the student book page where the word is defined and explored so they can read the word in context to deepen their understanding.

At *smp.org/LivinginChrist* you will also have access to an online test bank, which provides hundreds of questions for each course, beyond what is provided in the units. You can use test questions as they are presented or modify them for your students' learning needs.

# Introducing *The Church: Christ in the World Today*

This course leads the students toward a deeper understanding of the Church as the means to encountering the living Jesus. The course explores the origin, the human and divine elements, and the ongoing mission of the Church. Additionally, the students explore the Church's ongoing efforts to gather all into the People of God through the ecumenical movement and interreligious dialogue. Over the course of the eight units, the students reflect on their role in the Church and Christ's invitation to actively participate in and contribute to the life of the Church.

The eight units in this course center on eight important questions or concepts about the Church. Each unit builds on the knowledge, skills, and understanding of the previous one. Within each unit the knowledge, skills, and understanding also build as it progresses. The eight units are as follows:

- Unit 1: What Do We Mean When We Talk about "Church"?
- Unit 2: What Is the Origin of the Church?
- Unit 3: The Church Is a Mystery
- Unit 4: The Church Is One, Holy, Catholic, and Apostolic
- Unit 5: The Church Carries Out Its Mission
- Unit 6: The Church Is a Light to All People
- Unit 7: The Church Interprets the Signs of the Time in Light of the Gospel
- Unit 8: God Calls Us to Live as Disciples in the Church

# The Structure of Each Unit in This Teacher Guide

This teacher guide offers the teacher one path through each unit, referring the students to the student book, the Bible, resources on the Saint Mary's Press Web site *(smp.org/LivinginChrist),* and other Internet resources.

The path for each unit has the goal of leading all the students to comprehend four "understandings" with the related knowledge and skills. This curriculum model assumes that you will adjust your teaching according to the needs and capabilities of the students in your class. You do not have to complete every learning experience provided, and we hope you substitute your own ideas for those in the guide when needed.

Each unit has three basic parts: the Overview, the Learning Experiences, and handouts.

## The Overview

The Overview is a snapshot of the whole unit. It provides the following information:

- the concepts the students should understand by the end of the unit
- the questions the students should be able to answer by the end of the unit
- a brief description of the summary assessments (final performance tasks) offered, which will show that the students understand the most important concepts
- a summary of the steps in the Learning Experiences section (Each step in the unit builds on the one before but must be adjusted to fit your schedule and the needs of the students. The use of *steps* is more flexible than is a structure based on 60-minute periods, for example.)
- a list of background material on content and methods that can be found on the Saint Mary's Press Web site *(smp.org/LivinginChrist)*
- a list of articles from the student book covered in the unit
- a list of Scripture passages used
- a list of vocabulary that comes from the student book and from the learning experiences in the teacher guide

## Learning Experiences

The instruction and learning occur in this section. Each unit contains a similar process for instruction.

### Preassess Student Knowledge of the Concepts

Each unit opens with one or more options for preassessing what the students already know about a topic. It is useful to know this information as you prepare to present new material.

Preassessing the students' knowledge can help you to determine how to use your time effectively throughout the unit. It is not worth your time to teach the students what they already know or to teach above their heads. Students learn most effectively when new concepts build on what they already know. More often, you have a mixed group knowledge-wise, which is good, because the students can help one another.

Unit 1 offers a more comprehensive questionnaire to help you see where the students are coming from religiously and in terms of knowledge and belief. This preassessment will help you to make choices throughout the unit. Based on what you learn in your preassessment in unit 1, you may decide to spend more or less time on given topics.

## Present the Final Performance Tasks to the Students

A final performance task is a type of summary assessment, which means that it is a means of determining what the students understand, know, and can do after a period of instruction such as a unit. (The unit test is also a summary assessment.)

In addition to providing a unit test, we encourage you to assess (determine) student understanding of the four most important concepts in each unit by assigning one of the short projects called final performance tasks. Through these projects the students can demonstrate their understanding of the main concepts. This assignment allows you to have another snapshot of what the students understand.

For example, the four understandings for unit 1 are:

- God created all the world as essentially good.
- The Scriptures use figurative and symbolic language to convey religious truth, as exemplified in Genesis, chapters 1–11.
- Original Sin entered the world when Adam and Eve chose to reject a God-centered life in favor of a self-centered life.
- We need the grace of redemption in order to be healed of the effects of Original Sin.

The handout "Final Performance Task Options for Unit 1" (Document #: TX001436) in the teacher guide outlines the assignment options. Note that for all the options, the students must show their understanding of these concepts. The first final performance task option has the students conversing with Saint Paul about the Church in his time and now. The second option asks them to write a blog, authored by Saint Paul, to the members of the Church in his time. A traditional unit test is also provided.

We suggest that you explain the performance task options early in the unit so the students can focus on the knowledge and skills they can use for the final performance task they choose. This also helps to decrease the number of the "Are we learning anything today?" or "Why do we have to learn this?" questions by giving the students the big picture of where they are headed and how they will get there.

## Provide Learning Experiences for the Students to Deepen Their Understanding of the Main Concepts

This teacher guide uses the term *learning experiences* rather than *activities* to emphasize that much of what goes on in the classroom should contribute to student learning, such as explaining assignments; presenting new material; asking the students to work individually, in pairs, or in groups; testing the students; and asking them to present material to their peers.

Each step in the teacher guide leads the students toward deeper understanding of the four key understandings of a unit. At times learning experiences are grouped into a single step because they work toward the same goal.

At other times a step includes only one learning experience. If you have a better way of achieving a step goal, by all means use it. However, if new vocabulary or content is introduced in a step you have chosen to skip, you may want to go over that material in some way, or remove that material from the unit test.

Throughout the steps, references are made to student book articles, resources at *smp.org/LivinginChrist,* and other Internet resources. Often the teacher guide addresses the content in the student book early in the unit and then asks the students to uncover a deeper meaning with various learning experiences throughout. When applicable the book refers to *smp.org/LivinginChrist* for resources at your fingertips.

The goal of this course is for the students to gain a deeper understanding of the material. But what is understanding? The understanding we want the students to gain is multifaceted. Understanding encompasses several of the "facets of understanding," used by Jay McTighe and Grant Wiggins in their book *Understanding by Design:*

> We have developed a multifaceted view of what makes up a mature understanding, a six-sided view of the concept. When we truly understand we

**Explain**    ***Can explain***—via generalizations or principles, providing justified and systematic accounts of phenomena, facts, and data; make insightful connections and provide illuminating examples or illustrations.

**Interpret**    ***Can interpret***—tell meaningful stories; offer apt translations; provide a revealing or personal historical dimension to ideas and events; make the object of understanding personal or accessible through images, anecdotes, analogies, and models.

**Apply**    ***Can apply***—effectively use and adapt what we know in diverse and real contexts—we can "do" the subject.

**Perceive**    ***Have perspective***—see and hear points of view through critical eyes and ears; see the big picture.

**Empathize**    ***Can empathize***—find value in what others might find odd, alien, or implausible; perceive sensitively on the basis of prior direct experience.

*Have self-knowledge*—show metacognitive awareness; perceive the personal style, prejudices, projections, and habits of mind that both shape and impede our own understanding; are aware of what we do not understand; reflect on the meaning of learning and experience.

Note that Saint Mary's Press has created icons for each facet of understanding. When three or more facets are present, there will be an "understand" icon. When relevant, all facets of understanding should be addressed in each unit. If you are used to Bloom's Taxonomy, see *smp.org/LivinginChrist* for a comparison of both models of understanding and learning.

## Provide a Day or Partial Day for the Students to Work on the Final Performance Tasks

This guide encourages you to give the students time in class to work on their final performance tasks if you have assigned them. You do not, however, have to wait until the end of the unit. Not only does this day give the students time to work in groups if needed or to do some research, but it also gives you the opportunity to identify any students who may be having trouble with the assignment and allows you to work with them during class time.

## Give the Students a Tool to Help Them Reflect on Their Learning

The handout "Learning about Learning" (Document #: TX001159; see Appendix) is a generic way to help the students think about what they have learned during the entire unit. This process, whether done this way or in another fashion, is valuable for several reasons:

- The students do not get much time to reflect while they are moving through each unit. Looking over the unit helps them to make connections, revisit any "aha!" moments, and identify which concepts remain difficult for them to understand.
- We give students a gift when we help them learn how they learn best. Insights such as "I didn't get it until we saw the video," or "Putting together the presentation required that I really knew my stuff" can be applied to all the disciplines they are studying.

Feel free to have the students discuss the handout questions in pairs at times for variety.

## Handouts

All the handouts in the teacher guide, as well as the unit tests, are available on the Saint Mary's Press Web site at *smp.org/LivinginChrist,* as PDFs, as Word documents, or in Rich Text Format (RTFs), for downloading, customizing, and printing. The handouts found at the end of each unit in this guide are simply for teacher reference.

## Appendix

The teacher guide has one appendix, which consists of a handout that is used in each unit. The handout is also available at *smp.org/LivinginChrist* for downloading, customizing, and printing.

# Thank You

We thank you for putting your confidence in us by adopting the Living in Christ series. Our goal is to graduate students who are in a relationship with Jesus Christ, are religiously literate, and understand their faith in terms of their real lives.

Please contact us and let us know how we are doing. We are eager to improve this curriculum, and we value your knowledge and expertise. E-mail us at *LivinginChrist@smp.org* to offer your feedback.

# Unit 1    What Do We Mean When We Talk about "Church"?

## Overview

In this unit the students come to understand that the Church is unlike any other reality on earth, as the Church is both within history and beyond history. She is both human and divine. In the Church we meet God.

### Key Understandings and Questions

Upon completing this unit, the students will have a deeper understanding of the following key concepts:

- The media and society communicate mixed messages about the meaning of the Catholic Church.
- The word *church* comes from the Greek and Latin for "convocation or assembly" but can also refer to a liturgical assembly, a local parish community, or the gathering of the faithful worldwide.
- The Acts of the Apostles and the Pauline letters give us insight into the way the early Church understood itself.
- The models of the Church illustrate its many dimensions and functions.

Upon completing the unit, the students will have answered the following questions:

- What is my understanding of Church, and how has society and the media affected my understanding?
- What does the word *church* actually mean?
- How did the first members and leaders of the Church understand it?
- Why can the Church seem different depending on the situation in which we encounter it?

### Student Book Articles

This unit draws on articles from *The Church: Christ in the World Today* student book and incorporates them into the unit instruction. Whenever the teaching steps for the unit require the students to refer to or read an article from the student book, the following symbol appears in the margin: (📖). The articles covered in the unit are from "Section 1: The Church: Christ's Continued Presence and Work in the World," "Section 4: The Lived Mission of the Church," and "Section 5: The Church and Young People," and are as follows:

- "The Meaning of Church" (article 1, pp. 10–12)
- "The Holy Spirit Gifts the Church" (article 9, pp. 32–36)
- "The Mission of the Apostles" (article 10, pp. 39–42)
- "Spreading the Gospel" (article 11, pp. 42–44)
- "Persecution and Martyrdom" (article 12, pp. 45–47)
- "The Church Is the People of God" (article 13, pp. 50–52)
- "The Church Is the Body of Christ" (article 14, pp. 53–57)
- "The Church Is the Temple of the Holy Spirit" (article 15, pp. 57–59)
- "The Church and Hierarchy" (article 39, pp. 150–153)
- "Called by God to Belong to the Church" (article 52, pp. 199–202)
- "Christ Enriches Us through Participation in the Life of the Church" (article 53, pp. 202–206)
- "Called to Community" (article 54, pp. 206–210)

## How Will You Know the Students Understand?

The following resources will help you assess the students' understanding of the key concepts covered in this unit:

- handout "Final Performance Task Options for Unit 1" (Document #: TX001436)
- handout "Rubric for Final Performance Tasks for Unit 1" (Document #: TX001437)
- handout "Unit 1 Test" (Document #: TX001444)

## The Suggested Path to Understanding

This unit in the teacher guide provides you with one learning path to take with the students, to enable them to begin their study of the Church. It is not neces-sary to use all the learning experiences provided in the unit; however, if you substitute other material from this course or your own material for some of the material offered here, be sure that you have covered all relevant facets of understanding and that you have not missed any skills or knowledge required for later units.

 **Step 1:** Preassess what the students already know about the Church and its founding.

 **Step 2:** Follow the assessment by presenting to the students the handouts "Final Performance Task Options for Unit 1" (Document #: TX001436) and "Rubric for Final Performance Tasks for Unit 1" (Document #: TX001437).

**Perceive** | **Step 3:** Launch student discussion about the terms *catholic, church, Christian, religion, spirituality,* and *role of the Church,* building off step 1.

**Apply** | **Step 4:** Explore and critique messages about the Catholic Church that are presented in print media.

**Empathize** | **Step 5:** Assign the students to develop an ad campaign based on the questions Catholics and non-Catholics have about the Church, targeting areas of misinformation, concern, and ignorance.

**Reflect** | **Step 6:** Guide the students in examining their self-understanding of the early Church through exploring New Testament images of Church.

**Explain** | **Step 7:** Explore the models of the Church as explained by Avery Dulles.

**Interpret** | **Step 8:** Provide a small-group hands-on experience with each of the five models of Church.

**Perceive** | **Step 9:** Explore the models of Church in light of current Church events, using copies of local (diocesan) or national newspapers to find news articles featuring each model.

**Explain** | **Step 10:** Provide the students with a general historical perspective on the growth and development of the Church and some of the people and events that continue to influence the Church today.

**Understand** | **Step 11:** Now that the students are closer to the end of the unit, make sure they are all on track with their final performance tasks, if you have assigned them.

**Reflect** | **Step 12:** Provide the students with a tool to use for reflecting about what they learned in the unit and how they learned.

## Background for Teaching This Unit

Visit *smp.org/LivinginChrist* for additional information about these and other theological concepts taught in this unit:

- "The Church" (Document #: TX001514)
- "The Two Basic Sacraments of Christ and Church" (Document #: TX001515)

The Web site also includes information on these and other teaching methods used in the unit:

- "Media Literacy" (Document #: TX001516)
- "Using Small-Group Hands-On Experiences" (Document #: TX001517)

## Scripture Passages

Scripture is an important part of the Living in Christ series and is frequently used in the learning experiences for each unit. The Scripture passages featured in this unit are as follows:

- Acts of the Apostles 4:3–37 (the early Church)
- Acts of the Apostles 6:1–7 (the need for assistants)
- Colossians 1:18 (Christ is the head of the Church)
- 1 Corinthians 3:7–9 (we are God's coworkers)
- 1 Corinthians 3:16–17 (we are the temple of God)
- 1 Corinthians 12:12–20,27 (one body, many parts)
- Ephesians 2:19–22 (no longer strangers)
- Ephesians 4:11–16 (diversity of gifts)
- Galatians 3:27–28 (what faith has brought us)
- Romans 11:17–18,24 (the Gentiles' salvation)
- Romans 12:4–5 (many parts in one body)
- John 10:1–11 (the Good Shepherd)
- John 15:1–5 (the vine and the branches)
- Matthew 5:13–16 (the similes of salt and light)
- Matthew 28:16–20 (the commissioning of the Disciples)
- Matthew 16:13–20 (Peter's confession about Jesus)
- 1 Peter 2:5–7,9–10 (God's House and People)
- 1 Peter 5:2–4 (advice to presbyters)

## Vocabulary

The student book and the teacher guide include the following key terms for this unit. To provide the students with a list of these terms and their definitions, download and print the handout "Vocabulary for Unit 1" (Document #: TX001438).

| | | |
|---|---|---|
| age of reason | diocese | martyr |
| aspiration | evangelization | mystical |
| blasphemy | Gentile | Sacred Chrism |
| Body of Christ | Hellenistic | Theology of the Body |
| catholic | infallibility | |
| chalice | *katholikos* | Transubstantiation |
| charism | *Kyriake* | Trinitarian |
| charismatic | liturgy | virtue |
| community | Magisterium | |

# Learning Experiences

**Explain**

## Step 1

*Preassess what the students already know about the Church and its founding.*

**Teacher Note**

If this is the beginning of a new class, this learning experience could be used as an icebreaker. Lead a milling exercise during which the students move around among one another, sharing with one person at a time. With their first partner, they should share what they wrote down for *catholic*. With a new partner, they should share what they wrote down for *church*. With a third partner, they should share what they wrote down for *Christian*. Then have all the students return to their seats, and ask some volunteers to share some ideas.

1. Prepare for this learning experience by gathering pens or pencils and sheets of blank paper, one of each for each student.

2. Begin by writing the words *catholic, church,* and *Christian* on the board, and explaining that these three words can carry different meanings to different people or groups of people.

3. Have the students form pairs. Distribute a pen or pencil and a sheet of blank paper to each student. Then direct the students to quickly write down what first comes to mind when they see or hear each of these words.

4. Ask for volunteers to share some associations with the class. Record them on the board.

5. Give the students a few moments of quiet to review what the class currently understands about each of the three terms. You may want to point out some obvious differences and let them know that as the course unfolds, they will be learning much more about them.

6. Explain that the meaning of these words will be made clearer throughout the course. You may, however, wish to share the following definitions (from *Saint Mary's Press® Glossary of Theological Terms*, by John T. Ford, 2006) with the class before moving on to the next step:

- **catholic.** This term (from the Greek *katholikos*, meaning "universal" or "according to the whole") was first used by Ignatius of Antioch (early second century AD) to describe the *unity* of *local churches* under their local *bishops*. "Catholic" is also one of the four *marks of the Church* in the *Nicene Creed ("one, holy, catholic,* and *apostolic").* "Catholic" has come to be associated with a particular way of being *Christian* that emphasizes the *doctrines* and practices of the early Church and the celebration of the *Sacraments.* (See *Catechism of the Catholic Church [CCC],* 750.)

- **Catholic Church.** In the broadest sense, all *Churches* that profess the *Nicene Creed* consider themselves "Catholic." In addition, a number of Churches that accept the *doctrines* and practices of the early Church and celebrate the *Sacraments* consider themselves "Catholic"—for example, *Anglicans* and *Old Catholics.* The *Roman Catholic Church* considers itself "Catholic" because it possesses the fullness of Christ's presence, the fullness of Christ's doctrine, the fullness of *sacramental* life, and the full means of *salvation,* and because its *mission* is to the entire world. (See *CCC,* 830–831.)

- **Christian.** This term (from the Greek word *christos,* meaning "anointed") indicates that a *person* is a follower of *Christ* and has been *anointed* at *Baptism* and *Confirmation.* According to the Acts of the Apostles (11:26), the *disciples* of *Jesus* were first called Christians in Antioch. In contemporary usage, all those who profess to follow Christ are called Christians. (See *CCC,* 1289.)

- **church.** This word (derived from the Greek *Kyriake,* meaning "the Lord's house") has multiple meanings: (1) the building where *Christians* gather for *worship;* (2) a specific Christian *denomination,* such as *Anglicans, Lutherans, Methodists, Presbyterians,* and so on; (3) the whole body of Christians; and (4) *ecclesiastical authority* in contrast to civil authority, as in the contrast between Church and State. (See *CCC,* 781–810, for a fuller understanding of what Catholics mean by "Church.")

**Understand**

## Step 2

Follow the assessment by presenting to the students the handouts "Final Performance Task Options for Unit 1" (Document #: TX001436) and "Rubric for Final Performance Tasks for Unit 1" (Document #: TX001437).

This unit provides you with two ways to assess that the students have a deep understanding of the most important concepts in the unit: having a conversation with Saint Paul about the Church in his time and now, or writing a blog authored by Saint Paul to the members of the Church in his time. Refer to "Using Final Performance Tasks to Assess Understanding" (Document #: TX001011) and "Using Rubrics to Assess Work" (Document #: TX001012) at *smp.org/ LivinginChrist* for background information.

1. Prepare for this learning experience by downloading and printing the handouts "Final Performance Task Options for Unit 1," (Document #: TX001436) and "Rubric for Final Performance Tasks for Unit 1" (Document #: TX001437).

2. Begin by distributing the handouts. Give the students a choice as to which performance task they choose and add additional options if you so choose.

3. Review the directions, expectations, and rubrics in class, allowing the students to ask questions. You may want to say something to this effect:

> **Teacher Note**
>
> You will want to assign due dates for the final performance tasks.
>
> If you have done these performance tasks, or very similar ones, with students before, place examples of this work in the classroom. During this introduction explain how each is a good example of what you are looking for, for different reasons. This allows the students to concretely understand that there is not only one way to succeed.

➤ If you wish to work alone, you may choose option 1 or option 2. If you wish to work with one or two other people, you may choose option 1.

➤ Near the end of the unit, you will have one full class period as a workday for your final performance task. However, keep in mind that you should be working on, or at least thinking about, your chosen task *throughout* the unit, not just at the end. Please do not wait for this class workday to begin your final performance task.

4. Explain the types of tools and knowledge the students will gain throughout the unit so that they can successfully complete the final performance task.

5. Answer questions to clarify the end point toward which the unit is headed. Remind the students as the unit progresses that each learning experience builds the knowledge and skills they will need to show you that they understand the Church as the means to encountering the living Jesus as well as their role in the Church and Christ's invitation to actively participate and contribute to the life of the Church.

Article 1

Perceive

## Step 3

Launch student discussion about the terms *catholic, church, Christian, religion, spirituality,* and *role of the Church,* building off step 1.

The purpose of this learner-to-learner learning experience is for the students to discover, through discussion and observation, their knowledge of the definitions of some common terms in the Catholic faith.

1. As background for this learning experience, have the students read student book article 1, "The Meaning of Church."

2. Begin by writing the following terms on the board:

   • church *(ekklesia)*
   • religion

- catholic
- Christian
- Protestant
- spirituality
- role of the Church in the world
- convocation or assembly
- Body of Christ

3. Divide the large group into small groups of two or three, and then assign each small group one of the terms listed on the board.

4. Have the small groups work to define the term, discuss its significance, and present the term to the class using a demonstration or skit.

Articles
13, 14,
15

Apply

# Step 4

*Explore and critique messages about the Catholic Church that are presented in print media.*

1. Prepare for this learning experience by downloading and printing the handout "What Are They Saying?" (Document #: TX001439), one for each student, and gathering five different articles from newspapers, magazines, and journals that report on or discuss the Catholic Church from a variety of perspectives.

> **Teacher Note**
>
> Each student in each small group will need a different article. Therefore, if you have four small groups, you will need four copies of each of the five articles.

2. As background have the students read student book articles 13–15, "The Church Is the People of God," "The Church Is the Body of Christ," and "The Church Is the Temple of the Holy Spirit."

3. Begin with a question-and-answer session or discussion. Refer to "Media Literacy" (Document #: TX001516) at *smp.org/LivinginChrist* for background information. Discuss the following topics:

- role and influence of the media
- importance of reading the media critically
- how media relates to personal values
- responding to media

4. Distribute the handout and a copy of one of the articles to each student.

5. Give the students time to read the articles individually and to complete the handout.

6. Now have the students form small groups of five, each group member having read a different article. This way each small group can discuss all five articles.

7. Direct the small groups to summarize the articles, compare perceptions of the Church, discuss the accuracy of information presented in the articles, and develop at least two questions they would like to see answered during this course.

8. After the small-group discussion, gather the students back into the large group for a summary discussion of what they have learned from the reading and the small-group work. Take note of the students' questions to make sure they are addressed at an appropriate time during the semester.

## Step 5

*Assign the students to develop an ad campaign based on the questions Catholics and non-Catholics have about the Church, targeting areas of misinformation, concern, and ignorance.*

The students use either a digital media or a traditional print media to help people understand Catholic beliefs and practices more clearly. After producing an ad campaign, the students reflect on aspects of Catholic identity that can best help our culture today.

1. Prepare for this learning experience by ensuring the students will have access to the media center or computer lab. Also gather any art supplies you would like the students to use if they choose to create a traditional print media ad.

2. Write the following questions on the board and instruct the students to take out their notebooks to begin answering them:

   • What are three positive ways Catholic beliefs or practices are seen in the media or popular culture?

   • Why are these seen as positive?

   • What are three negative ways Catholic beliefs or practices are seen in the media or popular culture?

   • Why are these seen as negative?

   Give the students 5 to 7 minutes to write out their responses.

3. When time is up, divide the class into small groups of four. Invite the group members to listen to one another's reflections, noting the similar positive and negative ways the Catholic Church is perceived in our culture. Give the small groups 5 to 7 minutes to discuss their observations within the groups.

4. Ask each small group to share with the large group two positive and two negative ways Catholic life is seen in the media or popular culture. List these on the board and lead a discussion with the class using the following questions:

   ➤ Why are these seen as positive qualities?

   ➤ Why is the Church seen in a negative way?

5. Make a transition in the learning experience with the following remarks:

   ➤ We can see Catholic life is perceived in both positive and negative ways in our culture. Some of these perceptions, especially the negative ones, may have been influenced by misjudgments and misunderstandings, by bad examples on the part of Catholics, or by simple ignorance on the part of others toward Catholics. How can we help others to come to a fuller understanding of the Catholic faith? One way would be to grow in our own understanding of our faith and then to devise ways to explain it creatively and clearly to others. Here's a way to do this.

6. Next, instruct the students to individually respond to the following question:

   ➤ What are three Catholic beliefs or practices that seem to be easily misunderstood or misinterpreted?

7. After the students have prepared their three Catholic beliefs or practices that seem easily misunderstood or misinterpreted, invite them to begin naming them as you list them on the board. Then ask:

   ➤ What is the Church's teaching on these beliefs or practices?

8. Go through a number of the Catholic beliefs or practices that the students have identified, and on the board, next to those items, write down what the Church holds true about them. If the students are unsure about the Church's teaching, refer them to a Catholic sourcebook or Web site, such as Saint Mary's Press *(www.smp.org/OnlineResources/ CatholicQuickView)*.

9. To introduce the ad campaign project, give the following instructions:

   ➤ Now that we have begun to clarify for ourselves what the Church teaches and why, you are to create a creative and clear means to communicate these values to others. Imagine that you have been hired to create three different billboards or posters to promote the Catholic Church. The ads should explain some of the beliefs of the Church (refer to the list of misunderstandings and "re-understandings" listed on the board). You may prepare your ads on paper or in a digital media. Each ad in the campaign must do the following:

     • address one key element of the Church's teaching or mission or identity and cite one section of Church teaching to briefly highlight it (for example, a line from the Scriptures or a quotation from the *Catechism of the Catholic Church*)

- include at least one strong visual element and one design component
- include a slogan or motto about the Church or what she stands for in the modern world

You may choose to use some magazine ads to show the students how ads are constructed and how we associate strong reactions to images and slogans. Distribute any needed art supplies, and tell the students they have 30 minutes to complete their ad campaigns, or you may decide to assign the creation of the ad campaigns as homework.

10. Once the students have produced their ads, spend time in class letting each student present. As a follow-up to this learning experience, you may direct the students to prepare a one-page written reflection on this question: What are three key aspects of the Catholic faith that, even if misunderstood by some, can contribute to the vitality of our culture today, and how?

Articles 10, 11, 12

## Step 6

*Guide the students in examining their self-understanding of the early Church through exploring New Testament images of Church.*

This learning experience introduces the students to the images of Church that emerged from the New Testament and then highlights the Church's qualities toward which these images point. As a final exercise, the students consider contemporary metaphors that reveal other aspects of the Church's identity. There is a PowerPoint available at smp.org/LivinginChrist that you can use to explore this topic with your students.

1. Prepare for this learning experience by downloading and printing copies of the handout "New Testament Images of Church" (Document #: TX001440), one for each student.

2. As background have the students read student book articles 10–12, "The Mission of the Apostles," "Spreading the Gospel," and "Persecution and Martyrdom." Remind them to bring their Bibles to class.

3. Review the ads the students created in step 5, and then ask:

   ➤ Your ad campaigns tried to help explain specific Church beliefs or practices in a compact way. But, what image or symbolic picture do you think best describes the Church's overall identity today? Why?

4. As the students name particular images or symbols, write them on the board under the heading "Images of Church Today." Identify, with the students' help, the qualities of the symbols and images that seem positive, negative, or neutral.

5. Make a transition to the early Church's use of images with the following comment:

   ➤ Just as we did with our ads, the early Church used images or symbols or illustrations from their experience to convey an understanding of their identity as followers of Christ, both to themselves and to the world. Let us examine the images the earliest Christians used and what these images express about their understanding of being the Church.

6. Distribute the copies of the handout, which includes particular images of the Church along with the Scriptures that refer to them. The students will need to access the New Testament to complete this exercise. Read the instructions on the handout, and then direct students to complete it.

7. When the students have completed the handout, have them form small groups of three or four and compare responses regarding the qualities of the Church that are being expressed in each image. (For example, how is the Church like a bride? Both are unconditionally loved and both are beautiful in the eyes of the husband.)

8. While the small groups are working, write on the board all eight images of the Church listed on the handout:

   • the Church as the People of God
   • the Church as light and salt
   • the Church as the Body of Christ
   • the Church as the Bride of Christ
   • the Church as the Temple of God
   • the Church as the flock
   • the Church as the field or olive grove
   • the Church as the building or household of God

9. When all the small groups have compared responses to the eight images, each member should come to the board and write out the qualities of Church expressed in those images.

10. When all the small groups have had a chance to write on the board, review each model and the qualities of the Church contained in each model. Then pose the following questions for the students to reflect on and write about on the handout:

    ➤ What types of images or qualities of the Church were most attractive to the early followers of Christ? Why?

    ➤ What type of images or qualities of the Church are most attractive to you as a follower of Christ today? Why?

11. Conclude by having the students choose one of the following creative writing prompts to respond to in class or as homework:

- Name two more images, symbols, or illustrations from our modern world and explain how they express at least two of the New Testament qualities of the Church.
- Distribute two everyday objects (a button, a key, a safety pin, a nail clipper, a water bottle, etc.) to each student, and then ask the students to describe what two New Testament qualities of Church the objects could represent.

Articles 10, 11, 12

## Step 7

*Explore the models of the Church as explained by Avery Dulles.*

1. Prepare for this learning experience by downloading and printing the handouts "Models of the Church Chart" (Document #: TX001441) and "Matching Quiz: Models of the Church" (Document #: TX001442), one of each for each student. There is a PowerPoint available at smp.org/LivinginChrist that you can use to explore this topic with your students.

2. As background have the students read student book articles 10–12, "The Mission of the Apostles, " "Spreading the Gospel," and "Persecution and Martyrdom." Also make sure they are familiar with the Acts of the Apostles in the New Testament.

3. Briefly review step 6 with the students regarding the biblical images of Church. Remind them that these images emerged out of the biblical faith tradition as a way of describing their new lives in the Risen Jesus. Continue your remarks along these lines:

   ➤ In addition to these biblical images, other images or "models" of the Church have been proposed to help us understand the Church's identity as well as her mission in the world throughout history. These models were first presented in a book called *The Models of Church*, by Father (later Cardinal) Avery Dulles, a Jesuit priest. Father Dulles illustrates five models of the Church that he says emerged from the ministry of Jesus and early Church life and then continued to weave themselves throughout the Church's history, affecting how Catholics thought about and lived out their lives as members of the Church. Before we begin talking about Dulles' models of the Church, let's begin by defining the word *model* itself and discussing how models can be used as a means of understanding a complex experience.

4. Write the word *model* on the board and invite the class to offer definitions for the word. If not offered by the students, make sure the following points

are addressed: a representation, an example, a symbol, a pattern used to explain a larger concept.

5. Present the following guidelines for using models in any field:

   ➤ All models offer some useful information for understanding the subject at hand.

   ➤ No one model is complete in itself; all models offer unique perspectives and must be used together to deepen our understanding of the subject.

   ➤ The subject is always bigger than the models describe.

6. Distribute the handout "Models of the Church Chart" (Document #: TX001441) and share the following:

   ➤ We will be discussing the individual models as listed on the handout, with a few additional elements that we will add in the space provided. You might be wondering where these images came from and why these images were chosen and not others. Father Dulles looked at the ministry of Jesus and the early life of the Church and noticed five specific ways that seemed to mark the life of the Church: he called them Church as Institution, Church as Mystical Body or Communion, Church as Herald, Church as Servant, and Church as Sacrament. Let us review each model, provide a scriptural understanding of each image, and, finally, identify one example of this experience in the early Church.

7. Present the models on the handout, including the following additional points. Allow time with each model for discussion and questions.

   • Church as Institution

      ○ Focus: Church as visible society with formal structures and organization (official teachings, Sacrament system, etc.)

      ○ Strengths: provides strong sense of identity for members, clarity of beliefs, and sense of stability and continuity in the midst of a changing world

      ○ Weaknesses: can put too much emphasis on rules and traditions, can seem too concerned about status quo, can be slow to change

   • Church as Mystical Body / Communion

      ○ Focus: relationships of persons who are gathered in God through Jesus: horizontal (with others) and vertical (with God) dimensions maintained

      ○ Strengths: faith life in the Holy Spirit developed through strong, intimate relationships, gives evidence of the enduring Body of Christ image of Church

      ○ Weaknesses: can become too inwardly focused on relationships and without a sense of outreach to others, can minimize need for appropriate Church leadership

- Church as Herald
  - Focus: power of the Word of God to challenge, comfort, heal, and encourage the world that God's Word (Jesus) is active in the world, Church as messenger of Jesus that brings his Gospel to all
  - Strength: clear mission for the Church to proclaim and live out the Word of God in the world, especially in creative use of media and the arts
  - Weakness: can be perceived as too "preachy" and too focused on getting to know just the text of the Word of God (the Bible) and not the Word of God as Jesus in our lives

- Church as Servant
  - Focus: Church's identification with Jesus as the one who was "[among us] as one who serves" (Luke 22:27); direct service to all people is how the Church most embodies Christ
  - Strength: clear sense of mission to transform human society into an image of the Kingdom of God through direct service (corporal and spiritual works of mercy)
  - Weakness: could obscure the ultimate meaning of the service as preparation for the spiritual work for the coming Kingdom of God

- Church as Sacrament
  - Focus: summarizes other models; brings together the Church's institutional sense of itself as being a special sign to the world of Christ's faithful, transforming presence; Church celebrates those unique signs of Christ's presence called Sacraments so she can herself become a better Sacrament of Jesus in the world through her heralding, servant, and Spirit-led community building. We are called to become more and more what Christ is forming her to be.
  - Strengths: a strong sense of Christ's gift of himself in the Sacraments for the life of the Church and for the world, Church meant to be visible manifestation of Christ in the world
  - Weaknesses: can become too ritualistic or formulaic in its Sacraments, can focus too much on the sign or gesture and miss the point of the Sacraments as meant to nourish the Church

8. When you have finished reviewing the models of the Church with the students, distribute the handout "Matching Quiz: Models of the Church" (Document #: TX001442) and have the students complete it individually.

9. Invite the students to share their answers from the quiz. Answer any questions they might have about the models.

10. Direct the students to compose a response of at least one paragraph for each of the following questions:

➤ Which model of Church are you most drawn to and why?

➤ Which model of Church are you least drawn to and why?

11. After the students have had time to prepare an initial response to the two questions, invite them to group together with other students who selected the same model as the one to which they were most drawn. Ask different students to explain why they feel drawn to that model.

Articles 9, 39, 52, 53, 54

## Step 8

*Provide a small-group hands-on experience with each of the five models of Church.*

In this learning experience, the students partake in different exercises at stations that represent each of the five models of the Church. This allows them to gain clarity and a deeper understanding of each of the models.

1. Prepare for this learning experience by gathering the following supplies:

- a roll of masking tape
- five sheets of poster board
- a box of markers
- five small gift boxes
- small slips of paper, one for each student
- pens or pencils, one for each student
- pads of ten sticky notes, one pad for each student
- index cards, one for each student
- sheets of white drawing paper, one for each student
- black markers, one for each student in the largest of the small groups

    Create five areas in the classroom to be used for various stations. You might move desks together in circles to create five separate areas, or you might completely remove the desks and mark five distinct areas on the floor with masking tape. Distribute the supplies to each station, according to the instructions for each station in part 4. Also create a printed version of the instructions for each station as outlined in part 4.

2. As background for this learning experience, have the students read student book articles 9, 39, and 52–54, "The Holy Spirit Gifts the Church" "The Church and Hierarchy," "Called by God to Belong to the Church," "Christ Enriches Us through Participation in the Life of the Church," and "Called to Community." Be sure they bring their Bibles to class as well.

3. Divide the class into five small groups and share the following directions:

➤ Each small group will be sent to a station to complete an exercise. When time is called, each small group will rotate to another station. This will continue until each small group has completed all five stations. You will have approximately 10 minutes at each station.

4. Present the following directions for each station. You will also want to have a printed version of the directions at each station.

**Station 1: Institution**
Read student book article 39, "The Church and Hierarchy." Use poster board and markers to create an organizational chart of the hierarchy of the Church and how it works, including all ministries in the Church. Work as a group and produce one chart. Do not worry about the accuracy of the information at this point; focus on demonstrating previous learning, making discoveries, and being curious about information you have not yet learned.

> **Teacher Note**
>
> It might be helpful to prompt the students to start with Peter.

**Station 2: Mystical Communion** (Body of Christ)
Read student book article 9, "The Holy Spirit Gifts the Church." Each student takes turns sharing with the group one gift he or she possesses that contributes to the Church (e.g., compassion, musical talent, intelligence). Then he or she writes the name of the gift in marker on the outside of the gift box. Each person takes at least three turns to share their gifts and write them on the gift box. Then each person writes on a small piece of paper a brief prayer of petition to Jesus. Each group member then shares his or her prayer with the group and places it inside the gift box. At the end of the turn at this station, the group places its gift box at the front of the room or on the prayer table.

**Station 3: Sacrament**
Each student takes a stack of sticky notes and writes one response per sticky note as to how she or he sees Jesus present throughout the Church and the world. Each student should write at least ten responses. After writing on the notes, each student posts them individually around the entire classroom (floors, walls, ceilings). During the large-group follow-up sharing, the entire class will read the sticky notes that have been posted around the room.

**Station 4: Herald**
Each student conducts a Scripture hunt to find a passage that contains a statement calling the People of God to live in peace and unity. Each student in the group must find a different passage and write down the quotation and reference on an index card. The group then posts all the index cards on a wall in the classroom in the shape of a cross.

**Station 5: Servant**

Each student is to draw and label a collage of pictures of all the places throughout the world where the Church is present in the midst of suffering. Encourage the students to use black markers on white paper, as these colors are associated with the uniforms of servants.

5. When all the groups have completed all five stations, have the students share insights they gained at each station. You can also use this time to highlight some of the projects created at each station.

| Perceive | **Step 9**<br><br>Explore the models of Church in light of current Church events, using copies of local (diocesan) or national newspapers to find news articles featuring each model. |
|---|---|

1. Prepare for this learning experience by obtaining copies of a local diocesan newspaper (perhaps your school library subscribes to the diocesan paper and maintains back issues) or access to an online version of the newspaper. Links are available at *smp.org/LivinginChrist.* Also have available four sheets of blank paper for each pair of students.

2. Begin by sharing the following with the class:

   ➤ In the previous two learning experiences, we explored what the models of Church are, how they are related to Christ, and what their strengths and weaknesses are. Now we are going to examine where and how these models are present in the life of the Church today.

3. Have the students form pairs. Distribute to each student a copy of a local diocesan newspaper (or provide individual Internet access for the online version.)

4. Share the following directions with the class:

   ➤ We have examined five models of Church. Working with your partners, you are to find news stories that demonstrate four of those models. Allow 10 to 15 minutes for the students to look for and read the articles.

5. Once the pairs have found their articles, distribute four sheets of paper to each pair, and instruct the pairs to identify and prepare the following for each of the four stories found:

   • the title of the story and the date of the publication
   • which model of Church is represented in the article and how
   • a fifty-word summary of the article

6. Conclude by having the pairs present to the class the topic of their story and the model of Church they believe it represents and why.

## Step 10

*Provide the students with a general historical perspective on the growth and development of the Church and some of the people and events that continue to influence the Church today.*

1. Prepare for this learning experience by creating index cards, two for each student, with key events in the history of the Church written or printed on them (a list of key events is provided on the handout "Key Events in Church History" (Document #: TX001443). Also create century markers (e.g., 00, 50, 100, 200, or use identified eras or centuries), either on sheets of paper posted around the room or written on the board or a sheet of newsprint, to create a timeline. You will also need resource materials (arrange to use the computer lab or library, or have the resources available in the classroom).

2. Distribute the index cards to the students and ask them to research and write on the back of the card a paragraph or a bulleted list that gives the specific dates and explains the significance of the person, event, or document in the life of the Church. Direct the students to include the resource(s) used in the research.

3. Move around the room to assist any students who might need help.

4. When the students are done researching, have them put their cards in the appropriate place on the timeline.

5. Now divide the class into two groups. Have the students in one group take their places next to the information they researched. Invite the remaining students to move along the timeline and take note of the information that is available to them at this time. Encourage them to ask questions of those who did the research on any specific topic.

6. Have the students change roles to give everyone an opportunity to study the timeline.

7. Gather the students back into the large group to process what they have just done. Ask what they noticed or what stood out as they completed this exercise. Allow a few minutes for the students to journal before closing with a brief discussion. Tell the students that there will be a learning experience later on in the course that will build on what they are learning now.

## Step 11

Now that the students are closer to the end of the unit, make sure they are all on track with their final performance tasks, if you have assigned them.

If possible, devote 50 to 60 minutes for the students to ask questions about the tasks and to work individually or in their small groups.

1. Remind the students to bring to class any work they have already prepared so that they can work on it during the class period. If necessary, reserve the library or media center so the students can do any book or online research. Download and print the handouts "Final Performance Task Options for Unit 1" (Document #: TX001436) and "Rubric for Final Performance Tasks for Unit 1" (Document #: TX001437). Review the final performance task options, answer questions, and ask the students to choose one if they have not already done so.

2. Provide some class time for the students to work on their performance tasks. This then allows you to work with the students who need additional guidance with the project.

## Step 12

Provide the students with a tool to use for reflecting about what they learned in the unit and how they learned.

This learning experience provides the students with an excellent opportunity to reflect on how their understandings of the Church have developed throughout the unit.

1. To prepare for this learning experience, make copies of the handout "Learning about Learning" (Document #: TX001159; see Appendix), one for each student.

2. Distribute the handout, and give the students about 15 minutes to answer the questions quietly. Invite them to share any reflections they have about the content they learned as well as their insights into the way they learned.

# Final Performance Task Options for Unit 1

## Important Information for Both Options

The following are the main ideas you are to understand from this unit. They should appear in this final performance task so your teacher can assess whether you learned the most essential content:

- The media and society communicate mixed messages about the meaning of the Catholic Church.
- The word *church* comes from the Greek and Latin for "convocation or assembly" but can also refer to a liturgical assembly, a local parish community, or the gathering of the faithful worldwide.
- The Acts of the Apostles and the Pauline letters give us insight into the way the early Church understood itself.
- The models of the Church illustrate its many dimensions and functions.

## Option 1: A Conversation with Saint Paul: The Church Then and Now

Two students will create a 5- to 7- minute skit, with one student performing the role of Saint Paul and the other student the interviewer. The dialogue will compare and contrast Paul's experience of the Church with that of a believer in the Church in our modern society. Follow these guidelines in creating your skit:

- Create a positive and compelling "dialogue with Saint Paul" skit that explains how the images or models of the Church contributed to the life of the early Church as well as the life of the Church today.
- Address some of the negative issues or images of the Church that existed with the early Church as well as with the Church today.
- The Saint Paul character must do the following:
  - Describe his experiences (both positive and negative) of communicating the Gospel in his world.
  - Give advice for communicating the Church's message today.
  - Talk about the models of the Church in his era and the role of the Holy Spirit in shaping the Church.
  - Describe his hopes for the Church and his concern about possible dangers to her growth, both then and now.
  - Pose questions to the interviewer about the Church today
- The interviewer must do the following:
  - Describe the positive and negative aspects of how the Church is perceived today.
  - Describe how the images of the Church are at work in the Church today.
  - Describe for Saint Paul what is similar and what is different about the Church since Saint Paul's experience of it.
  - Ask questions but also answer questions posed by Saint Paul.

# Rubric for Final Performance Tasks for Unit 1

| Criteria | 4 | 3 | 2 | 1 |
|---|---|---|---|---|
| **Assignment includes all items requested in the directions.** | Assignment not only includes all items requested, but they are completed above expectations. | Assignment includes all items requested. | Assignment includes more than half of the items requested. | Assignment includes less than half of the items requested. |
| **Assignment shows understanding of the concept *the media and society communicate mixed messages about the meaning of the Catholic Church.*** | Assignment shows unusually insightful understanding of this concept. | Assignment shows good understanding of this concept. | Assignment shows adequate understanding of this concept. | Assignment shows little understanding of this concept. |
| **Assignment shows understanding of the concept *the word* church *comes from the Greek and Latin for "convocation or assembly" but can also refer to a liturgical assembly, a local parish community, or the gathering of the faithful worldwide.*** | Assignment shows unusually insightful understanding of this concept. | Assignment shows good understanding of this concept. | Assignment shows adequate understanding of this concept. | Assignment shows little understanding of this concept. |
| **Assignment shows understanding of the concept *the Acts of the Apostles and the Pauline letters give us insight into the way the early Church understood itself.*** | Assignment shows unusually insightful understanding of this concept. | Assignment shows good understanding of this concept. | Assignment shows adequate understanding of this concept. | Assignment shows little understanding of this concept. |
| **Assignment shows understanding of the concept *the models of the Church illustrate its many dimensions and functions.*** | Assignment shows unusually insightful understanding of this concept. | Assignment shows good understanding of this concept. | Assignment shows adequate understanding of this concept. | Assignment shows little understanding of this concept. |
| **Assignment uses proper grammar and spelling.** | Assignment has no grammar or spelling errors. | Assignment has one grammar or spelling error. | Assignment has two grammar or spelling errors. | Assignment has more than two grammar or spelling errors. |

- Your skit can be performed live in class or can be videotaped and then brought to class. The dialogue does not need to be memorized (improvisational dialogue is encouraged), but you must submit a detailed, typed script.
- The purpose of the skit is to help the class to gain a deeper understanding of the Church's important role in the life of a culture (Saint Paul's or our own) that is not always sympathetic to the Catholic Christian faith.
- The skit must make reference to at least two biblical images of the Church as well as three models of the Church in both Saint Paul's era our modern era.
- The skit must have some kind of concluding idea or theme.
- You may include costumes, props, maps, music, and so on, to "hook" your audience. This shows ingenuity and creativity in helping us to remember the key ideas of the performance.

# Option 2: Saint Paul Writes a Blog to Church Members

You are to write a blog to demonstrate your understanding of the Church during Saint Paul's era. Writing as Saint Paul, you are to describe the events, conflict of ideas (models of the Church), and concerns of the Church and the assembly during the era of the early Church. Follow these guidelines in writing your blog:

- Write as if you are Saint Paul, describing the events, conflicts, and concerns of the Church and the assembly during the early Church in as much detail as is necessary to capture the spirit of the times and to demonstrate your learning during this unit.
- Create fictional usernames, along with picture icons, and blog back and forth with the characters about your (Saint Paul's) vision for the Church as well as their (other users') differing visions of the Church. Include elements of the five models of the Church throughout your blogs. (*Note: This is a pretend blog where you create the entire blogging session to demonstrate the knowledge you have gained from this unit.*)
- Include the following terms and demonstrate their meanings in your blog: *catholic, church, Christian, religion, spirituality,* and *assembly.*
- Conclude your blog with something Saint Paul might have written if he were blogging today.

# Vocabulary for Unit 1

**age of reason:**  The age at which a person can be morally responsible. This is generally regarded to be the age of seven.

**aspiration:**  A short prayer meant to be memorized and repeated throughout the day. The word comes from the Latin *aspirare*, "to breathe upon." In this way we can heed Saint Paul's injunction to pray without ceasing and continually turn our thoughts toward God.

**blasphemy:**  Speaking, acting, or thinking about God, Jesus Christ, the Virgin Mary, or the saints in a way that is irreverent, mocking, or offensive.

**Body of Christ:**  A term that when capitalized designates Jesus' Body in the Eucharist, or the entire Church, which is also referred to as the Mystical Body of Christ.

**catholic:**  Along with One, Holy, and Apostolic, *Catholic* is one of the four marks of the Church. *Catholic* means "universal." The Church is catholic in two senses. She is catholic because Christ is present in her and has given her the fullness of the means of salvation and also because she reaches throughout the world to all people.

**chalice:**  The cup used during the Mass that holds the wine before the Consecration and the Blood of Christ after the Consecration. It represents the cup used at the Last Supper and is a symbol of Jesus' sacrifice and eternal life.

**charism:**  A special gift or grace of the Holy Spirit given to an individual Christian or community, commonly for the benefit and building up of the entire Church.

**charismatic:**  The word refers to a person gifted with the charism or graces of the Holy Spirit such as healing, prophecy, and speaking in tongues. Because self-deception is always possible, the charisms claimed by such a person must be verified by the Church.

**community:**  A body of individuals that is unified.

**diocese:**  A specific community of believers under the leadership of a bishop, also known as a "particular" or "local" Church. It is usually determined on the basis of geography but may also be determined by language or culture.

**evangelization:**  The proclamation of the Good News of Jesus Christ through words and witness.

**Gentile:**  A non-Jewish person. In the Scriptures the Gentiles were the uncircumcised, those who did not honor the God of the Torah. In the New Testament, Saint Paul and other evangelists reached out to the Gentiles, baptizing them into the family of God.

**Hellenistic:**  Of or relating to Greek history, culture, or art after Alexander the Great.

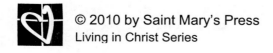

**infallibility:** The gift given by the Holy Spirit to the Pope and the bishops in union with him to teach on matters of faith and morals without error.

*katholikos:* Greek, meaning "universal" or "according to the whole."

*Kyriake:* Greek, meaning "the Lord's house."

**liturgy:** The Church's official, public, communal prayer. It is God's work, in which the People of God participate. The Church's most important liturgy is the Eucharist, or the Mass.

**Magisterium:** The Church's living teaching office, which consists of all bishops, in communion with the Pope.

**martyr:** A person who suffers death because of his or her beliefs. The Church has canonized many martyrs as saints.

**mystical:** Having a spiritual meaning or reality that is neither apparent to the senses nor obvious to the intelligence; the visible sign of the hidden reality of salvation.

**Sacred Chrism:** Perfumed olive oil that has been consecrated. It is used for anointing in the Sacraments of Baptism, Confirmation, and Holy Orders.

**Theology of the Body:** The name given to Pope John Paul II's teachings on the human body and sexuality delivered via 129 short lectures between September 1979 and November 1984.

**Transubstantiation:** In the Sacrament of the Eucharist, this is the name given to the action of changing the bread and wine into the Body and Blood of Jesus Christ.

**Trinitarian:** Of or relating to the Trinity or the doctrine of the Trinity.

**virtue:** A habitual and firm disposition to do good.

# What Are They Saying?

Name _____

Date _____

You are to explore and critique messages about the Church that are presented in print media. Use this handout to make notes about the articles you read. This will help you later when you present your findings.

**What Are They Saying?**

What is being said about the Catholic Church? What are the pictures that are included, if any? What is your first impression upon reading the article?

Who will be reading the article? What seems to be the purpose of the article?

From what perspective is the author writing? How do you know this?

What does the author of the article say about the Church? Do you share this understanding of the Church? Why or why not?

What is your response to the article? How does this article help you to clarify your understanding of the Church?

# New Testament Images of Church

For each of the eight New Testament images of Church listed in the first column, select one of the Scripture passages listed in the second column and then summarize in the third column what that Scripture passage says about that image. In the last column, list at least two qualities of the Church expressed in that image.

| New Testament Image of Church | Scripture Passage | Meaning of Scripture Passage | Qualities of the Church |
|---|---|---|---|
| **People of God** | Acts of the Apostles 10:34–36<br>1 Peter 2:9–10 | | |
| **Light and Salt** | Matthew 5:13–15 | | |
| **Body of Christ** | 1 Corinthians 12:12–20,27<br>Romans 12:4–5<br>Ephesians 4:11–16<br>Colossians 1:18<br>Galatians 3:27–28 | | |
| **Bride of Christ** | 1 Corinthians 6:15–17<br>2 Corinthians 11:2<br>Ephesians 5:25–26,29<br>Ephesians 5:31–32<br>Colossians 2:19 | | |

Document #: TX001440

| | | | |
|---|---|---|---|
| **Temple of God** | 2 Corinthians 6:16<br>1 Corinthians 3:16–17<br>Ephesians 2:21–22 | | |
| **Flock** | 1 Peter 5:2–4<br>John 10:1–11 | | |
| **Field / Olive Grove** | 1 Corinthians 3:7–9<br>Romans 11:17–18,24 | | |
| **Building / Household of God** | Acts of the Apostles 4:11<br>1 Peter 2:5–7<br>Galatians 4:6<br>Revelation 21:14<br>Ephesians 2:19–20 | | |

# Reflection Questions

1. What types of images or qualities of Church were most attractive to the early followers of Christ? Why would you say so? (Use the back of this sheet if necessary for your answer.)

2. What types of images or qualities of the Church are most attractive to you as a follower of Christ today? Why would you say so?

Document #: TX001440

# Models of the Church Chart

| Model | Institution |
|---|---|
| **Key Words** | teach, sanctify, govern<br>Magisterium<br>The Church authority comes from Apostolic Tradition. |
| **Signs and Functions** | Pope, bishops, priests<br>*Catechism of the Catholic Church*<br>Canon Law<br>diocesan directories |
| **Members** | all those who formally recognize themselves in relationship to an official Church community and Church teachings |
| **Connection to Jesus** | Matthew 16:13–20 |
| **Early Church** | Acts of the Apostles 6:1–7 |
| **Model** | Mystical Body / Communion |
| **Key Words** | People of God<br>fellowship<br>unity and diversity of gifts in community<br>Christ is the Head<br>Church is the Body |
| **Signs and Functions** | prayer groups<br>intimate relationship |
| **Members** | all who share in the body of Christ through the grace of the Holy Spirit |
| **Connection to Jesus** | John 15:5 |
| **Early Church** | Acts of the Apostles 4:32–37 |
| **Model** | Herald |
| **Key Words** | Word of God<br>conversion<br>witness<br>salvation |
| **Signs and Functions** | Bible studies<br>evangelization<br>missions<br>media |

Document #: TX001441

| | |
|---|---|
| **Members** | all those who give witness to their life in Christ and see the Word of God as key |
| **Connection to Jesus** | Matthew 28:16–20 |
| **Early Church** | Acts of the Apostles 2:37–41 |
| **Model** | Servant |
| **Key Words** | service to the world<br>dialogue<br>liberation<br>justice<br>peace<br>prophetic |
| **Signs and Functions** | hospitals<br>Saint Vincent de Paul Society<br>Catholic Campaign for Human Development<br>Habitat for Humanity<br>Catholic Relief Services |
| **Members** | all who serve the needs of others as Christ did;<br>"Whatever you did for one of these least brothers of mine, you did for me."<br>(Matthew 25:40) |
| **Connection to Jesus** | John 13:3–15 |
| **Early Church** | Acts of the Apostles 5:12–16 |
| **Model** | Sacrament |
| **Key Words** | grace<br>nourished by the Sacraments<br>"Be what you have received." |
| **Signs and Functions** | liturgy<br>light and salt for the world (to be a sign of Christ)<br>communal prayer<br>source of grace |
| **Members** | all who share in the liturgical life of the Church so as to be transformed by grace to be a sign of Christ in the world |
| **Connection to Jesus** | Luke 21:19–20 |
| **Early Church** | Acts of the Apostles 2:42–47 |

Chart adapted from notes provided by Dr. Philip Verhalen, STL, based on *Models of Church,* by Avery Dulles, SJ (Garden City, NY: Doubleday, 1974).

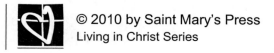

© 2010 by Saint Mary's Press
Living in Christ Series

Document #: TX001441

# Matching Quiz

## Models of the Church

Match each of the following statements with one of Dulles' five models of the Church.

**Institution**    **Mystical Communion**    **Herald**    **Servant**    **Sacrament**

1. _____ Jesus said, "Go, therefore, and make disciples of all nations" (Matthew 28:19).

2. _____ The Church is meant to be a visible manifestation, a sign of Christ in the world.

3. _____ After Jesus washed the disciples' feet, he told them, "I have given you a model to follow, so that as I have done for you, you should also do" (John 13:15).

4. _____ This model highlights the variety of people who make up the Church and emphasizes that it is the Spirit that makes us belong to one another.

5. _____ This model emphasizes the role of Church leadership to be clear in passing on Church teaching, governing the Church in love, and providing means for people to grow in holiness.

6. _____ A weakness of this model is that it could focus too much on its own relationships and not enough on outreach to others.

7. _____ Jesus said, "You are Peter, and upon this rock I will build my church" (Matthew 16:18).

8. _____ This model has a clear mission of bringing the Word of God to the world.

9. _____ This model focuses on justice, peace, and liberation as signs of the Kingdom of God.

10. _____ Jesus said: "I am the vine, you are the branches. Whoever remains in me and I in him will bear much fruit" (John 15:5).

© 2010 by Saint Mary's Press
Living in Christ Series

Document #: TX001442

# Key Events in Church History

- Acts of the Apostles
- Council of Constantinople
- Pope John Paul II
- Arian Controversy
- Council of Jerusalem
- the Crusades
- Saint Augustine
- Council of Nicaea
- Pope Leo XIII
- Avignon Papacy
- John Henry Newman
- *Dogmatic Constitution on the Church* (*Lumen Gentium*, 1964)
- *Baltimore Catechism*
- early persecutions
- Martin Luther
- Pope Benedict XVI
- Emperor Nero
- Saint Bernard of Clairvaux
- Epistles
- mendicant orders
- Book of Kells
- Essenes
- Papal Inquisition

- catacombs
- *filioque*
- Pentecost
- Saint Catherine of Siena
- Gospels
- Pope Pius XII
- Charlemagne
- Great Schism
- reformation
- suppression of Jesuits
- Gutenberg Bible
- Saint Columba
- Saint Hildegard of Bingen
- Saint Thomas Aquinas
- conversion of Paul
- Saint Jerome
- Council of Trent
- Constantine
- Ascension
- Vatican I
- Council of Chalcedon
- Pope John XXIII
- Vatican II

# Unit 1 Test

## Part 1: Multiple Choice

Write your answers in the blank spaces at the left.

1. _____ The Acts of the Apostles and the _____ letters give us insight into the way the early Church understood itself.

    A. Psalm
    B. Judaic
    C. Pauline
    D. Davidic

2. _____ The word _____ comes from the Greek and Latin for "convocation or assembly" but can also refer to a liturgical assembly, a local parish community, or the gathering of the faithful worldwide.

    A. liturgy
    B. church
    C. counsel
    D. diocese

3. _____ The _____ of the Church illustrate its many dimensions and functions.

    A. tenets
    B. dogma
    C. models
    D. hierarchy

4. _____ The _____ communicate mixed messages about the meaning of the Catholic Church.

    A. hymns and readings
    B. rules and regulations
    C. Vatican and Diocese
    D. media and society

5. _____ The _____ is the People of God.

    A. nation
    B. Church
    C. priesthood
    D. Scriptures

**6.** ____    The _____ is the Body of Christ.

   A. priest
   B. crucifix
   C. Church
   D. Bride

**7.** ____    _____ is the act of witnessing to the saving message of Christ through the sacrifice of one's life.

   A. Martyrdom
   B. Christianity
   C. Confirmation
   D. Treason

**8.** ____    As Catholics we are called to _____.

   A. sing
   B. pay taxes
   C. community
   D. avoid wine

**9.** ____    From all eternity God planned to form a(n) _____ as a means of drawing together the whole human race.

   A. banquet hall
   B. ark
   C. table of plenty
   D. church

**10.** ____    The Trinity is one God in three _____.

   A. houses
   B. acts
   C. pieces
   D. Persons

**11.** ____    The Greek term _____ means "universal" or "according to the whole."

   A. *ipsos*
   B. *heracles*
   C. *petros*
   D. *katholikos*

Document #: TX001444

**12.____** The term _____ has come to be associated with a particular way of being Christian that emphasizes the doctrines and practices of the early Church and the celebration of the Sacraments.

    **A.** Catholic
    **B.** Protestant
    **C.** devout
    **D.** Gnostic

**13. ____** The teachings recognized as central to Church teaching, defined by the Magisterium, and accorded the fullest weight and authority are called _____.

    **A.** Commandments
    **B.** CC & Rs
    **C.** prayers
    **D.** dogmas

**14.____** *Kyriake* is the Greek word for _____, meaning "the Lord's house."

    **A.** Psalm
    **B.** Heaven
    **C.** Throne
    **D.** Church

**15.____** The word _____ refers to a specific community of believers under the leadership of a bishop.

    **A.** club
    **B.** diocese
    **C.** fold
    **D.** fellowship

# Part 2: Matching

Match each statement in column 1 with a term from column 2. Write the letter that corresponds to your choice in the space provided. (*Note:* There are two extra items in column 2.)

## Column 1

**1.**_____ This term was first used by Saint Ignatius of Antioch in the second century. Today it refers to the members, the churches, the institutions, the hierarchy, the clergy, and the teachings of the Church founded by Jesus Christ and given to the Apostles.

**2.** _____ Also known as a "particular" or "local" Church, this is the regional community of believers, who commonly gather in parishes, under the leadership of a bishop.

**3.** _____ This is the Church's official, public, communal prayer. It is God's work, in which the People of God participate.

**4.** _____ The account of God's saving hand at work in human history and experience.

**5.** _____ The term refers to the entire community of God's People around the world.

**6.**_____ This term means "to represent, indicate, or typify beforehand; prefigure."

**7.**_____ This is a sacred text for both Christian and Jewish people.

**8.**_____ God called Israel his _____.

**9.**_____ When a person consciously and deliberately rejects a dogma of the Church.

**10.**_____ This is the word for God's promise to mankind.

## Column 2

**A.** heresy

**B.** foreshadow

**C.** Sacred Scriptures

**D.** Psalms

**E.** catholic

**F.** liturgy

**G.** covenant

**H.** Chosen People

**I.** Old Testament

**J.** diocese

**K.** church

**L.** Sacrament

# Part 3: Short Answer

Answer each of the following questions in paragraph form on a separate sheet of paper.

1.  Explain how God had planned to give the gift of Church to mankind from all time.

2.  Write about what a covenant with God means, and give at least two examples of mankind's Covenant with God.

3.  When Jesus instituted the Church, he called all people, not just the rich and the powerful. Explain how the Church is universal in light of Jesus' call.

# Unit 1 Test Answer Key

## Part 1: Multiple Choice

1. C
2. B
3. C
4. D
5. B
6. C
7. A
8. C
9. D
10. D
11. D
12. A
13. D
14. D
15. B

## Part 2: Matching

1. E
2. J
3. F
4. C
5. K
6. B
7. I
8. H
9. A
10. G

## Part 3: Short Answer

1. Calling together human beings is central to the Father's plan of salvation, as he wishes to gather us as his own People, the People of God, in order to save us. Jesus Christ, the only Son of God, who is himself fully God, established the Church when he proclaimed and ushered in the Kingdom of God. Even before the Church was instituted, the Father's eternal plan of calling together a holy people had already been taking shape in history. The Father's call to the people of Israel to enter into a covenant relationship with him was the clearest preparation for the Church.

2. A covenant is a solemn agreement between God and a human being in which mutual commitments are made. It is a promise. Examples are God's Covenant with Abraham (he would father a nation), God's Covenant with Noah (no more floods, with the rainbow as a sign), God's Covenant with Israel (the Chosen People of God), and Christ's Covenant with us (if we follow him, we will find eternal salvation).

3. Jesus' message was intended for all people. He directed his message to the poor, and proclaimed that the nations would be judged on how well they took care of people who were hungry and thirsty (see Matthew 25:31–46). Jesus also directed his message toward sinners, calling them to repentance and assuring them of the Father's great mercy. Jesus' followers were not the rich and powerful, but were fishermen. He told them they would now be fishers of men (see Mark 1:17). He told his followers that whatever they did for the least of his people, they did for him.

Document #: TX001445

# Unit 2   What Is the Origin of the Church?

## Overview

This unit helps the students to understand that the Catholic Church is not a creation of mankind but was instituted by the Holy Trinity: ordained by God the Father, founded by Jesus Christ the Son, and guided and empowered by the Holy Spirit.

## Key Understandings and Questions

Upon completing this unit, the students will have a deeper understanding of the following key concepts:

- Jesus instituted the Church to continue his mission; it is a community planned by God the Father, beginning with God's promise to Abraham.
- The Holy Spirit revealed the Church at Pentecost.
- The Holy Spirit inspired the Apostles' mission.
- The Holy Spirit gifts the Church for its mission and is present in and through it.

Upon completing the unit, the students will have answered the following questions:

- Did Jesus mean to found a Church?
- What happened at Pentecost?
- How were the Apostles brave enough to spread the Gospel after Jesus' death, Resurrection, and Ascension?
- What is the Holy Spirit's role in the Church today?

## Student Book Articles

This unit draws on articles from *The Church: Christ in the World Today* student book and incorporates them into the unit instruction. Whenever the teaching steps for the unit require the students to refer to or read an article from the student book, the following symbol appears in the margin: (⬛). The articles covered in the unit are from "Section 1: The Church: Christ's Continued Presence and Work in the World," and are as follows:

- "God's Call to Israel Foreshadows the Church" (article 2, pp. 13–14)
- "Christ Instituted the Church" (article 3, pp. 15–19)
- "Introducing the Holy Spirit" (article 4, pp. 21–23)
- "Pentecost: The Church Revealed to the World" (article 5, pp. 23–24)

- "The Meaning of Pentecost" (article 6, pp. 25–26)
- "The Holy Spirit Animates, Sanctifies, and Builds the Church" (article 7, pp. 27–29)
- "Life according to the Holy Spirit" (article 8, pp. 30–32)
- "The Holy Spirit Gifts the Church" (article 9, pp. 32–36)
- "The Mission of the Apostles" (article 10, pp. 39–42)
- "Spreading the Gospel" (article 11, pp. 42–44)

## How Will You Know the Students Understand?

The following resources will help you assess the students' understanding of the key concepts covered in this unit:

- handout "Final Performance Task Options for Unit 2" (Document #: TX001446)
- handout "Rubric for Final Performance Tasks for Unit 2" (Document #: TX001447)
- handout "Unit 2 Test" (Document #: TX001452)

## The Suggested Path to Understanding

This unit in the teacher guide provides you with one learning path to take with the students, to enable them to begin their study of Jesus by deepening their understanding of the Church. It is not necessary to use all the learning experiences provided in the unit; however, if you substitute other material from this course or your own material for some of the material offered here, be sure that you have covered all relevant facets of understanding and that you have not missed any skills or knowledge required for later units.

 **Step 1:** Preassess what the students already know about the early Church and the role of the Holy Spirit in the Church.

 **Step 2:** Follow this assessment by presenting to the students the handouts "Final Performance Task Options for Unit 2" (Document #: TX001446) and "Rubric for Final Performance Tasks for Unit 2" (Document #: TX001447).

 **Step 3:** Present the idea of covenants as God's promises to mankind as you help the students to understand that, from the beginning, God the Father had planned to have Jesus the Son found the Church.

 **Step 4:** Have the students create an advertisement about God's invitation to us: the call to abundant life.

| Apply | **Step 5:** Guide the students in creating movie posters announcing the coming of the Holy Spirit to reveal the Church at Pentecost. |

| Apply | **Step 6:** Investigate the Pentecost account, the effect the Holy Spirit had on the development of the early Church, and ways the Holy Spirit can be experienced today. |

| Perceive | **Step 7:** Conduct an all-play exercise illustrating the power and guidance of the Holy Spirit during the Apostles' mission to spread the Gospel. |

| Empathize | **Step 8:** Engage the students in a quest research exercise on the Council of Jerusalem. |

| Apply | **Step 9:** Lead the class in developing a comic book that illustrates Paul's missionary journeys and early Church expansion and a map of Paul's journeys. |

| Perceive | **Step 10:** Ask the students to translate the Gifts of the Holy Spirit into kid-friendly language and apply them to everyday life. |

| Understand | **Step 11:** Now that the students are closer to the end of the unit, make sure they are all on track with their final performance tasks, if you have assigned them. |

| Reflect | **Step 12:** Provide the students with a tool to use for reflecting about what they learned in the unit and how they learned. |

## Background for Teaching This Unit

Visit *smp.org/LivinginChrist* for additional information about these and other theological concepts taught in this unit:

- "The Holy Spirit" (Document #: TX001519)
- "Biblical Covenants" (Document #: TX001518)

The Web site also includes information on these and other teaching methods used in the unit:

- "Using the A to Z Method" (Document #: TX001520)
- "Using Final Performance Tasks to Assess Understanding" (Document #: TX001011)
- "Using Rubrics to Assess Work" (Document #: TX001012)

## Scripture Passages

Scripture is an important part of the Living in Christ series and is frequently used in the learning experiences for each unit. The Scripture passages featured in this unit are as follows:

- Acts of the Apostles 2:1–13 (the coming of the Spirit)
- Acts of the Apostles 2:14–42 (Peter's speech at Pentecost)
- Acts of the Apostles 9:1–30 (Saul's conversion)
- Acts of the Apostles 13:1–52 (the mission of Barnabas and Saul)
- Acts of the Apostles 15:1–41 (Council of Jerusalem)
- Acts of the Apostles, chapters 16–28 (the mission of Paul to the ends of the earth)
- 2 Corinthians 3:6 (the Spirit gives life)
- Genesis, chapter 15 (the Covenant with Abram)
- Isaiah 11:2 (the Spirit of the Lord)
- Romans 8:14–17 (children of God through adoption)

## Vocabulary

The student book and the teacher guide include the following key terms for this unit. To provide the students with a list of these terms and their definitions, download and print the handout "Vocabulary for Unit 2" (Document #: TX001448).

| | |
|---|---|
| animate | hierarchy |
| Ascension | Holy Spirit |
| charism | infallibility |
| charismatic | intercession |
| Communion | Magisterium |
| covenant | Pentecost |
| evangelization | petition |
| foreshadow | sanctify |
| Gentile | Trinitarian |
| Hellenistic | |

# Learning Experiences

Explain

## Step 1

*Preassess what the students already know about the early Church and the role of the Holy Spirit in the Church.*

This learning experience helps the students to explore what they already know about the early Church and the role of the Holy Spirit through identifying words that are associated with the early Church and the Holy Spirit.

1. Beginning with the student closest to you, assign each student a letter of the alphabet beginning with *A* and continuing in the order of the alphabet (you may chose to omit *Q* and *X*). If you have less than twenty-six students, assign the letters as directed and then allow the class to provide responses for the remaining letters. If you have more than twenty-six students, repeat letters for students.

2. Ask the students to stand. Beginning with the student assigned letter *A* (or *A1*), ask the students to share something they know about the early Church or the role of the Holy Spirit in the Church that begins with the letter they have been assigned. The students may sit down after they complete their turn.

   Here are some examples of words the students might name:

   - *A:* **ashes** (In the early Church, catechumens received ashes on Ash Wednesday [the first day of Lent] in preparation for their Baptism, which occurred at the Easter Vigil.)
   - *B:* **Baptism** (In the early Church, catechumens were welcomed into the Church at the Easter Vigil and received all three Sacraments of Christian Initiation at the same time.)
   - *C:* **catacombs** (In the early Church, Christians hid in catacombs to avoid being martyred for their faith.)
   - *H:* **hierarchy** (In the early Church, as is true today, the Holy Spirit helped to guide the formation and leadership of the Church.)
   - *W:* **worship** (In the early Church, the Mass was informal and resembled an *agape* service.)

3. If a student struggles to come up with a word for her or his letter, allow the class to offer suggestions. You may also choose to allow the students to identify additional words that begin with an assigned letter after they have provided the first word.

4. Do not comment on the information the students share. Rather, use this learning experience to determine the type and depth of information you must teach in this unit, based on the knowledge level the students demonstrate. Any information that must be corrected or elaborated upon can be built into future lesson plans.

## Step 2

*Follow this assessment by presenting to the students the handouts "Final Performance Task Options for Unit 2" (Document #: TX001446) and "Rubric for Final Performance Tasks for Unit 2" (Document #: TX001447).*

This unit provides you with two ways to assess that the students have a deep understanding of the most important concepts in the unit: creating a poster presentation that emphasizes the ongoing role of the Holy Spirit in the life of the Church or creating a children's storybook that tells the story of the early Church. Refer to "Using Final Performance Tasks to Assess Understanding" (Document #: TX001011) and "Using Rubrics to Assess Work" (Document #: TX001012) at *smp.org/LivinginChrist* for background information.

1. Prepare for this learning experience by downloading and printing the handouts "Final Performance Task Options for Unit 2" (Document #: TX001446) and "Rubric for Final Performance Tasks for Unit 2" (Document #: TX001447), one of each for each student.

2. Distribute the handouts. Give the students a choice as to which performance task they choose and add more options if you so choose.

3. Review the directions, expectations, and rubric in class, allowing the students to ask questions. You may want to say something to this effect:

   ➤ You may work with no more than two other people on option 1. If you want to work on your own, you may choose either option 1 or option 2.

   ➤ Near the end of the unit, you will have one full class period to work on your final performance task. Please keep in mind, however, that you should be working on this task throughout the course of the unit. Please do not wait until this class period to begin work on your final performance task.

### Teacher Note

You will want to assign due dates for the final performance tasks.

If you have done these performance tasks, or very similar ones, with students before, place examples of this work in the classroom. During this introduction explain how each is a good example of what you are looking for, for different reasons. This allows the students to concretely understand that there is not only one way to succeed.

4. Explain the types of tools and knowledge the students will gain throughout the unit so that they can successfully complete the final performance task.

5. Answer questions to clarify the end point toward which the unit is headed. Remind the students as the unit progresses that each learning experience builds the knowledge and skills they will need to show you that they understand how Jesus instituted the Church to continue his mission and the role of the Holy Spirit both in the early Church and in the Church today.

Articles
2, 3

# Step 3

*Present the idea of covenants as God's promises to mankind as you help the students to understand that, from the beginning, God the Father had planned to have Jesus the Son found the Church.*

1. Prepare for this learning experience by gathering blank sheets of paper and pens or pencils, one of each for each student.

2. As background, have the students read student book articles 2 and 3, "God's Call to Israel Foreshadows the Church" and "Christ Instituted the Church." Also remind the students to bring their Bibles to class. There is a PowerPoint available at *smp.org/LivinginChrist* that you can use to explore this topic with your students.

3. Begin by explaining the following points:

   ➤ A covenant is a formal alliance or agreement made by God with individuals, communities, or humanity in general. Two examples of biblical covenants are the Covenant between God and Noah, in which God promised never to destroy the earth with a flood again, and the Covenant between God and Abram, in which God made a Covenant with Abram that he would bless Abram's descendants, making them more numerous than the stars. This was an unconditional Covenant, granted by God to Abram without any action required on Abram's part.

   ➤ God also made a Covenant with the nation of Israel when he spoke to Moses on Mount Sinai, setting the nation of Israel apart from all other nations as God's Chosen People, if they would be obedient to his Divine Law. This is a conditional Covenant; it remains true only if Israel is obedient to God. If Israel disobeys, God will punish the people. The Mosaic Covenant is also referred to as the Old Covenant.

   ➤ The Old Covenant was replaced by the New Covenant in Christ. In the New Covenant, Jesus Christ promised that his sacrifice on the Cross would atone for the sins of all who put their faith in him.

4. Next, have the students form pairs. Distribute a sheet of paper and a pen or pencil to each student, and then direct the pairs to work together to find the following Bible passages and make notes about what sort of promises God makes, and what covenants he enters into with specific people:

- Genesis 9:11
- Genesis, chapter 15
- Exodus, chapters 19–24
- Luke 22:20
- 1 Corinthians 11:25
- 2 Corinthians 3:6
- Hebrews 8:8,13; 9:15; 12:24
- Matthew 26:28

5. Have each pair brainstorm other covenants that have been entered into throughout history. Have each pair come up with examples of two covenants they have made in their lives. Then have them discuss whether these were conditional or unconditional covenants, and how that status affected the value of those promises in their minds.

6. Gather the students back together and ask for feedback about what God's promises have been to mankind and how mankind has responded to those promises.

7. You may also choose to ask for feedback about personal covenants the students have entered and how those have fared. Remind the students to share only what is appropriate and safe to share.

Article 4

 Interpret

## Step 4

*Have the students create an advertisement about God's invitation to us: the call to abundant life.*

In this learning experience, the students consider ways God's invitation comes to us in the ordinary events of our lives and then create an advertisement that reflects that invitation.

1. Prepare for this learning experience by gathering sheets of blank paper, two for each pair of students.

2. As background have the students read student book article 4, "Introducing the Holy Spirit."

3. Begin by leading a lecture and discussion using the following talking points:

➤ What is an invitation?

➤ How do we respond? Why?

➤ We are called into life through our birth.

➤ Baptism and Confirmation and vocation are also calls to life. How so?

➤ Community is vital (the Trinity was made in God's image: relationship, interdependence).

➤ God, through Jesus, enters human history and enters creation. Why? So that we might become fully alive.

➤ The Church invites each of us to abundant life. How?

➤ Our "yes" to God's invitation transforms us. How?

4. Have the students form pairs. Distribute two sheets of paper to each pair. Direct them to use the first sheet to write a script for a 30-second radio commercial that demonstrates how God is inviting young people their age to a full life. The script should have at least two speaking parts and should present circumstances that are a part of the lives of young people (e.g., illness of a family member, struggling student, volunteer opportunities, enjoying the companionship of a new friend).

5. On the second sheet of paper, the students should each write a brief essay identifying specific aspects of their lives. Have them address the following questions:

➤ How is God inviting you through these specific circumstances right now?

➤ How are you accepting the invitation?

6. Have the students perform their scripts for the class or make recordings to share with the class.

Articles
5, 6,
7

## Step 5

*Guide the students in creating movie posters announcing the coming of the Holy Spirit to reveal the Church at Pentecost.*

1. Prepare for this learning experience by gathering sheets of newsprint, one for each small group of two or three, as well as markers, magazines (for cutting out images), scissors, and glue.

2. As background have the students read student book articles 5–7, "Pentecost: The Church Revealed to the World," "The Meaning of Pentecost," and "The Holy Spirit Animates, Sanctifies, and Builds the Church."

3. Divide the class into small groups of two or three and assign each group to create a "Coming Soon" movie poster for Pentecost and the founding of the Church. Explain that the movie posters should include the following:

- image of wind and tongues of fire
- the phrases "founding of the Church" and "gifts of languages"
- comments from reviewers praising Pentecost and the founding of the Church

4. Distribute the art supplies and direct the small groups to be as creative as possible in creating their movie posters. They can draw images, cut out images from the magazines, or download images if computers and printers are available.

5. When the students have completed their movie posters, have them share them with the class, explaining their ideas and visions. You may choose to post the posters around the room for the remainder of the unit.

> **Teacher Note**
>
> You may want to bring in movie posters (video rental stores often have posters they will give away) or print old movie posters from the Internet for examples. Old horror or science-fiction movie posters are good for showing over-the-top advertising, as are posters extolling the virtues of movies in CinemaScope and Technicolor.

Articles
8, 9

Apply

## Step 6

*Investigate the Pentecost account, the effect the Holy Spirit had on the development of the early Church, and ways the Holy Spirit can be experienced today.*

1. Prepare for this learning experience by downloading and printing the handout "The Power of the Holy Spirit in the Acts of the Apostles" (Document #: TX001449), one for each student.

2. As background have the students read student book articles 8 and 9, "Life according to the Holy Spirit" and "The Holy Spirit Gifts the Church." Remind the students to bring their Bibles to class.

3. Begin by inviting the students to share what they know about Pentecost and the role of the Holy Spirit in the development of the early Church.

4. When the students have shared what they know about Pentecost and the role of the Holy Spirit in the early Church, have the class read aloud Acts of the Apostles 2:1–41. You may either assign parts to students ahead of time or simply have each student read one or two verses.

5. Explain that in the reading there are three signs of the coming of the Holy Spirit at Pentecost: fire, wind, and new languages. Have the students identify what qualities each of these elements possesses that would make it a

good sign of the Holy Spirit. Here are some possible answers the students might come up with:

- Fire, wind, and language are all powerful, uncontrollable forces; likewise, the Holy Spirit is powerful and uncontrollable.

- Fire, wind, and language all have the potential for promoting life or causing harm; likewise, the Holy Spirit is meant to be a source of life, but ignoring the Spirit will cause harm. All these forces are ultimately sources of transformation; the Holy Spirit transforms the disciples into witnesses for Christ.

- Fire, wind, and language all have Old Testament connections to God: the burning bush, the wind that blew over the formless waste of creation, the tiny whisper that spoke to Elijah in the cave. In this account these signs take on newer meanings of the Spirit's power.

6. Next, have a volunteer read Acts of the Apostles 1:8 aloud. Then ask the students the following question:

   ➤ What does Jesus say about the coming of the Holy Spirit?

   *"You will receive power when the Holy Spirit comes on you" (Acts of the Apostles 1:8).*

7. Now pose the following questions to the class:

   ➤ What does the world see as powerful?

   *money, fame, weapons, education, beauty, political influence*

   ➤ What is the power or strength of the Holy Spirit?

   *love, faith, God*

8. Share the following with the class:

   ➤ The Holy Spirit's power, like fire, wind, and language, is meant to transform our lives with the life of the Risen Christ. In fact, each Pentecost element can correspond to an aspect of our lives that the Holy Spirit can transform: the fire can represent our inner life, the wind can represent the world around us, and the new languages can represent our relationships with others. Let us examine how the Spirit transformed the followers of Jesus in the Acts of the Apostles on each of three levels and where we might see these transformations happening in our world today.

9. Divide the class into small groups of three and make sure each small group has a Bible available. Distribute the handout and have each member of the group fill out one of the sections on the first part—power of the Spirit in our inner life (fire), power of the Spirit around us (wind), and power of the Spirit in relationships (new languages)—based on the Acts of the Apostles reading. Once each student has completed his or her section, the group members should then collaborate to complete the handout together.

10. When all the groups have completed the first part of the handout, ask the students the following questions and invite their reflections for a few minutes:

> ➤ Does the Holy Spirit still move people today in ways similar to those of the Acts of the Apostles? In other words, are people still transformed in their inner lives (fire), are people still sensing the Spirit in the world (wind), and are people still experiencing the Spirit in relationships (new languages)? Explain.

11. Now direct the students to individually refer back to the handout and select one of the three areas—fire, wind, or new languages—and then address in writing the question about the Spirit's power in the world today. Instruct the students to write directly on their handouts.

Articles 10, 11

Perceive

## Step 7

*Conduct an all-play exercise illustrating the power and guidance of the Holy Spirit during the Apostles' mission to spread the Gospel.*

In this exercise the students have a hands-on experience listening to the guidance of the Holy Spirit as they work their way through the world and try to spread the Good News like the Apostles did when building the early Church.

1. As background for this learning experience, have the students review student book articles 10 and 11, "The Mission of the Apostles" and "Spreading the Gospel," which they read in unit 1.

2. Begin by assigning the following roles to six volunteers:

   - Holy Spirit (one student)
   - Apostle (one student)
   - disciples (four students)

3. Have the Apostle stand at one end of the room and the Holy Spirit at the other. Between them, place chairs and desks in an obstacle course, through which the Apostle and the disciples will have to make their way.

4. Blindfold the Apostle and the disciples and station the four disciples at the side of the obstacle course in various spots. Direct the remaining students to stand along the course and down at the end.

5. Share the following instructions with the class:

> ➤ The object of the game is for the Holy Spirit to guide the Apostle and the disciples to the Church (the end of the room where the Holy Spirit is standing) by directing the Apostle and disciples through the obstacle

course with spoken instructions. As the Apostle works his or her way through the course, the Holy Spirit will give guidance about navigating the obstacles, and also telling the Apostle when to reach out to touch a disciple.

➤ When a disciple is touched, she or he steps onto the course with the Apostle and follows along, listening to the voice of the Holy Spirit.

➤ Students who are positioned along the way and at the end now become the voice of the world, trying to lead the Apostle and disciples astray, not by yelling but simply by speaking and distracting those on the course. (One effective way to do this is to have one or more students call the disciples by name and convince the disciples to listen to them, as they are the voice of the disciples' conscience.)

➤ The exercise ends when the Apostle and all four disciples have found their way to the Holy Spirit.

6. When the students finish the exercise, ask the Apostle and disciples what the experience was like for them. Then invite the rest of the class to share what they feel the exercise demonstrates about how the Holy Spirit led the early Church and how the Holy Spirit calls to us today. Ask the students to share what "voices" in the world they think are drowning out the voice of the Holy Spirit.

7. Conclude by explaining that it can be challenging to follow Christ and the Holy Spirit when all the voices in the world around us are drowning out their guidance. We have to be attentive to listening to Christ and the Holy Spirit. Before moving on to the next step, you may wish to invite the students to silent reflection and prayer.

**Empathize**

## Step 8

*Engage the students in a quest research exercise on the Council of Jerusalem.*

Conducting a quest means seeking information, typically by researching an idea, concept, or fact. Quest activities can be utilized in a variety of ways and formats and can be facilitated by the use of the Internet, library, interviews, scavenger hunts, or any other means of gathering information regarding a topic.

1. Explain to the students that they will be conducting a quest research exercise on the Council of Jerusalem. They are to work in pairs or groups of three to uncover as much accurate information as possible about the Council of Jerusalem.

2. Explain that each pair or group is to, at a minimum, identify the following:

- date and location of the Council of Jerusalem
- topics and decisions addressed by the Council
- key people of the Council and their positions on the topics and decisions

3. When the students have completed the research, they are to create a skit portraying the Council of Jerusalem. Each student in each group is responsible for choosing a character from the Council that he or she would like to portray in the skit.

4. Allow each pair or small group to perform its skit for the class. When all the skits have been performed, have the class review the key points of their research:

- date and location of the Council of Jerusalem
- topics and decisions addressed by the Council
- key people of the Council and their positions on the topics and decisions

5. For homework have each student turn in ten typed bullet points about his or her character. (This may or may not be a graded assignment; you decide.)

> **Teacher Note**
>
> If the students have access to the Internet in the classroom or in a computer lab, this exercise can be conducted during class time; otherwise, it should be completed outside of the class as a homework assignment.

**Apply**

## Step 9

Lead the class in developing a comic book that illustrates Paul's missionary journeys and early Church expansion and a map of Paul's journeys.

This is a way for the students to familiarize themselves with the geography and culture of the Greco-Roman world in which the Church was first established. After they have created the comic book, the students will make a map detailing Paul's journeys. There is a PowerPoint available at *smp.org/LivinginChrist* that you can use to explore this topic with your students.

1. Prepare for this learning experience by downloading and printing copies of the handout "Paul, The Missionary Adventurer: The Comic Book Version" (Document #: TX001450), one for each student. Also be sure that each student has a copy of the New Testament and maps of Paul's missionary journeys (located in the colored index section of *The Catholic Youth Bible®*), as well as several sheets of blank paper and black or blue pens and pencils for drawing their comics and writing out answers to reflection questions.

2. Distribute the handout, which has the directions for creating the pages of the comic book. Review the directions with the students.

3. Assign sections of the Acts of the Apostles as identified on the handout to each student.

4. Distribute the paper, pens, and pencils, and give the students 10 to 15 minutes to create their comic books according to the sections they were assigned. Encourage the students to be creative. It is important to emphasize, for students who are not artistic, that the important part of the comic book is the story; they will not be graded on their artwork.

5. When the students have completed their assigned sections, photocopy all the pages and assemble them into a book (or scan the drawings and create a digital copy of the book that the students can download). Distribute the copies of the comic book to the class or display the digital comic book on a projector.

6. Before reading the comic book as a class, write the following reflection questions on the board:

   • What model of the Church seems to dominate in the early Church? Explain.

   • What successes does the early Church experience, and why and how do they occur?

   • What struggles does the early Church experience, and why and how do they occur?

7. Now, together as a class, read the students' comic book account of Paul's journeys.

8. Refer to the reflection questions on the board and invite the students to share in their responses.

9. As a final reflection, ask the students to write out answers to the following questions:

   ➤ What are two successes of the Church today that are similar to successes of the early Church? Explain.

   ➤ What are two struggles of the Church today that are similar to struggles of the early Church? Explain.

## Step 10

*Ask the students to translate the Gifts of the Holy Spirit into kid-friendly language and apply them to everyday life.*

1. Prepare for this learning experience by downloading and printing copies of the handout "Gifts of the Holy Spirit" (Document #: TX001451), one for each student. Remind the students to bring their Bibles to class.

2. Begin by having volunteers read aloud Isaiah 11:1–3 and 1 Corinthians 12:27–31. Ask the rest of the students to follow along in their own Bibles.

3. Distribute the handout and direct the students to complete it individually.

4. When all the students have completed the handout, have them each pair with another student and share their answers.

5. Now gather the class together and invite volunteers to share their answers. Allow for any questions the students might have. Conclude by emphasizing that the Gifts of the Holy Spirit produce virtue in a person's life (fruit of the Holy Spirit).

## Step 11

*Now that the students are closer to the end of the unit, make sure they are all on track with their final performance tasks, if you have assigned them.*

If possible, allow 50 to 60 minutes for the students to ask questions about the tasks and to continue working on them.

1. Remind the students to bring to class any work they have already prepared or completed so that they can work on it during the time allotted. If necessary, reserve the library, computer lab, or media center so the students can do any book or online research. Download and print the handouts "Final Performance Task Options for Unit 2" (Document #: TX001446) and "Rubric for Final Performance Tasks for Unit 2" (Document #: TX001447). Review the final performance task options, answer questions, and ask the students to choose one if they have not already done so.

2. Provide some class time for the students to work on their performance tasks. This then allows you to work with the students who need additional guidance with the project.

**Reflect**

# Step 12

*Provide the students with a tool to use for reflecting about what they learned in the unit and how they learned.*

This learning experience provides the students with an excellent opportunity to reflect on how their understandings of God and the Trinity have developed throughout the unit.

1. To prepare for this learning experience, download and print the handout "Learning about Learning" (Document #: TX001159; see Appendix), one for each student.

2. Distribute the handout, and give the students about 15 minutes to answer the questions quietly. Invite them to share any reflections they have about the content they learned as well as their insights into the way they learned.

# Final Performance Task Options for Unit 2

## Important Information for Both Options

The following are the main ideas you are to understand from this unit. They should appear in this final performance task so your teacher can assess whether you learned the most essential content:

- Jesus instituted the Church to continue his mission; it is a community planned by God the Father, beginning with God's promise to Abraham.

- The Holy Spirit revealed the Church at Pentecost.

- The Holy Spirit inspired the Apostles' mission.

- The Holy Spirit gifts the Church for its mission and is present in and through it.

## Option 1: The Spirit Lives!

You are a member of the newly confirmed whose continued participation in the parish youth group is to share what you have learned in your Confirmation preparation with those just beginning the process. You are to create a poster presentation that emphasizes the ongoing role of the Holy Spirit in the life of the Church that will open conversation among a group of twelve to fifteen teens who are preparing for the Sacrament of Confirmation. Your goal is to help these teens to understand that the role of the Holy Spirit continues from the early Church through today. Follow these guidelines in creating your poster presentation:

- Create an outline of key points to cover in the presentation.

- Incorporate quotations, pictures, symbols, and diagrams to give your audience a visual representation of your key points.

- Write two open-ended questions to foster communication among the members of the group and to give them an opportunity to develop a deeper understanding of the role of the Holy Spirit in the life of the Church.

- Write a three-paragraph personal reflection on each of your questions.

Document #: TX001446

# Option 2: History of the Early Church

## Children's Storybook

Create a children's storybook to demonstrate your understanding of what you have learned from this unit regarding the early Church, the role of the Holy Spirit in the early Church, and the significance of the Council of Jerusalem. Follow these guidelines in creating your storybook:

- Create three five-page chapters with text and a picture on each page.

- Include a cover page (title and your name), dedication page, and back cover page.

- Include citations for any quoted material (i.e., Scripture passages or quotations from the *Catechism of the Catholic Church*).

© 2010 by Saint Mary's Press
Living in Christ Series                                           Document #: TX001446

# Rubric for Final Performance Tasks for Unit 2

| Criteria | 4 | 3 | 2 | 1 |
|---|---|---|---|---|
| **Assignment includes all items requested in the directions.** | Assignment not only includes all items requested, but they are completed above expectations. | Assignment includes all items requested. | Assignment includes more than half of the items requested. | Assignment includes less than half of the items requested. |
| **Assignment shows understanding of the concept *Jesus instituted the Church to continue his mission; it is a community planned by God the Father, beginning with God's promise to Abraham.*** | Assignment shows unusually insightful understanding of this concept. | Assignment shows good understanding of this concept. | Assignment shows adequate understanding of this concept. | Assignment shows little understanding of this concept. |
| **Assignment shows understanding of the concept *the Holy Spirit revealed the Church at Pentecost.*** | Assignment shows unusually insightful understanding of this concept. | Assignment shows good understanding of this concept. | Assignment shows adequate understanding of this concept. | Assignment shows little understanding of this concept. |
| **Assignment shows understanding of the concept *the Holy Spirit inspired the Apostles' mission.*** | Assignment shows unusually insightful understanding of this concept. | Assignment shows good understanding of this concept. | Assignment shows adequate understanding of this concept. | Assignment shows little understanding of this concept. |
| **Assignment shows understanding of the concept *the Holy Spirit gifts the Church for its mission and is present in and through it.*** | Assignment shows unusually insightful understanding of this concept. | Assignment shows good understanding of this concept. | Assignment shows adequate understanding of this concept. | Assignment shows little understanding of this concept. |
| **Assignment uses proper grammar and spelling.** | Assignment has no grammar or spelling errors. | Assignment has one grammar or spelling error. | Assignment has two grammar or spelling errors. | Assignment has more than two grammar or spelling errors. |

© 2010 by Saint Mary's Press
Living in Christ Series

# Vocabulary for Unit 2

**animate:** To give life to.

**Ascension:** The "going up" into Heaven of the Risen Christ forty days after his Resurrection.

**charism:** A special gift or grace of the Holy Spirit given to an individual Christian or community, commonly for the benefit and building up of the entire Church.

**charismatic:** The word refers to a person gifted with the charism or graces of the Holy Spirit such as healing, prophecy, and speaking in tongues. Because self-deception is always possible, the charisms claimed by such a person must be verified by the Church.

**Communion:** Refers to receiving the Body and Blood of Christ. In general, your companionship and union with Jesus and other baptized Christians in the Church. This union has its origin and high point in the celebration of the Eucharist. In this sense the deepest vocation of the Church is Communion.

**covenant:** A personal, solemn promise of faithful love that involves mutual commitments and creates a sacred relationship.

**disciples:** The general term for any student or follower of a particular teacher. In the New Testament, the disciples are understood as the seventy-two who received instruction from Jesus. In modern usage, the term is generally applied to all the baptized.

**evangelization:** The proclamation of the Good News of Jesus Christ through words and witness.

**foreshadow:** To represent or prefigure a person before his or her life or an event before it occurs.

**Gentile:** A non-Jewish person. In the Scriptures the Gentiles were the uncircumcised, those who did not honor the God of the Torah. In the New Testament, Saint Paul and other evangelists reached out to the Gentiles, baptizing them into the family of God.

**Hellenistic:** Of or relating to Greek history, culture, or art after Alexander the Great.

**hierarchy:** In general, the line of authority in the Church; more narrowly, the Pope and the bishops, as successors of the Apostles, in their authoritative roles as leaders of the Church.

**Holy Spirit:** The Third Person of the Blessed Trinity, understood as the perfect love between God the Father, and the Son, Jesus Christ, who inspires, guides, and sanctifies the life of believers.

**infallibility:** The gift given by the Holy Spirit to the Pope and the bishops in union with him to teach on matters of faith and morals without error.

**intercession:** A prayer on behalf of another person or group.

**Magisterium:** The Church's living teaching office, which consists of all bishops, in communion with the Pope.

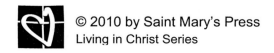

**Pentecost:**  The fiftieth day following Easter, which commemorates the descent of the Holy Spirit on the early Apostles and disciples.

**petition:**  A prayer form in which one asks God for help and forgiveness.

**sanctify, sanctification:**  To make holy; sanctification is the process of becoming closer to God and growing in holiness, taking on the righteousness of Jesus Christ with the gift of sanctifying grace.

**Trinitarian:** Of or relating to the Trinity or the doctrine of the Trinity.

Document #: TX001448

# The Power of the Holy Spirit in Acts of the Apostles

Refer to the New Testament to complete the parts of the chart that refer to the sections of Acts of the Apostles.

| Power of the Holy Spirit | Acts of the Apostles | Effect of the Holy Spirit in Acts of the Apostles | Effect of the Holy Spirit Today |
|---|---|---|---|
| **The "fire": the Spirit in the inner life** | 4:8,31<br><br>5:32<br><br>6:10<br><br>16: 6,7 | | |
| **The "wind": the Spirit around communities and in the world** | 6:3,5,10<br><br>8:29,40<br><br>10:19,44–47<br><br>11:12–16<br><br>15:8 | | |
| **The "new languages": being led by the Spirit in relationships** | 2:14,33<br><br>10:38<br><br>11:27<br><br>13:2<br><br>20:23<br><br>21:11 | | |

After reviewing the experiences of the Holy Spirit in Acts of the Apostles and filling in the above chart, select one of the three areas of the Holy Spirit's effect (inner life, world around us, or relationships) and give an example of where you believe the Spirit is at work today and explain why.

Living in Christ Series

Document #: TX001449

# Paul, the Missionary Adventurer: The Comic Book Version

You will be assigned one (or two) of the following passages from Acts of the Apostles to work with. After reading your assigned passage, you will create a comic book or graphic novel illustrating Paul's missionary journey.

| | | |
|---|---|---|
| Acts of the Apostles 9:1–22 | Acts of the Apostles 17:16–34 | Acts of the Apostles 23:1–11 |
| Acts of the Apostles 9:23–30 | Acts of the Apostles 18:1–28 | Acts of the Apostles 23:12–35 |
| Acts of the Apostles 13:1–12 | Acts of the Apostles 19:1–20 | Acts of the Apostles 24:1–27 |
| Acts of the Apostles 13:13–52 | Acts of the Apostles 19:21–40 | Acts of the Apostles 25:1–12 |
| Acts of the Apostles 14:1–18 | Acts of the Apostles 20:1–12 | Acts of the Apostles 25:13–27 |
| Acts of the Apostles 14:19–28 | Acts of the Apostles 20:13–38 | Acts of the Apostles 26:1–32 |
| Acts of the Apostles 15:1–41 | Acts of the Apostles 21:1–26 | Acts of the Apostles 27:1–44 |
| Acts of the Apostles 16:1–24 | Acts of the Apostles 21:27–40 | Acts of the Apostles 28:1–10 |
| Acts of the Apostles 16:25–40 | Acts of the Apostles 22:1–21 | Acts of the Apostles 28:11–31 |
| Acts of the Apostles 17:1–15 | Acts of the Apostles 22:22–30 | |

Follow these guidelines to create your comic book or graphic novel:

- Read the assigned section(s) and write a brief summary of the main action in these verses.

- Draw a ½-inch border around the edge of one sheet of paper.

- Fold the paper into quarters and then unfold it and lay it flat.

- Write the chapter and verse of your assigned passage in the upper right corner of the paper.

- In each quadrant of the paper, draw or sketch the main action of your section, adding appropriate dialogue or commentary in each panel. Stick figures are acceptable. Make your drawings heavy and dark so they photocopy well. Do not draw in the border area.

- Submit the booklet upon completion, with your name clearly written on it.

© 2010 by Saint Mary's Press
Living in Christ Series

Document #: TX001450

# Gifts of the Holy Spirit

Name_____ Date_____

The Gifts of the Holy Spirit are graces given to us by the Holy Spirit to help us to respond to God's call to holiness. They empower humanity with grace, power, and tools that support spiritual growth, happiness, and the wisdom to build just societies. In ancient times the Gifts of the Holy Spirit were recognized as understanding, knowledge, counsel, piety, fortitude, wisdom, and fear of the Lord.

On the lines in the chart below, write words or phrases to explain each of the seven Gifts of the Holy Spirit. Use language that is part of your own vocabulary.

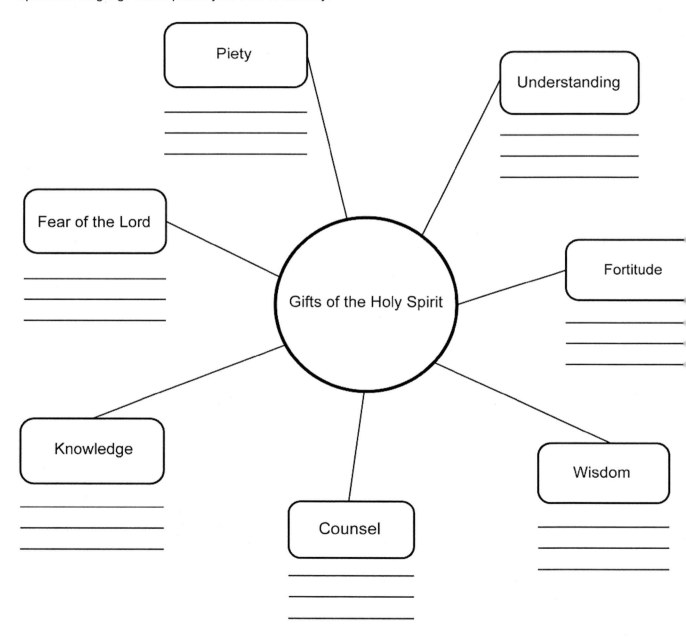

# Unit 2 Test

## Part 1: True or False

Write *true* or *false* in the space next to each statement.

1. _____ *Ekklesia* is the New Testament Greek word for *Christ*.

2. _____ *Diocese* is another word for *parish*.

3. _____ Even before the Church was instituted, God had an eternal plan for calling together a holy people.

4. _____ Once Christ was born, the Old Testament no longer had any value.

5. _____ The Scriptures are God's revelation of himself to mankind.

6. _____ God promised Moses that he would father a great nation, Israel.

7. _____ A covenant is a land lease between Israelites and Egyptians.

8. _____ God gave the Israelites the Ten Commandments on Mount Sinai.

9. _____ Jesus Christ was a Jew.

10. _____ Jesus' message of salvation was intended for Israelites only.

11. _____ Jesus' listeners learned about the Kingdom not only from his words but also from his actions.

12. _____ The Epistles are the wives of the Apostles.

13. _____ Saint Paul was the first Pope, given the role by Jesus.

14. _____ "Upon this rock I will build my Church" (Matthew 16:18), said Jesus, referring to Peter.

15. _____ The choice of the Twelve Apostles reflects the Twelve Tribes of Israel, God's Chosen People.

16. _____ Jesus called the most talented and powerful people to follow him.

17. _____ The Cardinal of Cologne sits in the Chair of Saint Peter.

18. _____ Jesus was assumed into Heaven during the Assumption.

19. _____ The Apostles were to become fishers of men (see Mark 1:17).

20. _____ Jesus established the Church through his preaching: "This is the time of fulfillment. The kingdom of God is at hand" (Mark 1:15).

# Part 2: Definitions

Define each of the following terms in a complete sentence or two on a separate sheet of paper.

hierarchy

ecumenism

redemption

covenant

Pentecost

Transubstantiation

liturgy

heresy

Jesus Christ

sanctify

virtue

# Part 3: Short Answer

Answer each of the following questions in paragraph form on a separate sheet of paper.

1.   Describe the Holy Spirit.

2.   Describe what happened on the day of Pentecost.

3.   How do the events at Pentecost contrast with the Tower of Babel?

# Unit 2 Test Answer Key

## Part 1: True or False

1. False
2. False
3. True
4. False
5. True
6. False
7. False

8. True
9. True
10. False
11. True
12. False
13. False
14. True

15. True
16. False
17. False
18. False
19. True
20. True

## Part 2: Definitions

**hierarchy:** In general, the line of authority in the Church; more narrowly, the Pope and the bishops, as successors of the Apostles, in their authoritative roles as leaders of the Church.

**ecumenism:** The movement to restore unity among all Christians.

**redemption:** From the Latin *redemptio,* meaning "a buying back"; referring, in the Old Testament, to Yahweh's deliverance of Israel and, in the New Testament, to Christ's deliverance of all Christians from the forces of sin.

**covenant:** A solemn agreement between human beings or between God and a human being in which mutual commitments are made.

**Pentecost:** The fiftieth day following Easter, which commemorates the descent of the Holy Spirit on the early Apostles and disciples.

**Transubstantiation:** In the Sacrament of the Eucharist, this is the name given to the action of changing the bread and wine into the Body and Blood of Jesus Christ.

**liturgy:** The Church's official, public, communal prayer. It is God's work, in which the People of God participate. The Church's most important liturgy is the Eucharist, or the Mass.

**heresy:** The conscious and deliberate rejection of a dogma of the Church.

**Jesus Christ:** The Son of God, the Second Person of the Trinity, who assumed human nature. Jesus in Hebrew means "God saves" and was the name given the historical Jesus at the Annunciation. *Christ,* the Greek translation of the word *Messiah,* means "the anointed one," and is a title the Church gave Jesus after his full identity was revealed.

**sanctify, sanctification:** To make holy; sanctification is the process of becoming closer to God and growing in holiness, taking on the righteousness of Jesus Christ with the gift of sanctifying grace.

**virtue:** A habitual and firm disposition to do good.

# Part 3: Short Answer

1. The Holy Spirit is the third Divine Person of the Holy Spirit, not revealed to mankind until Pentecost, after Jesus Christ had died, risen from the dead, and ascended into Heaven. The Holy Spirit and Christ are inseparable in their mission. Being human, Christ had to die at some point. God sent the Holy Spirit to dwell with mankind for all time. The Holy Spirit animates, sanctifies, and builds the Church. A life lived according to the Holy Spirit is full of love and joy instead of a life of selfishness, conflict, and a blind focus on short-term pleasure. The Holy Spirit teaches us to pray.

2. At the moment of Pentecost, Jesus Christ poured out the Holy Spirit upon the Church. We look at the significance of Pentecost as the Revelation of the Church, the Holy Spirit, and the Trinity. At Pentecost the Church was revealed to the world. Suddenly, a noise like a driving wind filled the house, and tongues as of fire rested on each of the Apostles, and they were filled with the Holy Spirit. Thereafter, they spoke to the crowd, and the crowd heard them, each in their own native language. Peter explained that the glorified Jesus himself was pouring the Holy Spirit upon the Apostles and enabling them to miraculously speak in such a way that they could be understood by all members of the audience. Peter instructed his listeners to repent and be baptized so their sins would be forgiven, so they too would receive the Holy Spirit. Three thousand people were baptized that day (see Acts of the Apostles 2:37–41).

3. At the time of the Tower of Babel, the whole world spoke one language (see Genesis 11:1). When some of the people attempted to build a tower up to the sky to "make a name for themselves" (Genesis 11:4), God scattered them throughout the earth, confusing their languages so they could no longer communicate. At Pentecost, however, the Holy Spirit enabled people speaking various languages to hear the same message. At the Tower of Babel, God put up barriers to understanding; at Pentecost he broke them down. Without the ability of the Holy Spirit to help the Apostles to communicate, the salvation message of Jesus Christ would have been understood by only a few. The Holy Spirit enables all to hear Christ's message of salvation.

# Unit 3

# The Church Is a Mystery

## Overview

In this unit the students come to a fuller understanding of the mystery of the Church and the purpose of that Church here on earth.

### Key Understandings and Questions

Upon completing this unit, the students will have a deeper understanding of the following key concepts:

- The Church is both visible and spiritual.
- The Church is a sign and instrument of communion with God and the unity of the whole human race.
- The mission of the Church is to share the Good News of Jesus Christ, preserve it, and be a means of salvation.
- We encounter the living Christ in the Church.

Upon completing the unit, the students will have answered the following questions:

- How can the Church be a divine and human institution?
- What can we learn from the Church about how to live as a human race?
- What is the mission of the Church?
- Where do we find Jesus Christ in the Church?

### Student Book Articles

This unit draws on articles from *The Church: Christ in the World Today* student book and incorporates them into the unit instruction. Whenever the teaching steps for the unit require the students to refer to or read an article from the student book, the following symbol appears in the margin: (📖). The articles covered in the unit are from "Section 2: The Church Is One, Holy, Catholic, and Apostolic," "Section 3: The Church's Salvation and Mission," and "Section 4: The Lived Mission of the Church," and are as follows:

- "Why Is the Church Holy?" (article 20, pp. 80–83)
- "The Fullness of Truth and Salvation" (article 33, pp. 126–129)
- "The Evangelical Counsels" (article 44, pp. 169–172)
- "The Mission of the Laity" (article 45, pp. 172–175)
- "The Work and Vocation of the Laity" (article 46, pp. 176–179)

## How Will You Know the Students Understand?

The following resources will help you assess the students' understanding of the key concepts covered in this unit:

- handout "Final Performance Task Options for Unit 3" (Document #: TX001454)
- handout "Rubric for Final Performance Tasks for Unit 3" (Document #: TX001455)
- handout "Unit 3 Test" (Document #: TX001461)

## The Suggested Path to Understanding

This unit in the teacher guide provides you with one learning path to take with the students, to enable them to understand the Church as a mystery. It is not necessary to use all the learning experiences provided in the unit; however, if you substitute other material from this course or your own material for some of the material offered here, be sure that you have covered all relevant facets of understanding and that you have not missed any skills or knowledge required for later units.

 **Step 1:** Preassess what the students already understand about the Church as mystery using the handout "The Top Ten Things" (Document #: TX001457).

 **Step 2:** Follow this assessment by presenting to the students the handouts "Final Performance Task Options for Unit 3" (Document #: TX001454) and "Rubric for Final Performance Tasks for Unit 3" (Document #: TX001455).

 **Step 3:** Introduce and help the students to understand the visible and spiritual reality of the Church.

 **Step 4:** Have the students reflect on their experiences of the Church as visible and spiritual.

 **Step 5:** Guide the students in identifying descriptions of the Church in the *Catechism of the Catholic Church* and in working to understand the Church as a sign and instrument of communion with God and the unity of the whole human race.

 **Step 6:** Help the students to uncover how Pope John Paul II's ministry was a sign of unity through his extensive travels, World Youth Days, and relationship with the people of the world.

**Step 7:** Lead the students in analyzing the school's mission statement to better understand the importance of mission and the role members of a community play in fulfilling that mission.

 **Step 8:** Have the students explore primary source documents to better understand the mission of the Church: to share the Good News of Jesus Christ, preserve it, and be a means of salvation.

 **Step 9:** Help the students to explore ways in which we encounter the Living Christ in the Church.

 **Step 10:** Review the key concepts of the unit (Church as mystery, human and divine, visible and spiritual, charged with carrying out the mission of Christ) through discussion and an exercise.

 **Step 11:** Now that the students are closer to the end of the unit, make sure they are all on track with their final performance tasks, if you have assigned them.

 **Step 12:** Provide the students with a tool to use for reflecting about what they learned in the unit and how they learned.

## Background for Teaching This Unit

Visit *smp.org/LivinginChrist* for additional information about these and other theological concepts taught in this unit:

- "The Visible and the Invisible Church" (Document #: TX001537)
- "The Church as the Body of Christ and Sacrament" (Document #: TX001521)

The Web site also includes information on these and other teaching methods used in the unit:

- "Using Primary Sources" (Document #: TX001313)
- "Preassessment Informs Teaching" (Document #: TX001008)

## Scripture Passages

Scripture is an important part of the Living in Christ series and is frequently used in the learning experiences for each unit. The Scripture passages featured in this unit are as follows:

- Acts of the Apostles 16:15,31–33; 18:8 (Baptism in the early Church)
- Ephesians 5:25–26 (Christ loved the Church and gave himself up for her)
- John 3:1–8 (Nicodemus visits Jesus)
- John 14:6 (the way, the truth, and the life)
- Mark 10:17–22 (the rich man)
- Mark 16:15–16 (Jesus commissions the disciples)
- Matthew 7:12 (the Golden Rule)
- Matthew 13:24–30 (the Parable of the Weeds among the Wheat)
- Matthew 19:23–26 (for God all things are possible)
- Philippians 2:6–8 (Jesus became obedient to the point of death)

## Vocabulary

The student book and the teacher guide include the following key terms for this unit. To provide the students with a list of these terms and their definitions, download and print the handout "Vocabulary for Unit 3" (Document #: TX001456).

| | |
|---|---|
| chastity | evangelical counsels |
| celibacy | *mysterium* |
| conversion | *sacramentum* |
| domestic | vow |

# Learning Experiences

### Teacher Note

If the students seem to remember and understand about the early Church fairly well, you may want to consider these options:

- Decide whether you want to skip this unit, which is all about the early Church as a mystery, and move directly into unit 4, "The Church Is One, Holy, Catholic, and Apostolic." If you decide to do so, it is suggested that you still have the students complete the handout "The Mission of the Church" (Document #: TX001458), regarding Church documents, as this will show a clear understanding of the topic.

- Summarize from the student book some of the material about the Church as mystery and the call to discipleship from articles 20, 33, and 45, "Why Is the Church Holy?" "The Fullness of Truth and Salvation," and "The Mission of the Laity," and see how well the students pick up the four major concepts presented there. If they do well, you may want to skip the learning experiences in this unit and spend more

*continued*

**Explain**

## Step 1

Preassess what the students already understand about the Church as mystery using the handout "The Top Ten Things" (Document #: TX001457).

1. Prepare for this learning experience by downloading and printing the handout "The Top Ten Things" (Document #: TX001457), one for each student. Also gather pens or pencils, one for each student.

2. Begin by distributing the handout and the pens or pencils and instructing the students to complete the handout individually. Allow 3 to 5 minutes for the students to complete the handout.

3. When all the students have completed the handout, ask for volunteers to share their responses. You may choose to list on the board the characteristics the students identify.

4. Explain to the students that in this unit they will come to a fuller understanding of the mystery of the Church (divine and human), and the purpose of that Church here on earth.

**Understand**

## Step 2

Follow this assessment by presenting to the students the handouts "Final Performance Task Options for Unit 3" (Document #: TX001454) and "Rubric for Final Performance Tasks for Unit 3" (Document #: TX001455).

This unit provides you with two ways to assess that the students have a deep understanding of the most important concepts in the unit: creating a video presentation that emphasizes that through our Baptism we are each called to spread the Good News of Jesus Christ or creating posters that examine the face of Christ in the world today. Refer to "Using Final Performance Tasks to Assess Understanding" (Document #: TX001011) and "Using Rubrics to Assess Work" (Document #: TX001012) at *smp.org/Livingin-Christ* for background information.

1. Prepare by downloading and printing the handouts "Final Performance Task Options for Unit 3" (Document #: TX001454) and "Rubric for Final Performance Tasks for Unit 3" (Document #: TX001455), one for each student.

2. Distribute the handouts. Give the students a choice as to which performance task they choose and add more options if you so choose. Review the directions, expectations, and rubric in class, allowing the students to ask questions. You may want to say something to this effect:

   ➤ You may work with no more than two other people on option 1. If you want to work on your own, you may choose either option 1 or option 2.

   ➤ Near the end of the unit, you will have one full class period to work on your final performance task. Please keep in mind, however, that you should be working on this task throughout the course of the unit. Please do not wait until this class period to begin work on your final performance task.

Article 20

**Apply**

**Step 3**

*Introduce and help the students to understand the visible and spiritual reality of the Church.*

> **Teacher Note**
>
> You will want to assign due dates for the final performance tasks.
>
> If you have done these performance tasks, or very similar ones, with students before, place examples of this work in the classroom. During this introduction explain how each is a good example of what you are looking for, for different reasons. This allows the students to concretely understand that there is not only one way to succeed.

Introduce the students to the idea that the Church is both visible and spiritual, using student book article 20, "Why Is the Church Holy?" Also have them read paragraphs 771 and 779 in the *Catechism of the Catholic Church (CCC)*. You may also want to use the PowerPoint "Visible and Spiritual Church" (Document #: TX001508) in this step.

1. Begin by addressing the following points with the class:

   ➤ The phrase "visible and invisible Church" means the Catholic Church is both human and divine. The Church is the Mystical Body of Christ, and Jesus Christ himself is both human and divine; therefore, the Church is human (the visible) and divine (the invisible).

   ➤ The Church is more than we can see. It is also a spiritual reality. The Church is visible and invisible in that it is on earth (visible) and in Purgatory and in Heaven (invisible). This is a mystery that we see with the eyes of faith only, but which builds on visible reality.

   ➤ The earthly structure of the Church exists for the sole purpose of sanctifying the members or making them holy. In the Church, humans can gather and unite as children of God.

   ➤ When we understand the true nature of the Church as human and divine, we see that she is not limited to her visible aspects, and we recognize the source of her holiness. The Church is holy because the most holy God created her. Christ, her bridegroom, loves her and gave up his life for her to make her holy (see Ephesians 5:25–26). He also joins himself to her as his body and gave the Holy Spirit to the Church (see *CCC,* 867).

2. Divide the class into small groups of two or three. Direct each small group to come up with several examples of things that are invisible but whose existence can be proven (e.g., wind, air, gravity, time, surface tension).

3. Now have the small groups develop experiments, using what is available in the classroom, to prove the existence of that which is invisible (e.g., blowing on bubbles to make them move, blowing on feathers to make them float, testing gravity, breaking surface tension, pulling paper through the air to see the air friction). Invite each small group to demonstrate its experiment for the class.

4. After each group has demonstrated for the class, explain that some things that are invisible can be tested, as in the experiments, but that other things are taken "on faith."

5. Conclude by emphasizing that although we cannot "prove" our beliefs with an experiment, the Scriptures and Tradition are God's Revelation to us of his existence and the existence of the Holy Trinity.

**Reflect**

## Step 4

*Have the students reflect on their experiences of the Church as visible and spiritual.*

1. Prepare for this learning experience by gathering sheets of blank paper, one for each student.

2. Begin with a brief question-and-answer discussion. Pose the following questions to the class:

   ➤ What does it mean to be visible?

   ➤ How does a group, organization, or society become visible?

   ➤ What does it mean to be spiritual?

   ➤ What kind of evidence would show the spiritual dimension of a group, organization, or society?

3. Write the following questions on the board:

   - How is the Church visible to you?
   - What do you do that helps make the Church visible to the world around you?
   - How would you describe the spiritual dimension of the Church?
   - How do you experience the spiritual dimension of the Church?

4. Instruct the students to take 15 minutes for quiet reflection with these questions. Distribute the sheets of paper and tell the students to write their responses to the questions. Assure them that they do not need to write the whole time. The most important part of this exercise is their taking time for deep personal reflection.

5. After the time of reflection, ask the questions one at a time and ask for two or three volunteers to share their responses.

6. Close by summarizing what the students have said. Students may have questions about the Church. Note their questions and explain that questions will be answered as we continue our study of the Church.

**Teacher Note**

You may want to play some quiet, instrumental music during the reflection time. Instrumental music is preferred, as lyrics can sometimes be distracting when students are trying to reflect.

Article
33

## Step 5

*Guide the students in identifying descriptions of the Church in the Catechism of the Catholic Church and in working to understand the Church as a sign and instrument of communion with God and the unity of the whole human race.*

1. Prepare for this learning experience by gathering copies of the *Catechism of the Catholic Church*, one for each small group of three or four, as well as a sheet of paper for each small group. There is a PowerPoint available at *smp.org/LivinginChrist* that you can use to explore this topic with your students.

2. Begin by having the students read student book article 33, "The Fullness of Truth and Salvation."

3. Divide the class into small groups of three or four. Distribute a sheet of paper and a copy of the *Catechism* to each group, and then instruct the groups to find and record descriptions of the Church in the *Catechism* (e.g., bride of Christ, light of the world). If you would like, you can point the students to paragraphs 781–801 as a starting point. Allow 5 to 7 minutes for this.

4. Once the small groups have identified several descriptions of the Church in the *Catechism,* have each group share a description and what they think it says about the Church. Record their answers on the board. Continue with the sharing until all descriptions of the Church have been presented.

5. Now have the small groups reread student book article 33, "The Fullness of Truth and Salvation." Direct them to identify places in the article that support or reiterate the descriptions of the Church the class identified from the *Catechism*. Allow 5 minutes for this.

6. When the small groups have finished rereading the article, lead a large-group discussion about what it means to say that the fullness of Jesus Christ's Church is found in the Catholic Church only. Be prepared for questions about whether the Church says that people of other faiths are not saved.

7. Conclude by emphasizing that the Church is a means of unity, not division, for all God's People. The Church's mission is to reach out to all people and to share the fullness of Jesus Christ.

**Step 6**

*Help the students to uncover how Pope John Paul II's ministry was a sign of unity through his extensive travels, World Youth Days, and relationship with the people of the world.*

In this learning experience, the students research five different aspects of the ministry of Pope John Paul II and how his ministry was a sign of unity. This will take several class periods, at least one for research, one for creating the presentations, and one for presenting.

1. Prepare for this learning experience by reserving the media center or computer lab so the students will have access to the Internet.

2. Divide the large group into small groups of five. These will be the "home" groups.

3. Within each home group, have each student choose one of the following letters: *A, B, C, D, E.*

4. Now have all of the *A*'s form a small group, all of the *B*'s form a small group, and so on. These will be the five "focus" groups.

5. Assign the following topics to the focus groups according to their corresponding letters of the alphabet:

   A. World Youth Day 2005
   B. relations with the Jewish community
   C. international travel
   D. ecumenism (outreach to other world religions)
   E. socioeconomic diversity (plea to the World Bank during the Jubilee Year 2000.)

6. Instruct each focus group to research its topic in relation to the ministry of Pope John Paul II. While conducting their research, they should be working to answer the question, How was the ministry of Pope John Paul II a sign of unity?

7. Each focus group is to develop a brief presentation to share with the home groups that presents the assigned ministry of Pope John Paul II and how it was a sign of unity. The presentations can be designed as PowerPoints or handouts and should include the following:

   • information about the ministry
   • significant development promoted by Pope John Paul II in relation to the ministry
   • at least two quotations from Pope John Paul II relating to the ministry
   • at least one photo of Pope John Paul II in relation to the assigned topic

8. Once the focus groups have completed their research and created their presentations, have the students return to their home groups and present to their group members.

9. Conclude by having a class discussion about the research and presentations. Ask one student from each focus group to summarize for the class what his or her group learned about its assigned ministry of Pope John Paul II and how that ministry was a sign of unity.

## Step 7

Lead the students in analyzing the school's mission statement to better understand the importance of mission and the role members of a community play in fulfilling that mission.

1. Prepare for this learning experience by making copies of the school's mission statement, one for each student. Also gather sheets of blank paper, one for each student.

2. Begin by explaining to the students that they will be looking at the mission statement for their school and what it means for those associated with the school.

3. Divide the class into small groups of four or five. Assign the following roles to the members of each group:

   - student
   - teacher
   - principal
   - parent

   For small groups of five, have two students play the student or teacher role.

4. Distribute a blank sheet of paper to each student and explain that each student is to take on the point of view of the role she or he has been assigned. The small groups should read through the school's mission statement twice and then each person should respond to the following questions (write these on the board), recording her or his answers:

   - What does the mission statement say is the purpose of our school?
   - How does the mission statement say the school accomplishes it purpose?
   - As a student, teacher, principal, or parent, what does the mission statement state or imply is my role in fulfilling the mission?

5. When the small groups have finished answering the questions, have the students combine with other students who took on the same role (i.e., teachers form a group, parents form a group, and so on). In the new groups, they are to complete the following statements (write these on the board):

   • As (students, parents, teachers, principal) our role in the mission of the school is . . .

   • We fulfill this role by . . .

6. Allow each group to share its completed statements with the class.

7. Conclude by sharing the following with the class:

   ➤ We have just looked at the mission of our school and what it means for the various members of our community. The Church has a much larger mission. In the next learning experience, we will explore what the mission of the Church is and what our role as the laity is in that mission.

Articles
44, 45,
46

## Step 8

Have the students explore primary source documents to better understand the mission of the Church: to share the Good News of Jesus Christ, preserve it, and be a means of salvation.

This learning experience guides the students in reading excerpts from several Church primary source documents that address the mission of the Church. Excerpts are provided, but you may also choose to direct the students to identify and read additional primary source documents. Some suggested additional resources include the *Catechism of the Catholic Church*, "Documents of II Vatican Council," papal statements for the annual World Mission Day, statements from the Conference of Catholic Bishops, and statements from the local ordinary.

1. Prepare for this learning experience by downloading and printing the handout "The Mission of the Church" (Document #: TX001458), one for each student.

2. As background have the students read student book articles 44–46, "The Evangelical Councils," "The Mission of the Laity," and "The Work and Vocation of the Laity."

3. Begin by asking the students to summarize the key points from the three student book articles. As a prompt, ask the class:

**Teacher Note**

Depending on the way language is used in your local setting, it might be important to point out that inclusive language is not used in most of these documents and that "men" means all persons, and that is the way it should be understood.

➤ What are the evangelical counsels and how do they relate to the work of priests and bishops?

➤ What is the mission and work of the laity?

4. Explain that we are blessed to have extensive writings available to us that address and explain the Church. For this learning experience, we will be looking at excerpts from several documents that address the mission of the Church in the world today and how it relates to us as the laity.

5. Distribute the handout "The Mission of the Church" (Document #: TX001458). Instruct the students to read the excerpts and answer the three questions under the heading "The Mission of the Church Reflection."

6. When the students have completed the reading and questions, divide the class into small groups of two or three and have them share their responses to the questions.

7. In their small groups, the students should then respond to the questions under the heading "The Laity Share in the Mission of the Church by . . ." Allow the groups 5 to 7 minutes to respond. Then have the groups share their responses with the rest of the class.

8. Conclude with a brief summary discussion. Encourage the students to share any questions they have about the mission of the Church, the most interesting insight they gained from this exercise, and what they feel is the most challenging part of the mission of the Church and the mission of the laity.

# Step 9

*Help the students to explore ways in which we encounter the Living Christ in the Church.*

1. Prepare for this learning experience by gathering sheets of blank paper, one for each small group of three or four and one for each student.

2. Begin by explaining to the students that Christ enriches us through participation in the life of the Church. Each of us, through Baptism, is called to the Church, to Christ. And, once knowing Christ, we are sent out into the world as disciples, with the help of the Holy Spirit. Being a disciple means being a part of Christ's mission and sharing our God-given talents for the sake of others.

3. Divide the class into small groups of three or four. Distribute a sheet of blank paper to each group and explain that each group is to spend 5 minutes brainstorming groups and activities in the Church through which they see the work of Christ and the mission of the Church being fulfilled. These groups and activities can be in their parish, the school, the local

community, or the world at large. Some examples include lectors, Eucharistic ministers, teachers and school staff, Knights of Columbus, religious orders, Catholic Relief Services, and so on.

4. Once the groups and activities have been identified, have the students return to their seats. Distribute a sheet of blank paper to each student and explain that each student is to select one of the groups or activities he or she would be interested in joining or learning more about and write an essay explaining why he or she chose that group or activity. The essay should consist of three paragraphs and should address the following:

   - what about this group or activity is inviting
   - how this activity or group promotes the mission of the Church
   - what gifts he or she has to share with the group or activity

   Allow 5 to 7 minutes for the students to write.

5. When the students finish writing, invite volunteers to read all or part of their essays aloud for the class.

## Step 10

Review the key concepts of the unit (Church as mystery, human and divine, visible and spiritual, charged with carrying out the mission of Christ) through discussion and an exercise. There is a PowerPoint available at smp.org/LivinginChrist that you can use to explore this topic with your students.

1. Prepare for this learning experience by downloading and printing the handout "'The Church Is Mystery' Word Search" (Document #: TX001459), one for each student. Also gather four sheets of newsprint, a marker, and a roll of masking tape. Additionally, you might consider using the PowerPoint "Key Concepts of Church" (Document #: TX001507) in this step.

2. Begin by distributing the handout and directing the students to complete the word search. The handout "'The Church Is Mystery' Word Search Solution" (Document #: TX001460) has the solution to the puzzle.

3. While the students work on the word search, write each of the following concepts on a separate sheet of newsprint and then post the four sheets around the room:

   - Church as mystery
   - Church as human and divine

- Church as both visible and spiritual
- Church charged with carrying out mission of Christ

4. Ask for four volunteers, one for each of the four concepts. The volunteers' job is to record on the newsprint what the class shares about each respective concept.

5. Invite the students to share what they have learned about each of the four concepts over the course of this unit. They do not have to respond in order, but they should raise their hands and wait to be called on.

6. Facilitate the sharing by calling on students and summarizing what they share so the recorder can write it down. When the students seem to be done sharing responses, summarize what they have shared and add any additional insight that is needed for the four concepts.

**Understand**

## Step 11

Now that the students are closer to the end of the unit, make sure they are all on track with their final performance tasks, if you have assigned them.

If possible, devote 50 to 60 minutes for the students to ask questions about the tasks and to work individually or in their small groups.

1. Remind the students to bring to class any work they have already prepared or completed so that they can work on it during the time allotted. If necessary, reserve the library, computer lab, or media center so the students can do any book or online research. Download and print the handouts "Final Performance Task Options for Unit 3" (Document #: TX001454) and "Rubric for Final Performance Tasks for Unit 3" (Document #: TX001455). Review the final performance task options, answer questions, and ask the students to choose one if they have not already done so.

2. Provide some class time for the students to work on their performance tasks. This then allows you to work with the students who need additional guidance with the task.

## Step 12

*Provide the students with a tool to use for reflecting about what they learned in the unit and how they learned.*

This learning experience provides the students with an excellent opportunity to reflect on how their understandings of God and the Trinity have developed throughout the unit.

1. To prepare for this learning experience, download and print the handout "Learning about Learning" (Document #: TX001159; see Appendix), one for each student.

2. Distribute the handout and give the students about 15 minutes to answer the questions quietly. Invite them to share any reflections they have about the content they learned as well as their insights into the way they learned.

# Final Performance Task Options for Unit 3

## Important Information for Both Options

The following are the main ideas you are to understand from this unit. They should appear in this final performance task so your teacher can assess whether you learned the most essential content:

- The Church is both visible and spiritual.

- The Church is a sign and instrument of communion with God and the unity of the whole human race.

- The mission of the Church is to share the Good News of Jesus Christ, preserve it, and be a means of salvation.

- We encounter the living Christ in the Church.

## Option 1: "We Are Called to Spread the Word" Video

You have been hired by the diocese to create a 3- to 5-minute video that demonstrates the Catholic understanding of evangelization. Before shooting the video, you are to create a storyboard that includes the music you will use, the scenes you will shoot, and the people you will interview to demonstrate Catholic understanding of evangelization. Follow these guidelines in creating your video:

- The final cut of the video should be no less than 3 minutes and no longer than 5 minutes.

- Use film, sound, dialogue, and photos to create this video. No graphic images or political themes may be used.

- You must obtain permission from all people who appear in this video. Let them know that your video will not be posted on the Internet; it will be used in the classroom only.

- You are not allowed to download video or photos from the Internet for this assignment; only original work may be used.

- You must own (on CD or as MP3s) all music, and you must credit the music properly at the end of the video.

- You will hand in a typed script of the movie, along with any copyright information (for the music or images). You must also include all permission slips signed by those appearing in the video.

Document #: TX001454

# Option 2: "We See the Face of Christ Today" Posters

Your school's campus ministry department has asked you to create two posters that will be used to invite students to become more active in campus ministry (the posters could be used to encourage students to take a more active role in liturgies, service opportunities, or retreat experiences). Follow these guidelines in creating your posters:

- Use 14-x-17-inch photocopy paper for both posters.

- On the first poster, create a large image of Jesus composed of a mosaic of photos of students from your school. (Use a school yearbook for the pictures, but do not use images of individual people. Instead, photocopy pages of pictures from each class in the school, as well as a page of staff photos, and then use sections from those pages.) Use two quotations from this unit as captions for this poster. In a short essay, explain how Christ can be encountered in your school.

- On the second poster, create a large image of Jesus composed of a mosaic of pictures of people from your local community or from around the world. (As before, do not use photos of individual people; rather, use photos that include groups of people in order to create the face of Jesus.) Use two quotations from this unit as captions for this image. In a short essay, explain one way Christ can be encountered in your community or around the world today through the Church.

# Rubric for Final Performance Tasks for Unit 3

| Criteria | 4 | 3 | 2 | 1 |
|---|---|---|---|---|
| **Assignment includes all items requested in the directions.** | Assignment not only includes all items requested, but they are completed above expectations. | Assignment includes all items requested. | Assignment includes more than half of the items requested. | Assignment includes less than half of the items requested. |
| **Assignment shows understanding of the concept *the Church is both visible and spiritual.*** | Assignment shows unusually insightful understanding of this concept. | Assignment shows good understanding of this concept. | Assignment shows adequate understanding of this concept. | Assignment shows little understanding of this concept. |
| **Assignment shows understanding of the concept *the Church is a sign and instrument of communion with God and the unity of the whole human race.*** | Assignment shows unusually insightful understanding of this concept. | Assignment shows good understanding of this concept. | Assignment shows adequate understanding of this concept. | Assignment shows little understanding of this concept. |
| **Assignment shows understanding of the concept *the mission of the Church is to share the Good News of Jesus Christ, preserve it, and be a means of salvation.*** | Assignment shows unusually insightful understanding of this concept. | Assignment shows good understanding of this concept. | Assignment shows adequate understanding of this concept. | Assignment shows little understanding of this concept. |
| **Assignment shows understanding of the concept *we encounter the living Christ in the Church.*** | Assignment shows unusually insightful understanding of this concept. | Assignment shows good understanding of this concept. | Assignment shows adequate understanding of this concept. | Assignment shows little understanding of this concept. |
| **Assignment uses proper grammar and spelling.** | Assignment has no grammar or spelling errors. | Assignment has one grammar or spelling error. | Assignment has two grammar or spelling errors. | Assignment has more than two grammar or spelling errors. |

© 2010 by Saint Mary's Press
Living in Christ Series

Document #: TX001455

# Vocabulary for Unit 3

**celibacy:** The state or condition of those who have chosen or taken vows to remain unmarried in order to devote themselves entirely to the service of the Church and the Kingdom of God.

**chastity:** The virtue by which people are able to successfully and healthfully integrate their sexuality into their total person; recognized as one of the fruits of the Holy Spirit. Also one of the vows of religious life.

**conversion:** A change of heart, turning away from sin and toward God.

**domestic:** Relating to household or family.

**evangelical counsels:** The call to go beyond the minimum rules of life required by God (such as the Ten Commandments and the Precepts of the Church) and strive for spiritual perfection through a life marked by a commitment to chastity, poverty, and obedience.

*mysterium:* The hidden reality of God's plan of salvation.

*sacramentum:* The visible sign of the hidden reality of salvation.

**vow:** A free and conscious commitment made to other persons (as in Marriage), to the Church, or to God.

Document #: TX001456

# The Top Ten Things

In the spaces provided, write ten things you know about the Church's divine and human characteristics.

1. _____

2. _____

3. _____

4. _____

5. _____

6. _____

7. _____

8. _____

9. _____

10. _____

Document #: TX001457

# The Mission of the Church

## From the *Catechism of the Catholic Church,* Numbers 737–738

The mission of Christ and the Holy Spirit is brought to completion in the Church, which is the Body of Christ and the Temple of the Holy Spirit. This joint mission henceforth brings Christ's faithful to share in his communion with the Father in the Holy Spirit. The Spirit *prepares* men and goes out to them with his grace, in order to draw them to Christ. The Spirit *manifests* the risen Lord to them, recalls his word to them and opens their minds to the understanding of his Death and Resurrection. He *makes present* the mystery of Christ, supremely in the Eucharist, in order to reconcile them, to *bring them into communion* with God, that they may "bear much fruit."[1]

Thus the Church's mission is not an addition to that of Christ and the Holy Spirit, but is its sacrament: in her wholly being and in all her members, the Church is sent to announce, bear witness, make present, and spread the mystery of the communion of the Holy Trinity.

Endnote Cited in Quotation from the *Catechism of the Catholic Church,* Second Edition
1.   John 15:8,16.

## From the *Pastoral Constitution on the Church in the Modern World (Gaudium et Spes),* Promulgated by Pope Paul VI, December 7, 1965, Numbers 45, 89, 92–93

While helping the world and receiving many benefits from it, the Church has a single intention: that God's kingdom may come, and that the salvation of the whole human race may come to pass. For every benefit which the People of God during its earthly pilgrimage can offer to the human family stems from the fact that the Church is "the universal sacrament of salvation," simultaneously manifesting and exercising the mystery of God's love.

For God's Word, by whom all things were made, was Himself made flesh so that as perfect man He might save all men and sum up all things in Himself. The Lord is the goal of human history, the focal point of the longings of history and of civilization, the center of the human race, the joy of every heart and the answer to all its yearnings. He it is Whom the Father raised from the dead, lifted on high and stationed at His right hand, making Him judge of the living and the dead. Enlivened and united in His Spirit, we journey toward the consummation of human history, one which fully accords with the counsel of God's love: "To reestablish all things in Christ, both those in the heavens and those on the earth" (Ephesians 11:10).

Since, in virtue of her mission received from God, the Church preaches the Gospel to all men and dispenses the treasures of grace, she contributes to the ensuring of peace everywhere on earth and to the placing of the fraternal exchange between men on solid ground by imparting knowledge of the divine and natural law. Therefore, to encourage and stimulate cooperation among men, the Church must be clearly present in the midst of the community of nations both through her official channels and through the full and sincere collaboration of all Christians—a collaboration motivated solely by the desire to be of service to all.

Document #: TX001458

By virtue of her mission to shed on the whole world the radiance of the Gospel message, and to unify under one Spirit all men of whatever nation, race or culture, the Church stands forth as a sign of that brotherhood which allows honest dialogue and gives it vigor.

Such a mission requires in the first place that we foster within the Church herself mutual esteem, reverence and harmony, through the full recognition of lawful diversity. Thus all those who compose the one People of God, both pastors and the general faithful, can engage in dialogue with ever abounding fruitfulness. For the bonds which unite the faithful are mightier than anything dividing them. Hence, let there be unity in what is necessary; freedom in what is unsettled, and charity in any case.

Mindful of the Lord's saying: "by this will all men know that you are my disciples, if you have love for one another" (John 13:35), Christians cannot yearn for anything more ardently than to serve the men of the modern world with mounting generosity and success. Therefore, by holding faithfully to the Gospel and benefiting from its resources, by joining with every man who loves and practices justice, Christians have shouldered a gigantic task for fulfillment in this world, a task concerning which they must give a reckoning to Him who will judge every man on the last of days.

## From the *Decree on the Missionary Activity of the Church (Ad Gentes),* Promulgated by Pope Paul VI, December 7, 1965, Numbers 1 and 10

Divinely sent to the nations of the world to be unto them "a universal sacrament of salvation," the Church, driven by the inner necessity of her own catholicity, and obeying the mandate of her Founder (cf. Mark 16:16), strives ever to proclaim the Gospel to all men. The Apostles themselves, on whom the Church was founded, following in the footsteps of Christ, "preached the word of truth and begot churches." It is the duty of their successors to make this task endure "so that the word of God may run and be glorified" (2 Thessalonians 3:1) and the kingdom of God be proclaimed and established throughout the world.

In the present state of affairs, out of which there is arising a new situation for mankind, the Church, being the salt of the earth and the light of the world (cf. Matt. 5:13–14), is more urgently called upon to save and renew every creature, that all things may be restored in Christ and all men may constitute one family in Him and one people of God.

The Church, sent by Christ to reveal and to communicate the love of God to all men and nations, is aware that there still remains a gigantic missionary task for her to accomplish. For the Gospel message has not yet, or hardly yet, been heard by two billion human beings (and their number is increasing daily), who are formed into large and distinct groups by permanent cultural ties, by ancient religious traditions, and by firm bonds of social necessity. Some of these men are followers of one of the great religions, but others remain strangers to the very knowledge of God, while still others expressly deny His existence, and sometimes even attack it. The Church, in order to be able to offer all of them the mystery of salvation and the life brought by God, must implant herself into these groups for the same motive which led Christ to bind Himself, in virtue of His Incarnation, to certain social and cultural conditions of those human beings among whom He dwelt.

# From "Message of His Holiness Benedict XVI for the 83rd World Mission Sunday 2009"

"The nations will walk in its light" (Revelation 21:24). The goal of the Church's mission is to illumine all peoples with the light of the Gospel as they journey through history towards God, so that in Him they may reach their full potential and fulfillment. We should have a longing and a passion to illumine all peoples with the light of Christ that shines on the face of the Church, so that all may be gathered into the one human family, under God's loving fatherhood.

# *On the Vocation and the Mission of the Lay Faithful in the Church and in the World (Christifideles Laici),* by Pope John Paul II, Number 36

In both accepting and proclaiming the Gospel in the power of the Spirit the Church becomes at one and the same time an "evangelizing and evangelized" community, and for this very reason she is made the servant of all. In her lay faithful participate in the mission of service to the person and society. Without doubt the Church has the Kingdom of God as her supreme goal, of which "she on earth is its seed and beginning," and is therefore totally consecrated to the glorification of the Father. However, the Kingdom is the source of full liberation and total salvation for all people: with this in mind, then, the Church walks and lives, intimately bound in a real sense to their history.

Having received the responsibility of manifesting to the world the mystery of God that shines forth in Jesus Christ, the Church likewise awakens one person to another, giving a sense of one's existence, opening each to the whole truth about the individual and of each person's final destiny. From this perspective the Church is called, in virtue of her very mission of evangelization, to serve all humanity. Such service is rooted primarily in the extraordinary and profound fact that "through the Incarnation the Son of God has united himself in some fashion to every person."

For this reason the person "is the primary route that the Church must travel in fulfilling her mission: the individual is the primary and fundamental way for the Church, the way traced out by Christ himself, the way that leads in variably through the mystery of the Incarnation and Redemption."

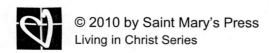

## The Mission of the Church Reflection

1. What did you learn about the mission of the Church to share the Good News of Jesus Christ? Where do you see this happening in our world today?

2. What did you learn about the mission of the Church to preserve the Good News of Jesus Christ? Where do you see this happening in our world today?

3. What did you learn about the mission of the Church to be a means of salvation? Where do you see this happening in our world today?

# The Laity Share in the Mission of the Church by . . .

For each question provide two or three examples of how the laity share in the mission of the Church.

1. How does the priestly office of the laity relate to the mission of the Church?

2. How does the prophetic office of the laity share in the mission of the Church?

3. How does the kingly office of the laity share in the mission of the Church?

© 2010 by Saint Mary's Press
Living in Christ Series

Document #: TX001458

# "The Church Is Mystery" Word Search

```
M I S S I O N E Y F I T C N A S U
P P E T A N N I V C T B H L Y Q P
M S I T P A B M H I S D O T L A E
C A E V A S U M R C A O S H I N C
A L E Q C H R I S T L Q E G M E I
T F C P H W P Z E U V M N I A Y L
H S N V E S T Y R K A I X L F Q O
O P E B S N Y H V S T N F C C D T
L I S K B N T A E G I I G J O J S
I R E K A M E E R R O S E G M G O
C I R E Y R L C P N T L R M N P
U T P R A D O S B O S R P A U O A
S U T Y X C P T T I S Y O C N I A
L A M R H F S W N E S T E E I T Y
C L L U U A J U O E R I P J T I L
N R R O J T G I S R M Y V C Y D O
H C E Z B H H P Z E K A L H J A H
H X O A V E G Q V A J I T A C R Z
F F H K T R Y O C V A D W S O T D
J U K Z Q O W T F X I K N T E X W
Z E L B I B R Q U N I T Y E D T P
Y S A C R A M E N T E D I R B G Y
```

| | | | |
|---|---|---|---|
| ACT | CREATOR | MISSION | SERVE |
| APOSTOLIC | FAMILY | MYSTERY | SON |
| BAPTISM | FATHER | OBEY | SPIRIT |
| BIBLE | GOD | PENTECOST | SPIRITUAL |
| BRIDE | GRACE | PEOPLE | TESTAMENT |
| CATHOLIC | HOLY | PRAY | TRADITION |
| CHASTE | INNATE | PRESENCE | TRUTH |
| CHOSEN | JESUS | SACRAMENT | UNITY |
| CHRIST | LIGHT | SALVATION | VISIBLE |
| CHURCH | MAKER | SANCTIFY | VOW |
| COMMUNITY | MINISTRY | SAVE | WORK |

Document #: TX001459

# "The Church Is Mystery" Word Search Solution

Document #: TX001460

# Unit 3 Test

## Part 1: Multiple Choice

Write your answers in the blank spaced provided at the left.

1. _____ Unlike any other organization, the Church is made up of a human component and a _____ component.

   A. divine or spiritual
   B. priestly or hierarchical
   C. biblical
   D. angelic

2. _____ The Church depends completely on the gift of _____ to be holy.

   A. the lives of the saints
   B. Baptism and reconciliation
   C. God's grace
   D. tithing

3. _____ There are three stages of sanctification: life on earth, Purgatory, and _____.

   A. expiation of sins
   B. penance
   C. Heaven
   D. wearing white linen

4. _____ _____, who by God's grace is perfectly holy, is the model toward which all other Church members strive.

   A. Saint Paul
   B. Elijah
   C. The Pope
   D. Mary

5. _____ The earthly structure of the Church exists for the sole purpose of making the members _____.

   A. holy
   B. guilt ridden
   C. better than others
   D. sinless

Document #: TX001461

**6.** _____  The holiness of the Church on earth is real but _____.

    **A.** purchased at a cost
    **B.** owned by priests
    **C.** imperfect
    **D.** only skin deep

**7.** _____  Because the Church sanctifies, it is natural that she embraces_____.

    **A.** babies
    **B.** all other religions
    **C.** heresy
    **D.** sinners

**8.** _____  _____ is the passing on of the authority to teach and interpret the Scriptures and Tradition to the bishops.

    **A.** Apostolic Succession
    **B.** Inspiration
    **C.** Faith and morals
    **D.** The Acts of the Apostles

**9.** _____  The Scriptures tell us that God loves all people and wills everyone to be _____.

    **A.** sinless
    **B.** saved
    **C.** Catholic
    **D.** religious

**10.** _____  The fullness of _____ is transmitted through the Scriptures and Tradition.

    **A.** the history of the whole world
    **B.** Revelation
    **C.** Covenant
    **D.** papal infallibility

# Part 2: Matching

Match each statement in column 1 with a term from column 2. Write the letter that corresponds to your choice in the space provided. (*Note:* There are two extra items in column 2.)

## Column 1

1. _____ A change of heart that turns us away from sin and toward God.

2. _____ Teachings recognized as central to Church teaching.

3. _____ The virtue by which people are able to successfully and healthfully integrate their sexuality into their total person; recognized as one of the fruits of the Holy Spirit.

4. _____ A free and conscious commitment made to other persons (as in Marriage), to the Church, or to God.

5. _____ The hidden reality of God's plan of salvation.

6. _____ Christ said that "no one can enter the kingdom of God without being born of water and _____" (John 3:5).

7. _____ A solemn agreement between human beings or between God and a human being.

8. _____ A short summary statement or profession of faith.

9. _____ On our path to holiness, all Christians are called to follow the _____ of chastity, obedience, and poverty.

10. _____ As a young person, you are called to _____ before Marriage.

## Column 2

A. evangelical counsels

B. abstinence

C. hyperventilation

D. dogma

E. covenant

F. conversion

G. chastity

H. *mysterium*

I. vow

J. Spirit

K. creed

L. Sacred Tradition

# Part 3: Short Answer

Answer each of the following questions in paragraph form on a separate sheet of paper.

1.  What does it mean to live a chaste life?

2.  What are your responsibilities as a member of the laity?

3.  What does Christ mean when he says to his disciples, "You are the salt of the earth"

    (Matthew 5:13), and why did he compare them to salt rather than another spice?

# Unit 3 Test Answer Key

## Part 1: Multiple Choice

1. A.
2. C.
3. C.
4. D.
5. A.

6. C.
7. D.
8. A.
9. B.
10. B.

## Part 2: Matching

1. F.
2. D.
3. G.
4. I.
5. H.

6. J.
7. E.
8. K.
9. A.
10. B.

## Part 3: Short Answer

1. Chastity is the healthy integration of our sexuality into our whole person; it is a virtue that is also one of the fruits of the Holy Spirit. To be chaste does not mean to deny or suppress our sexuality, but rather to order it in the right way. We are called to control our sexual desires, rather than have them control us. Married couples are called to chastity, to being faithful to one another. Young people are called to abstinence before Marriage, to a purity of heart, to avoidance of sexual fantasies and pornography. Living a chaste life is a huge challenge in this world where television, movies, and the Internet push us toward promiscuity, adultery, and the unchaste life. But with the help of God's grace, including the sacramental graces of Baptism and the Eucharist, this virtue can be developed. Priests and those consecrated to the religious life are called to live lives of chastity and of celibacy.

2. The laity are all members of the Church (except for those who have been ordained). The laity's primary role is in witnessing to God's love to the whole world. The laity is to be Christ's hands, feet, voice, and ears in sharing the Good News of the Gospel with friends, classmates, family members, and people in the community. The laity has both the right and the duty to help influence the world's social, political, and economic realities to reflect God's will. The laity's mission and the ministry of the hierarchy work together in continuing Christ's mission in the Church and the world.

3. Of all the spices, salt may be the most necessary and the tastiest. On its own, it has a very strong bite. But when mixed with other foods, its zest enhances the other flavors in the foods. Christ calls his disciples, and all Christians, to bring out the true flavor and goodness of the world, not only in ourselves but in others. When salt loses its flavor, it cannot enhance the flavor of anything else. Therefore, it is

important that we keep our flavor (our fervor for God, Christ, and the Holy Spirit, and our belief in salvation through the grace of God), for the benefit of the rest of the world.

# Unit 4   The Church Is One, Holy, Catholic, and Apostolic

## Overview

This unit guides the students in exploring and understanding the four marks of the Catholic Church: one, holy, catholic, apostolic. Knowledge of these four marks of the Church is vital for the students to have a clear understanding of what it means to be Catholic in the world today.

### Key Understandings and Questions

Upon completing this unit, the students will have a deeper understanding of the following key concepts:

- The Church is one: united in charity, in the profession of faith, in the common celebration of worship and Sacraments, and in the Apostolic Succession.
- The Church is holy because, although Church members sin, the Church as the Body of Christ is sinless.
- The Church is catholic because it exists for all people and is the means of salvation for all people.
- The Church is apostolic because Christ calls all Church members to share the Gospel of salvation.

Upon completing the unit, the students will have answered the following questions:

- What creates unity in the Church?
- How is the Church the means of salvation for all people?
- How does our own mission fit in with the mission of the Apostles?

### Student Book Articles

This unit draws on articles from *The Church: Christ in the World Today* student book and incorporates them into the unit instruction. Whenever the teaching steps for the unit require the students to refer to or read an article from the student book, the following symbol appears in the margin: (📖). The articles covered in the unit are from "Section 2: The Church is One, Holy, Catholic, and Apostolic," and are as follows:

- "The First Mark of the Church" (article 16, pp. 63–65)
- "Bonds of Unity" (article 17, pp. 66–69)
- "Why Is the Church Holy?" (article 20, pp. 80–83)
- "The Church Makes Us Holy through God's Grace" (article 21, pp. 84–86)

- "The Meaning of the Word *Catholic*" (article 25, pp. 98–99)
- "Catholicity: The Fullness of Christ in the Church" (article 26, pp. 100–102)
- "The Church's Relationship with All People" (article 27, pp. 102–106)
- "Universality and Diversity" (article 28, pp. 106–110)
- "The Apostles Continue Jesus' Mission" (article 29, pp. 112–114)
- "Apostolic Tradition" (article 30, pp. 114–117)
- "The Successors to Peter and the Apostles" (article 31, pp. 117–120)
- "The Apostolate of the Laity" (article 32, pp. 120–122)

## How Will You Know the Students Understand?

The following resources will help you assess the students' understanding of the key concepts covered in this unit:

- handout "Final Performance Task Options for Unit 4" (Document #: TX001463)
- handout "Rubric for Final Performance Tasks for Unit 4" (Document #: TX001464)
- handout "Unit 4 Test" (Document #: TX001469)

## The Suggested Path to Understanding

This unit in the teacher guide provides you with one learning path to take with the students, to enable them to deepen their understanding of the four marks of the Church. It is not necessary to use all the learning experiences provided in the unit; however, if you substitute other material from this course or your own material for some of the material offered here, be sure that you have covered all relevant facets of understanding and that you have not missed any skills or knowledge required for later units.

 **Step 1:** Preassess student knowledge of the four marks of the Church, using the carousel method.

 **Step 2:** Follow this assessment by presenting to the students the handouts "Final Performance Task Options for Unit 4" (Document #: TX001463) and "Rubric for Final Performance Tasks for Unit 4" (Document #: TX001464).

 **Step 3:** Present activities stations for teaching the students the four marks of the Church.

 **Step 4:** Introduce the Web quest to help the students to discover how faith is expressed around the world through the Church's being united in charity, in the profession of one faith, in the common celebration of worship and Sacraments, and in Apostolic Succession.

**Step 5:** Present material on the mark the Church is holy, using clips from the film *Champions of Faith* (2007, 65 minutes, not rated) from Catholic Media Exchange and an exercise with an examination of conscience.

 **Step 6:** Explore with the students the two meanings of the phrase "the Church is catholic" by having them identify symbols of the fullness of Christ and the means of salvation and by examining the Church's relationship with other faith traditions.

 **Step 7:** Introduce the students to our current successor to Peter, Pope Benedict XVI, and have them create a PowerPoint slideshow about his life.

 **Step 8:** Have the students create a PowerPoint of the successions of the Popes to help them to understand the concept of Apostolic Succession.

 **Step 9:** Conduct student reflections on their service in the school, parish, and community. How have they seen the face of Jesus in their service? How have the people they have ministered to in their service been the face of Jesus to them?

**Step 10:** Now that the students are closer to the end of the unit, make sure they are all on track with their final performance tasks, if you have assigned them.

**Step 11:** Provide students with a tool to use for reflecting about what they learned in the unit and how they learned.

## Background for Teaching This Unit

Visit *smp.org/LivinginChrist* for additional information about these and other theological concepts taught in this unit:

- "The Church Is One" (Document #: TX001522)
- "The Marks of the Church" (Document #: TX001523)

The Web site also includes information on these and other teaching methods used in the unit:

- "Web Quest" (Document #: TX001525)

## Scripture Passages

Scripture is an important part of the Living in Christ series and is frequently used in the learning experiences for each unit. The Scripture passages featured in this unit are as follows:

- Acts of the Apostles 1:15–26 (the choice of Judas's successor)
- Acts of the Apostles 2:14–21 (Peter's speech at Pentecost)
- Acts of the Apostles 9:36–42 (Peter restores Tabitha to life)
- Acts of the Apostles 15:1–34 (Council of Jerusalem)
- 1 Corinthians 12:4–6,14–31 (one body, many parts)
- Ephesians 2:19–22 (no longer strangers)
- Ephesians 4:4–6 (unity in the body)
- John 3:16 (for God so loved the world)
- John 14:6 (the Advocate)
- John 20:19–23 (appearance to the disciples)
- Matthew 13:24–30 (the Parable of the Weeds among the Wheat)
- Matthew 28:16–20 (the commissioning of the disciples)
- 1 Peter 3:15–16 (Christian suffering)
- Romans 11:28–29 (God's irrevocable call)

## Vocabulary

The student book and the teacher guide include the following key terms for this unit. To provide the students with a list of these terms and their definitions, download and print the handout "Vocabulary for Unit 4" (Document #: TX001465).

| | |
|---|---|
| actual grace | habitual grace |
| Apostles' Creed | icon |
| apostolate | iconostasis |
| apostolic | laypeople (laity) |
| Apostolic Succession | marks of the Church |
| bishop | Nicene Creed |
| catholic | sacramental graces |
| conversion | Sacrament of Holy Orders |
| creed | Sacred Tradition |
| ecclesial | sanctifying grace |
| episcopal | supernatural grace |
| grace | |

# Learning Experiences

## Step 1

*Preassess student knowledge of the four marks of the Church, using the carousel method.*

Visual, bodily-kinesthetic, and linguistic learners especially benefit from the utilization of this teaching method as they work with others to recall previous learning. This learning experience will help you to assess your students' knowledge and comprehension of the subject matter and can be used before, during, and after a lesson.

1. Prepare for this learning experience by gathering four sheets of newsprint, a black marker, a roll of masking tape, and four different-colored markers. Then write each of the four marks of the Church (One, Holy, Catholic, and Apostolic) on a separate piece of newsprint and post the sheets around the room (in the four corners, if possible).

2. Have the students count off by fours. Have the 1 students start at the sheet with the word *one*, the 2 students at the sheet with the word *holy,* and so on. Provide each group with a different-colored marker.

3. Have each group choose a scribe to write everything on their paper that their group can recall about their assigned mark of the Church as it relates to Catholicism.

4. Rotate the small groups clockwise after about 3 to 5 minutes. Have the groups place a checkmark next to the statements and information the previous group wrote that this group deems as correct responses. Have the groups put a line through any information they deem to be incorrect. Continue this process until all four groups have had a turn at each sheet of newsprint.

5. Conclude this learning experience by conducting a large-group discussion about the information written on each of the four sheets of newsprint.

**Understand**

## Step 2

Follow this assessment by presenting to the students the handouts "Final Performance Task Options for Unit 4" (Document #: TX001463) and "Rubric for Final Performance Tasks for Unit 4" (Document #: TX001464).

This unit provides you with two ways to assess that the students have a deep understanding of the most important concepts in the unit: creating a children's book that presents one of the four marks of the Church or creating a Power-Point presentation that examines all four marks of the Church. Refer to "Using Final Performance Tasks to Assess Understanding" (Document #: TX001011) and "Using Rubrics to Assess Work" (Document #: TX001012) at *smp.org/ LivinginChrist* for background information.

1.  Prepare for this learning experience by downloading and printing the handouts "Final Performance Task Options for Unit 4" (Document #: TX001463) and "Rubric for Final Performance Tasks for Unit 4" (Document #: TX001464), one for each student.

2.  Distribute the handouts. Give the students a choice as to which performance task they choose and add more options if you so choose. Review the directions, expectations, and rubric in class, allowing the students to ask questions. You may want to say something to this effect:

    ➤ If you wish to work alone, you may choose option 1 or option 2. If you wish to work with a partner, you may choose option 2.

    ➤ Near the end of the unit, you will have one full class period to work on your final performance task. Please keep in mind, however, that you should be working on this task throughout the course of the unit. Please do not wait until this class period to begin work on your final performance task.

---

**Teacher Note**

If you have done these performance tasks, or very similar ones, with students before, place examples of this work in the classroom. During this introduction explain how each is a good example of what you are looking for, for different reasons. This allows the students to concretely understand that there is not only one way to succeed.

Articles
16, 17,
20, 21,
25, 26,
27, 28,
29, 32

## Step 3

*Present activities stations for teaching the students the four marks of the Church.*

The following articles in the student book address the four marks of the Church. Throughout this unit the students will be directed to read these articles. For this learning experience, you may choose to simply make the students aware of the articles or you may direct them to read all of them. If you have the students read all the articles, be aware that later in the unit the students will be directed to reread or review them. The PowerPoint "Four Marks" (Document #: TX001509) may also be used with this step. There is a PowerPoint available at *smp.org/ LivinginChrist* that you can use to explore this topic with your students.

- "The First Mark of the Church" (article 16)
- "Bonds of Unity" (article 17)
- "Why Is the Church Holy?" (article 20)
- "The Church Makes Us Holy through God's Grace" (article 21)
- "The Meaning of the Word *Catholic*" (article 25)
- "Catholicity: The Fullness of Christ in the Church" (article 26)
- "The Church's Relationship with All People" (article 27)
- "Universality and Diversity" (article 28)
- "The Apostles Continue Jesus' Mission" (article 29)
- "The Apostolate of the Laity" (article 32)

1. Prepare for this learning experience by gathering four sheets of newsprint; a black marker; a roll of masking tape; several magazines, markers, pairs of scissors, and bottles of glue; mini-jars of Play-Doh, one for each student; and several sheets of blank paper, one of each for each student.

2. Using the sheets of newsprint, make signs for four stations around the room. Include the following instructions on each sign, post the signs in different areas of the room, and stock each station with the appropriate supplies:

   - Station 1 (One)

     ○ Create a group unity collage by cutting out pictures from magazines. Around the edges of the paper, write words that unify others.

     ○ Write a brief paragraph explaining how the Church works to unify the world.

   - Station 2 (Holy)

○ Using Play-Doh, create a variety of icons, images, and symbols that represent the holiness of the Church (statues, a crucifix, rosary beads, and so on).

○ Create a display with the objects and post signs to explain how each item represents the holiness of the Church.

- Station 3 (Catholic)

○ Create a Catholic slogan and design for a T-shirt or sweatshirt.

○ Write a three-to-five-sentence paragraph explaining how the slogan demonstrates what it means to be Catholic.

- Station 4 (Apostolic)

○ Create an individual service log of service performed while in high school.

○ Brainstorm the ways your school conducts service.

3. Divide the large group into four small groups for this exercise. Start each small group at a different station and then have the groups rotate clockwise until each small group has completed all four stations.

4. Conclude by conducting a large-group discussion. Verify that the students truly understand the basics of the four marks of the Church.

Articles
16, 17

Interpret

## Step 4

Introduce the Web quest to help the students to discover how faith is expressed around the world through the Church's being united in charity, in the profession of one faith, in the common celebration of worship and Sacraments, and in Apostolic Succession.

For this learning experience, you will use the Web quest exercise. See the article "Web Quest" (Document #: TX001525) at *smp.org/LivinginChrist* for more information on this learning method.

1. Prepare for this learning experience by verifying the Web site suggestions provided at *smp.org/LivinginChrist.* You will also want to identify supplementary resources that are available on campus or in the local community. If the students do not have laptops or computers in the classroom, arrange to use the computer lab or library. Also download and print the handout "The Church Is One" (Document #: TX001466), one for each student, and gather pens or pencils, one for each student.

2. As background have the students read student book articles 16 and 17, "The First Mark of the Church" and "Bonds of Unity."

3. Begin by presenting the four themes and inviting the students to provide a basic explanation of each theme:

   ➤ the Church united in charity

   ➤ the Church united in the profession of one faith

   ➤ the Church united in the common celebration of worship and Sacraments

   ➤ the Church united in Apostolic Succession

4. Divide the class into travel groups of four or five students and assign each travel group one of the four themes. If you have more than four groups, assign the same theme to multiple groups.

5. Distribute the handout and pens or pencils. Go through the directions with the students.

6. Provide useful Web addresses to the students and allow time for computer research and presentation preparation. If you choose to have the students complete all work during class time, you will want to allow two or three days for this exercise. Be sure to have available all needed art supplies.

7. When the groups have completed their research and created their presentations, allow class time for each travel group to present its "travel log."

8. Conclude the learning experience by leading a class discussion about what the students learned from their travel experiences and the presentations of the other groups.

Articles
20, 21

## Step 5

*Present material on the mark the Church is holy, using clips from the film* Champions of Faith *(2007, 65 minutes, not rated) from Catholic Media Exchange and an exercise with an examination of conscience.*

1. Prepare for this learning experience by obtaining a copy of the DVD *Champions of Faith* (2007, 65 minutes, not rated) from Catholic Media Exchange and a TV and DVD player, if you choose to start this learning experience by showing clips from the film. Also download and print a copy of the handout "An Examination of Conscience" (Document #: TX001467).

2. As background have the students read student book articles 20 and 21, "Why Is the Church Holy?" and "The Church Makes Us Holy through God's Grace."

3. As an optional start to this learning experience, you can show one or more clips of your choosing from *Champions of Faith* to illustrate failures in faith followed by redemption and healing. This inspiring video presents various Catholic baseball superstars as they share about their faith, an example of the successes and struggles of major league players as they strive to live out their faith.

4. If you do show clips from *Champions of Faith,* have a follow-up discussion with the students about how the video portrays "holiness."

5. Review with the class student book article 21, "The Church Makes Us Holy through God's Grace." As part of the review, have the class respond to the following questions:

    ➤ What is grace?

    ➤ How do we cooperate with the Holy Spirit's grace?

    ➤ What are the different types of grace?

6. Explain that we must be willing to make an effort to cooperate with grace and work toward holiness. One way we can cooperate is to examine our lives and see where we need to grow and where we are already cooperating with grace. We are going to spend time examining both of these things in our lives.

7. Invite the students to clear their desks and to sit comfortably. Explain that you are going to lead them in an examination of conscience. An examination of conscience is when we take time to reflect and pray about our relationship with God and identify the ways we need to strengthen the relationship and ask for forgiveness. An examination of conscience is not about feeling bad or guilty; it is about working to cooperate with grace and growing closer to God.

8. Lead the students in the examination of conscience on the handout "An Examination of Conscience" (Document #: TX001467). Pause after each question to provide the students time for reflection.

9. Follow the examination of conscience by explaining that as a class you are now going to reflect on the ways that you are cooperating with grace and God's will.

10. In the center of the board, write "Where I See Grace Working," leaving space around it for writing.

11. Invite the class to provide examples of where they see grace working around them. For this sharing they are to identify examples where they have witnessed grace working in the lives of those around them. These could be examples they have seen of people publicly living out their faith, making good choices, and performing works of mercy. Ask the students not to include names but to simply identify the situation. For example, "helping a classmate who is struggling with an assignment," "volunteering at church," "welcoming a new student to the school."

12. Conclude by emphasizing that the Church is holy and that we are called to holiness. To live holy lives, we have to work to cooperate with the Holy Spirit's grace in our lives.

Articles
25, 26,
27, 28

## Step 6

*Explore with the students the two meanings of the phrase "the Church is catholic" by having them identify symbols of the fullness of Christ and the means of salvation and by examining the Church's relationship with other faith traditions.*

1. Prepare for this learning experience by downloading and printing copies of the handout "Catholic / catholic" (Document #: TX001468), one for each student.

2. As background have the students read student book articles 25–28, "The Meaning of the Word *Catholic*," "Catholicity: The Fullness of Christ in the Church," "The Church's Relationship with All People," and "Universality and Diversity."

3. Begin by sharing the following with the class:

   ➤ The third mark of the Church we will look at is "catholic," with a lower-case *c*. When we say the Church is catholic, we are saying two things: first, that the Church possesses the fullness of Christ and has received from him the fullness of the means of salvation; and second, that the Church has been sent on a mission by Christ to all people in the world to gather all into the People of God.

4. Distribute the handout. Instruct the students to write the word *Catholic* with a capital *C* in the middle of the Church, leaving space around it for writing and drawing.

5. Next tell the students they are to draw images around the word *Catholic* that symbolize the Catholic Church possessing the fullness of Christ and the fullness of the means of salvation. They may want to consult the student book articles they read in preparation for this learning experience for ideas. Give the students 5 to 10 minutes to complete this.

6. When the students have finished drawing the symbols, invite volunteers to share the symbols they identified. You may need to correct or clarify any inaccuracies. Encourage the students to add symbols that are shared that they do not already have on their handout.

7. Share the following:

➤ As we know, the Church possesses the fullness of Christ and has received from him the fullness of the means of salvation. *Catholic* also means, though, that the Church has a mission from Christ to all the people in the world to gather all into the People of God. This means that the Church is for all people and all are invited.

8. Instruct the students to look again at the handout where they drew the symbols. Direct them to draw circles representing the faiths listed here. They should place the circles in proximity to the particular faiths' relation to the Church (i.e., overlapping with the Church, next to the Church, or separated from the Church). They may want to consult the student book articles they read in preparation for this learning experience for ideas. Give the students 5 to 10 minutes to complete this.

- other Christian communities
- Eastern Catholic Churches
- Judaism
- Islam
- Hinduism
- Buddhism

9. When the students have completed drawing the circles, invite volunteers to share where they placed the circles and why.

10. To conclude this learning experience, direct the students to now draw a large circle on the page, encompassing all the circles and images. Explain:

➤ On your handout you can see that the Church possesses the symbols you drew to represent the fullness of Christ and the means of salvation. The large circle you just drew represents the Church's mission to gather all people into the People of God. As you can see, there are faith traditions that are not a part of the Catholic Church. Even so, the mark of the Church as catholic means that all are invited into the fullness of Christ. The Church also recognizes that most faiths participate to some degree in the fullness of God's truth and divine life.

Articles
29, 30,
31

# Step 7

*Introduce the students to our current successor to Peter, Pope Benedict XVI, and have them create a PowerPoint slideshow about his life.*

1. Prepare for this learning experience by ensuring that the students will have access to the computer lab or media center. Also gather blank sheets of paper, one for each student.

2. As background have the students read student book articles 29–31, "The Apostles Continue Jesus' Mission," "Apostolic Tradition," and "The Successors to Peter and the Apostles."

3. Introduce the learning experience using these or similar words:

   ➤ One aspect of the Church's apostolic nature is the role of the Pope in the life of the Church. Let's examine the life of Pope Benedict XVI (formerly Cardinal Joseph Ratzinger) and how he became Pope.

4. Divide the class into small groups of four or five and assign each small group one of the following areas of Pope Benedict XVI's life:

   • his early life and upbringing in Germany
   • his life as a priest
   • his life as a bishop or cardinal and his work in the Vatican
   • his life as Pope, his hobbies, and his writings
   • his impact on the Church today

5. Direct the groups to create a PowerPoint slideshow summary and an accompanying handout that summarizes important information from the PowerPoint on the aspect of the life of Pope Benedict XVI they have been assigned. Many Web sites are available with timelines and biographical information about the Holy Father. The PowerPoint should contain a minimum of ten slides.

6. Another option with this exercise is to instruct the small groups to also create a simple game to accompany their PowerPoint presentation. The game can be played after the presentation to test the class on the content of the presentation.

7. When the small groups have finished creating the slideshows, have them present their finished products for the class. If you are using the game option, prepare for the games to be played after viewing the PowerPoint presentations.

## Teacher Note

If you are doing the lesson in a longer block, have two students in each small group prepare the PowerPoint slideshow and the other two or three students prepare the game.

8. When the students have finished showing the PowerPoint presentations (and playing the games, if this option was chosen), distribute a blank sheet of paper to each student and direct the students to individually complete the lesson by writing a reflection on the following questions:

> ➤ In reviewing the life of Joseph Ratzinger, what are three events that prepared him to accept the role of Pope? Explain each. (Think about his family life, his role as a priest, and his role as a cardinal for experiences that may have prepared him.)

> ➤ What qualities do Peter, the first bishop of Rome, and Pope Benedict XVI have in common in carrying out their apostolic roles?

**Apply**

## Step 8

*Have the students create a PowerPoint of the successions of the Popes to help them to understand the concept of Apostolic Succession.*

This experience has students using PowerPoint software to illustrate the successions of the Popes. If you do not wish to have students use PowerPoint, instruct them to create another kind of visual display.

1. Prepare for this learning experience by ensuring the students will have access to the computer lab or media center.

2. Instruct the students to conduct research on the Internet to discover information about and photos of the successions of the Popes in the Catholic Church. (A link to the Vatican Library Web site can be found at *smp.org/ LivinginChrist.*) Information about Pope Benedict XVI and his nine predecessors is available at the Vatican Web site. As part of their research, the students should identify the following:

   • important biographical information
   • years of his papacy
   • significant events of his papacy
   • important global events that coincided with his papacy

3. Assign the students the task of creating a PowerPoint slide show of at least ten photos, complete with narration that highlights information they identified in their research. Allow 20 to 30 minutes for the students to create their slides.

4. Allow time for the students to share their PowerPoints with the class.

Article
32

# Step 9

*Conduct student reflections on their service in the school, parish, and community. How have they seen the face of Jesus in their service? How have the people they have ministered to in their service been the face of Jesus to them?*

This learning experience guides the students in a bilevel journal reflection, having them use both words and images to identify how they have been impacted by the service they have done or witnessed.

1. Prepare for this learning experience by gathering sheets of blank paper, one for each student.

2. As background have the students read student book article 32, "The Apostolate of the Laity."

3. Distribute a sheet of paper to each student. Direct the students to position their sheets of paper in portrait mode and to draw a line down the paper, 3 inches from the left edge of the page.

4. Now invite the students to quietly reflect for a few moments on any service experiences they have had during high school. Encourage them to think about service they have done in their school, parish, and community. Allow 2 to 3 minutes for silent reflection.

5. Now, in the large portion of the paper, have the students write a reflection addressing the following prompts:

   ➤ How have you seen the face of Jesus in your service?
   ➤ How have the people you have ministered to in your service revealed the face of Jesus to you?

6. Conclude by having the students draw images and write words in the left 3 inches of the page to illustrate their feelings about and reactions to what they have written regarding their service.

## Step 10

*Now that the students are closer to the end of the unit, make sure they are all on track with their final performance tasks, if you have assigned them.*

If possible, devote 50 to 60 minutes for the students to ask questions about the tasks and to work individually or in their small groups.

1. Remind the students to bring to class any work they have already prepared so that they can work on it during the class period. If necessary, reserve the library or media center so the students can do any book or online research.

2. Provide some class time for the students to work on their performance tasks. This then allows you to work with the students who need additional guidance with the project.

## Step 11

*Provide the students with a tool to use for reflecting about what they learned in the unit and how they learned.*

This learning experience provides the students with an excellent opportunity to reflect on how their understandings of God and the Trinity have developed throughout the unit.

1. To prepare for this learning experience, download and print the handout "Learning about Learning" (Document #: TX001159; see Appendix), one for each student.

2. Distribute the handout, and give the students about 15 minutes to answer the questions quietly. Invite them to share any reflections they have about the content they learned as well as their insights into the way they learned.

# Final Performance Task Options for Unit 4

## Important Information for Both Options

The following are the main ideas you are to understand from this unit. They should appear in this final performance task so your teacher can assess whether you learned the most essential content.

- The Church is one: united in charity, in the profession of faith, in the common celebration of worship and Sacraments, and in the Apostolic Succession.

- The Church is holy because, although Church members sin, the Church as the Body of Christ is sinless.

- The Church is catholic because it exists for all people and is the means of salvation for all people.

- The Church is apostolic because Christ calls all Church members to share the Gospel of salvation.

## Option 1: Children's Book

You have been hired to write a children's book to explain one of the four marks of the Church. Follow these guidelines in composing your book:

- Explain one of the four marks of the Church in a way that is understandable to a child.

- Include both illustrations and text.

- Have a minimum of ten pages and a maximum of sixteen pages (excluding cover, title, and dedication pages).

## Option 2: PowerPoint Presentation

Create a PowerPoint presentation that teaches about the four marks of the Church. Follow these guidelines in creating your presentation:

- Feature text (typically bulleted), images, and music. (Be sure to cite the sources of the text, graphics, and music at the end of the slide show.)

- Include at least four relevant quotations from the *Catechism of the Catholic Church*.

- Create fifteen to twenty slides.

- Write a script for the presentation that you will turn in with the PowerPoint.

# Rubric for Final Performance Tasks for Unit 4

| Criteria | 4 | 3 | 2 | 1 |
|---|---|---|---|---|
| **Assignment includes all items requested in the directions.** | Assignment not only includes all items requested, but they are completed above expectations. | Assignment includes all items requested. | Assignment includes more than half of the items requested. | Assignment includes less than half of the items requested. |
| **Assignment shows understanding of the concept *the Church is one: united in charity, in the profession of faith, in the common celebration of worship and Sacraments, and in the Apostolic Succession.*** | Assignment shows unusually insightful understanding of this concept. | Assignment shows good understanding of this concept. | Assignment shows adequate understanding of this concept. | Assignment shows little understanding of this concept. |
| **Assignment shows understanding of the concept *the Church is holy because, although Church members sin, the Church as the Body of Christ is sinless.*** | Assignment shows unusually insightful understanding of this concept. | Assignment shows good understanding of this concept. | Assignment shows adequate understanding of this concept. | Assignment shows little understanding of this concept. |
| **Assignment shows understanding of the concept *the Church is catholic because it exists for all people and is the means of salvation for all people.*** | Assignment shows unusually insightful understanding of this concept. | Assignment shows good understanding of this concept. | Assignment shows adequate understanding of this concept. | Assignment shows little understanding of this concept. |
| **Assignment shows understanding of the concept *the Church is apostolic because Christ calls all Church members to share the Gospel of salvation.*** | Assignment shows unusually insightful understanding of this concept. | Assignment shows good understanding of this concept. | Assignment shows adequate understanding of this concept. | Assignment shows little understanding of this concept. |
| **Assignment uses proper grammar and spelling.** | Assignment has no grammar or spelling errors. | Assignment has one grammar or spelling error. | Assignment has two grammar or spelling errors. | Assignment has more than two grammar or spelling errors. |

# Vocabulary for Unit 4

**actual grace:** God's interventions and support for us in the everyday moments of our lives. Actual graces are important for conversion and for continuing growth in holiness.

**Apostles' Creed:** One of two creeds of faith that has a special place in the Church's life. The Apostles' Creed is a statement of Christian faith developed from the baptismal creed of the ancient Church of Rome.

**apostolate:** The Christian person's activity that fulfills the apostolic nature of the whole Church when he or she works to extend the Kingdom of Christ to the entire world. If your school shares the wisdom of its founder, its namesake, or the charism of the religious order that founded it, it is important to learn about this person or order and his or her charism, because as a graduate you will likely want to incorporate this charism into your own apostolate.

**apostolic:** To be founded on the Twelve Apostles.

**Apostolic Succession:** The uninterrupted passing on of apostolic preaching and authority from the Apostles directly to all bishops. It is accomplished through the laying on of hands when a bishop is ordained in the Sacrament of Holy Orders as instituted by Christ. The office of bishop is permanent, because at ordination a bishop is marked with an indelible, sacred character.

**bishop:** One who has received the fullness of the Sacrament of Holy Orders and is a successor to the Apostles.

**catholic:** Along with One, Holy, and Apostolic, *Catholic* is one of the four marks of the Church. *Catholic* means "universal." The Church is catholic in two senses. She is catholic because Christ is present in her and has given her the fullness of the means of salvation and also because she reaches throughout the world to all people.

**conversion:** A change of heart, turning away from sin and toward God.

**creed:** Based on the Latin *credo,* meaning, "I believe," a creed is an official presentation of the faith, usually prepared and presented by a council of the Church and used in the Church's liturgy. Two creeds occupy a special place in the Church's life: the Apostles' Creed and the Nicene Creed.

**ecclesial:** Of or relating to a church.

**episcopal:** Of or relating to bishops.

**grace:** The free and undeserved gift of God's loving and active presence in the universe and in our lives, empowering us to respond to his call and to live as his adopted sons and daughters. Grace restores our loving communion with the Holy Trinity, lost through sin.

**habitual grace:** Sanctifying grace is a habitual grace, meaning that it is a stable and supernatural disposition. It is always with us, helping us to live according to God's will. Habitual grace differs from actual grace and sacramental grace.

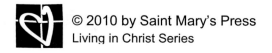 © 2010 by Saint Mary's Press
Living in Christ Series

Document #: TX001465

**icon:** Religious painting traditional among many Eastern Christians. Christian iconography expresses in image the same Gospel message that the Scriptures communicate by words.

**iconostasis:** A screen or partition with doors and tiers of icons that separates the bema, the raised part of the church with the altar, from the nave, the main part of the church, in Eastern Churches.

**laypeople (laity):** All members of the Church with the exception of those who are ordained as bishops, priests, or deacons. The laity share in Christ's role as priest, prophet, and king, witnessing to God's love and power in the world.

**marks of the Church:** The four essential features or characteristics of the Church: One, Holy, Catholic (universal), and Apostolic.

**Nicene Creed:** The formal statement or profession of faith commonly recited during the Eucharist.

**sacramental graces:** The gifts proper to each of the Seven Sacraments.

**Sacred Tradition:** From the Latin *tradere*, meaning "to hand on." Refers to the process of passing on the Gospel message. It began with the oral communication of the Gospel by the Apostles, was written down in the Scriptures, and is interpreted by the Magisterium under the guidance of the Holy Spirit.

**Sacrament of Holy Orders:** The Sacrament by which members of the Church are ordained for permanent ministry in the Church as bishops, priests, or deacons.

**sanctifying grace:** The grace that heals our human nature wounded by sin and restores us to friendship with God by giving us a share in the divine life of the Trinity. It is a supernatural gift of God, infused into our souls by the Holy Spirit, that continues the work of making us holy.

**supernatural grace:** Transcending the power of human intellect and will.

# The Church Is One

## Introduction

We say that the Church is one because the Church's example for unity and source of unity is the three Divine Persons in the Trinity: the Father, the Son, and the Holy Spirit. Unity does not mean uniformity, however, as the Church is diverse in many ways. The unity of the Church is sustained by God's love and can be seen through several bonds, including the profession of faith, common worship, and Apostolic Succession.

Unity among Christians has been threatened over time by heresies, schism, and other breaks. The results of these breaks can be seen today in the different Christian denominations that exist.

## What You Will Do

You will travel via the Internet to the Church in various places throughout the world. You and your fellow travelers will prepare a brief presentation to share with the class about what you learn about one of four themes:

- the Church united in charity

- the Church united in the profession of one faith

- the Church united in the common celebration of worship and Sacrament

- the Church united in Apostolic Succession

## Where You Will Begin Your Travels

The sites you visit will depend on the theme assigned to your travel group. The Web sites listed here will take you to many places that will introduce you to basic information. They may also point you to side trips that will enrich your experience. You are not limited to these Web sites for your travels.

- your own diocesan Web site

- the Web site for the religious order(s) that staff your school or local parish

- the Vatican Web site

- the United States Conference of Catholic Bishops Web site

- the Catholic News Service Web site

© 2010 by Saint Mary's Press
Living in Christ Series

- the Spring Hill College Theology Library Web site

- the Catholic Relief Services Web site

You may supplement what you learn on your Internet travels with print resources, recordings, or other artifacts that may be available in your school library, sacred vessels or liturgy aids from the school chapel, or other appropriate materials that you may be able to locate in the larger community.

# Your Travel Log

You will visit at least three different places in the world. You will keep a log of what you learn at each site. You must remember that the purpose of your travels is to investigate your theme as it is lived or expressed throughout the world. Therefore you and your travel group must visit the Church on different continents (or in different cultures). Your log will be titled with the theme of your assignment.

Each log entry will include the following:

- Web address

- evidence that this is a credible source for your information (sponsoring organization, author, and so on), especially important for some of the sites that are not on the list of suggested starting points

- what you learned

- how what you learned adds to your understanding of your assigned theme

# Telling the Story of Your Travels

Your travel group will meet to develop a way of sharing your travel experience, presenting what you learned, with the class. This may be a travel brochure, an oral presentation, a poster, a PowerPoint presentation, an annotated map, a display with explanation of artifacts, or another form of creative expression. You will provide each class member with a handout that highlights your theme.

Document #: TX001466

# An Examination of Conscience

## Love of God

- Is there anything that I am allowing to take God's place in my life?

- Do I pray regularly, and when I do pray, do I give my full attention to my prayer?

- Do I attend Mass and receive the Eucharist every week? Do I keep Sunday holy?

- Am I making a good effort to grow in my relationship with God by receiving the Sacrament of Penance and Reconciliation, by doing spiritual reading, and by going on retreats and participating in other spiritual practices?

- Am I always reverent to God in my words and actions?

## Love of Neighbor

- Have I treated anyone with disrespect, especially my parents, brothers and sisters, teachers, and other people in authority?

- Have I obeyed the rules and laws of my school, state, and country?

- Have I harmed another person intentionally or through my careless actions? Have I been unkind or cruel to others in thought, word, or deed?

- Have I harmed another person's dignity by engaging in gossip or spreading demeaning stories about the person?

- Have I protected my chastity at all times? Have I viewed pornography, engaged in lustful thoughts, or been sexually active in any way outside of marriage?

- Have I been truthful in all situations calling for the truth? Have I cheated or been dishonest in any way?

- Have I been envious of someone else in any way?

- Have I participated in or supported another person's sinful actions?

- Have I been of service to others whom I was in a position to help? Have I reached out in some way to people in need?

© 2010 by Saint Mary's Press
Living in Christ Series

Document #: TX001467

# Catholic / catholic

Living in Christ Series

Document #: TX001468

# Unit 4 Test

## Part 1: True or False

Write *true* or *false* in the space next to each statement.

1. _____ The New Testament is perfectly clear: there is only one Church, one Body of Christ, and it is characterized by oneness or unity.

2. _____ Christ gave the Church the gift of unity, a gift she cannot lose.

3. _____ Unity is the same as uniformity.

4. _____ Christ wants no diversity in the Church.

5. _____ There are different kinds of spiritual gifts but the same Spirit.

6. _____ The integrity of the Church's worship is guaranteed because the ritual has been passed down from the Apostles through bishops.

7. _____ As the successor to Paul, the Pope is the visible principle and foundation of the unity of the whole Church.

8. _____ The Pope leads the Church by domination and power.

9. _____ Church members are connected by both visible and invisible bonds of unity.

10. _____ People all over the world profess one faith by praying the Nicene Creed.

11. _____ The Apostles' Creed is a summary of the Apostles' faith, while the Nicene Creed has authority because it comes from the Church's first two ecumenical councils.

12. _____ The Creed summarizes truths about the Father, the Son, and the Holy Spirit, as well as belief in the Church and other essential beliefs.

13. _____ The Twelve Sacraments create bonds of unity within the Church, especially the Eucharist.

14. _____ The bishops and the Pope have received their authority by means of hierarchical succession through the Sacrament of Holy Orders.

15. _____ The Church honors Mary above all other saints.

16. _____ The word *Theotokos* means "God-bearer" in Greek.

17. _____ When Mary's earthly life was over, she was taken up, body and soul, into Heaven (the Assumption), where she already shares in the glory of her Son's Resurrection.

18. _____ Saint Paul emphasized that all his strength and authority was due to his education and upbringing.

19. _____ Jesus is the fullness of Divine Revelation.

20. _____ Apostolic Succession is a source of unity in the Church.

# Part 2: Matching

Match each statement in column 1 with a term from column 2. Write the letter that corresponds to your choice in the space provided. (*Note:* There are two extra items in column 2.)

## Column 1

1. _____ One of two creeds of faith that has a special place in the Church's life.

2. _____ The first of the four marks of the Church.

3. _____ The Bishop of Rome.

4. _____ Baptism, the Eucharist, and Confirmation are _____.

5. _____ Jesus was _____.

6. _____ One who has received the fullness of the Sacrament of Holy Orders and is a successor to the Apostles.

7. _____ Three faiths trace their faith back to Abraham: Christianity, Judaism, and _____.

8. _____ The Roman Catholic Church is also known as the _____ Church.

9. _____ Religious painting traditional among many Eastern Christians.

10. _____ The Church is _____ because she was founded on the Apostles.

## Column 2

A. Sacraments of Christian Initiation

B. bishop

C. hyperventilation

D. the Pope

E. Latin

F. Apostles' Creed

G. one

H. Hinduism

I. apostolic

J. Islam

K. icon

L. Jewish

Document #: TX001469

# Part 3: Fill-in-the-Blank

Use the word bank to fill in the blanks in the following sentences. (*Note:* There are two extra terms in the word bank.)

**WORD BANK**

| | |
|---|---|
| Apostles | Sacred Tradition |
| Trinity | one who is sent |
| Divine Revelation | divine authorship |
| Pharisees | Covenant |
| Sacrament of Holy Orders | forgive sins in Jesus' name (see John 20:22–23) |
| the Holy Spirit | Rome |

1. Bishops are the successors of the _____ through the fullness of the Sacrament of Holy Orders, which conveys sacred power to bishops through the laying on of hands.

2. With the help of _____, the Church preserves and hands on the teachings of the Apostles and their successors.

3. The Greek word *apostolos* literally means "_____."

4. Christ gave his Apostles great power and authority to serve in his name and act in his person. They had the authority to _____.

5. Jesus is the fullness of _____.

6. The handing on, or transmission, of the truths Jesus Christ taught is known as _____.

7. The Sacred Scriptures have _____ because the Apostles or their associates wrote them under the inspiration of the Holy Spirit.

8. The word _____ is not used in the Bible.

9. The _____ is an essential element of Apostolic Succession.

10. The Pope is the bishop of _____.

Document #: TX001469

# Part 4: Short Answer

Answer the following question in paragraph form on a separate sheet of paper.

1.  How are you as a layperson called to continue the mission of Christ and the Apostles?

Document #: TX001469

# Unit 4 Test Answer Key

## Part 1: True or False

| | | |
|---|---|---|
| 1. True | 8. False | 15. True |
| 2. True | 9. True | 16. True |
| 3. False | 10. True | 17. True |
| 4. False | 11. True | 18. False |
| 5. True | 12. True | 19. True |
| 6. True | 13. False | 20. True |
| 7. False | 14. False | |

## Part 2: Matching

| | | |
|---|---|---|
| 1. F | 5. L | 9. K |
| 2. G | 6. B | 10. I |
| 3. D | 7. J | |
| 4. A | 8. E | |

## Part 3: Fill-in-the-Blank

1. Apostles
2. the Holy Spirit
3. one who is sent
4. forgive sins in Jesus' name (see John 20:22–23)
5. Divine Revelation
6. Sacred Tradition
7. divine authorship
8. Trinity
9. Sacrament of Holy Orders
10. Rome

## Part 4: Short Answer

1. The source of the apostolate for all members of the Church is Christ. Our relationship with Christ affects our ability to spread the Good News. Whether ordained or lay, a person who wants to engage in the apostolate must be in union with Christ. Participating in the celebration of the Eucharist is the soul of the apostolate. The apostolate can take many forms for the laity because we live in the world, sharing the varied gifts given to us by the Holy Spirit. We are called to witness to God's love and power in the world, and to share the Good News of salvation through Christ with the world. Whether at school, at work, within our families, or among our friends—wherever we are—we are called to be witnesses and to tell others about Jesus Christ and his gift of salvation to the world.

© 2010 by Saint Mary's Press
Living in Christ Series

Document #: TX001470

# Unit 5 The Church Carries Out Its Mission

## Overview

This unit helps the students to understand the Church's missionary mandate to evangelize and share the Good News of Jesus Christ. The students reflect on the role of the hierarchy, religious congregations, the laity, and the family in fulfilling this missionary mandate.

## Key Understandings and Questions

Upon completing this unit, the students will have a deeper understanding of the following key concepts:

- The Church's people share a common mission.
- The hierarchy's unique role in the Church is to teach, govern, and sanctify the Church.
- Vowed religious further the Church's mission through their vows of chastity, poverty, and obedience.
- The laity's unique role in the Church is to proclaim Christ by word and example in the ordinary circumstances of the world.

Upon completing the unit, the students will have answered the following questions:

- What is the mission of the Church?
- How does the hierarchy contribute to this mission?
- How do religious communities contribute to this mission?
- How do single and married laypeople contribute to this mission?

## Student Book Articles

This unit draws on articles from *The Church: Christ in the World Today* student book and incorporates them into the unit instruction. Whenever the teaching steps for the unit require the students to refer to or read an article from the student book, the following symbol appears in the margin: (📖). The articles covered in the unit are from Section 3: "The Church's Salvation and Mission" and "Section 4: The Lived Mission of the Church," and are as follows:

- "The Church and Evangelization" (article 38, pp. 141–145)
- "The Church and Hierarchy" (article 39, pp. 150–153)
- "The Pope: Visible Head of the Church" (article 40, pp. 153–155)

- "The Role of the Bishops in the Church Hierarchy" (article 41, pp. 156–159)
- "The Priesthood" (article 42, pp. 160–163)
- "The Diaconate" (article 43, pp. 163–167)
- "The Mission of the Laity" (article 45, pp. 172–175)
- "The Work and Vocation of the Laity" (article 46, pp. 176–179)
- "The Consecrated Life: Religious Orders" (article 47, pp. 179–182)
- "Other Types of Consecrated Life" (article 48, pp. 182–184)

## How Will You Know the Students Understand?

The following resources will help you assess the students' understanding of the key concepts covered in this unit:

- handout "Final Performance Task Options for Unit 5" (Document #: TX001471)
- handout "Rubric for Final Performance Tasks for Unit 5" (Document #: TX001472)
- handout "Unit 5 Test" (Document #: TX001479)

## The Suggested Path to Understanding

This unit in the teacher guide provides you with one learning path to take with the students, to enable them to begin their study of the ways in which the Church carries out its mission. It is not necessary to use all the learning experiences provided in the unit; however, if you substitute other material from this course or your own material for some of the material offered here, be sure that you have covered all relevant facets of understanding and that you have not missed any skills or knowledge required for later units.

 **Step 1:** Preassess student knowledge of the hierarchy of the Church and each person's call to share in the mission of the Church.

 **Step 2:** Follow this assessment by presenting to the students the handouts "Final Performance Task Options for Unit 5" and (Document #: TX001471) "Rubric for Final Performance Tasks for Unit 5" (Document #: TX001472).

 **Step 3:** Have the students begin exploring the evangelical mission of the Church, which is shared by all Church members.

 **Step 4:** Have the students create a collage about the Church's mission of evangelization and the role of the baptized in that mission.

**Step 5:** Have the students begin exploring the evangelical Church's mission of evangelization and the difference between proselytizing and evangelizing.

 **Step 6:** Present a learning experience related to the hierarchy, ordained members of the Church.

 **Step 7:** Introduce the students to the local diocese or archdiocese organizations to familiarize them with the local Catholic faith community.

 **Step 8:** Present student book and other material about the role of the vowed religious in the Church's mission of salvation.

 **Step 9:** Present a learning experience related to the role of the laity in the Church's mission of salvation.

 **Step 10:** Introduce the concept of the family as the domestic church and help the students to identify ways their families have the qualities of a domestic church.

 **Step 11:** Now that the students are closer to the end of the unit, make sure they are all on track with their final performance tasks, if you have assigned them.

 **Step 12:** Provide the students with a tool to use for reflecting about what they learned in the unit and how they learned.

## Background for Teaching This Unit

Visit *smp.org/LivinginChrist* for additional information about these and other theological concepts taught in this unit:

- "Called to Holiness: Holiness in Modern Church Teaching" (Document #: TX001341)
- "The Domestic Church" (Document #: TX001527)

The Web site also includes information on these and other teaching methods used in the unit:

- "Using the Jigsaw Process" (Document #: TX001020)
- "Treating Sensitive Topics" (Document #: TX001335)

## Scripture Passages

Scripture is an important part of the Living in Christ series and is frequently used in the learning experiences for each unit. The Scripture passages featured in this unit are as follows:

- Acts of the Apostles 6:1–6 (the need for assistants)
- Mark 10:42–45 (the last shall be first)
- Matthew 28:19 (make disciples of all nations)
- Philippians 2:7–8 (becoming obedient to death)
- 1 Thessalonians 5:17 (pray without ceasing)
- 1 Timothy 3:8–13 (conduct of deacons)

## Vocabulary

The student book and the teacher guide include the following key terms for this unit. To provide the students with a list of these terms and their definitions, download and print the handout "Vocabulary for Unit 5" (Document #: TX001473).

| | |
|---|---|
| bishop | Latin Church, Latin Rite |
| candidacy | ministry |
| college of bishops | monk |
| collegial | presbytery, presbyterate |
| consecrated life | priesthood |
| discernment | province |
| domestic | (religious) brother |
| domestic church | (religious) sister |
| eremitic | secular |
| hermit | seminary study |
| hierarchy | Transitional Diaconate |
| Holy See | vicar |
| institute | vocation |

# Learning Experiences

**Explain**

## Step 1

*Preassess student knowledge of the hierarchy of the Church and each person's call to share in the mission of the Church.*

1. Prepare for this learning experience by gathering pens or pencils, one for each student, and downloading and printing the handout "Catholic Church Role Description" (Document #: TX001474), one for every two students. Also write the following terms on small slips of paper and place them in a container from which they can be drawn:

| | |
|---|---|
| pope | catechist |
| cardinal | youth minister |
| bishop | director of religious education |
| auxiliary bishop | music minister |
| monsignor | lector |
| priest | usher |
| parochial vicar | Eucharistic minister |
| religious sister | lay professional minister |
| nun | parish council member |
| brother | canonical lawyer |

2. Instruct the students to form pairs, and then have each pair draw a slip of paper from the container. Inform the students that they may not know much about the Church role they selected but that they should do their best with the assignment.

3. Distribute the pens or pencils and the handout. Allow the pairs 5 minutes to complete the handout together.

4. After 5 minutes have the partners pass their role description papers to another pair. All pairs then have 3 minutes to add to or correct the information they have been given.

5. Continue until the role description papers have been passed at least three times. At the end of the exercise, have the pairs share the role descriptions with the whole class.

**Teacher Note**

If you are concerned about confidentiality, you could collect the papers each time and distribute them to different pairs. Names need not be written on the handouts.

## Step 2

Follow this assessment by presenting to the students the handouts "Final Performance Task Options for Unit 5" (Document #: TX001471) and "Rubric for Final Performance Tasks for Unit 5" (Document #: TX001472).

This unit provides you with two ways to assess that the students have a deep understanding of the most important concepts in the unit: creating a mission chart or creating a mission brochure. Refer to "Using Final Performance Tasks to Assess Understanding" (Document #: TX001011) and "Using Rubrics to Assess Work" (Document #: TX001012) at *smp.org/LivinginChrist* for background information.

1. Prepare by downloading and printing the handouts "Final Performance Task Options for Unit 5" (Document #: TX001471) and "Rubric for Final Performance Tasks for Unit 5" (Document #: TX001472), one of each for each student.

2. Distribute the handouts. Give the students a choice as to which performance task they choose and add more options if you so choose. Review the directions, expectations, and rubric in class, allowing the students to ask questions. You may want to say something to this effect:

   ➤ Near the end of the unit, you will have one full class period to work on your final performance task. Please keep in mind, however, that you should be working on this task throughout the course of the unit. Please do not wait until this class period to begin work on your final performance task.

### Teacher Note

You will want to assign due dates for the final performance tasks.

If you have done these performance tasks, or very similar ones, with students before, place examples of this work in the classroom. During this introduction explain how each is a good example of what you are looking for, for different reasons. This allows the students to concretely understand that there is not only one way to succeed.

**Explain**

## Step 3

*Have the students begin exploring the evangelical mission of the Church, which is shared by all Church members.*

This exercise introduces students to the concept of evangelization and guides them in recognizing common and uncommon elements of the Church's evangelical mission.

1. Prepare for this learning experience by downloading and printing the handout "'Tools of Evangelization' Word Search" (Document #: TX001475), one for each student.

2. Begin by distributing the handout, which is a word search for terms related to evangelization, and directing the students to complete it individually. Allow 5 to 7 minutes for the students to complete the word search.

3. When the students are finished, lead a class discussion using the following questions:

   ➤ What words from the word search do you associate with the Church?

   ➤ What words from the word search seem odd to you in terms of evangelization and the Church?

   ➤ How can the media be a positive and a negative resource in terms of evangelization?

4. Conclude by sharing that evangelization is not limited to the time we are at church or church activities. We are called to evangelize in all parts of our lives.

Article
38

**Interpret**

## Step 4

*Have the students create a collage about the Church's mission of evangelization and the role of the baptized in that mission.*

This learning experience helps to open the students' minds (and, hopefully, hearts) to the concept that at Baptism they were given a role to play in spreading the Good News of Jesus Christ.

1. Prepare for this learning experience by gathering the following items for each student: a sheet of art paper, a magazine, a glue stick, a pair of scissors, and several markers. Also have available a roll of masking tape for posting the completed collages.

2. As background have the students read student book article 38, "The Church and Evangelization," if they haven't done so already.

3. Begin by leading a class discussion on the following questions:

   ➤ What are the three situations in which the Church is to evangelize in the world today, as presented in Pope John Paul II's encyclical "On the Permanent Validity of the Church's Missionary Mandate" (*Redemptoris Missio*, December 7, 1990)?

   ➤ What is the responsibility of the laity in terms of evangelization?

   ➤ How can a young person be an evangelist for other young people in both direct and subtle ways?

   ➤ What are the elements of evangelization as outlined in the encyclical?

4. Next explain that the students are each going to create a collage demonstrating how they can spread the Good News about God, Jesus Christ, and salvation to others. They will use magazine pictures as well as their own drawings. Each image on the collage should be labeled, identifying which element of evangelization it addresses from "On the Permanent Validity of the Church's Missionary Mandate" (*Redemptoris Missio*). The collage should contain a minimum of eight images and address at least three of the four elements of evangelization.

5. Distribute the art supplies and direct the students to begin working. Allow 10 to 15 minutes for the students to create their collages.

6. When the students finish their collages, have each person share her or his collage with the class.

7. Post the collages around the classroom as a reminder of the concepts the students just learned.

**Apply**

## Step 5

*Present student book material about the Church's mission of evangelization and the difference between proselytizing and evangelizing.*

This learning experience presents two options to help the students to distinguish between proselytizing and evangelizing. Proselytizing is using fear, guilt, intimidation, and negative ways (such as judging others) to get people to join a group or religion. Evangelizing is inviting others into a deep relationship with God or inviting others to consider joining the Catholic religion.

### Option 1

Have the students create small-group skits (or tableaus) to demonstrate the difference between these two concepts.

**Option 2**

Have the students share about a time when someone invited them to do something versus a time when someone used guilt or fear to get them to do something. How did the method the person used to get them to do the activity make them feel about that activity?

Conclude either option by clarifying that the Church calls us to evangelize, not to proselytize. A key element in evangelization is respect.

Articles
39, 40,
41, 42,
43

# Step 6

*Present a learning experience related to the hierarchy, ordained members of the Church.*

1. Prepare for this learning experience by gathering sheets of blank paper and art supplies, such as markers, scissors, colored paper, and glue, for each small group of two or three.

2. As background have the students read student book articles 39–43, "The Church and Hierarchy," "The Pope: Visible Head of the Church," "The Role of the Bishops in the Church Hierarchy," "The Priesthood," and "The Diaconate."

3. Begin with an account from *Vatican News Service* of the election of Pope Benedict XVI to introduce the Pope, the college of cardinals, and so on.

4. Divide the class into small groups of two or three and have them create a game (like chess or checkers or a card game, for example), using the members of the hierarchy of the Church as game pieces. Have the students keep in mind who trumps whom, who works in concert with others, who is lower on the totem pole, and so on.

5. Distribute the art supplies and paper, and allow the small groups 10 to 15 minutes to create their games. Direct the groups to also write directions for their games, explaining the role and responsibility of each member of the hierarchy and how that applies to the game.

6. When the groups have finished, have them present their games to the class.

7. If there is time, allow the groups to play one another's games.

## Step 7

*Introduce the students to the local diocese or archdiocese organizations to familiarize them with the local Catholic faith community.*

This step uses a scavenger hunt game to help the students become aware of the different roles for both consecrated and lay people in the administration of the local diocese or archdiocese.

1. Prepare for this learning experience by ensuring the students will have access to a diocese directory, either in hard copy or via the Internet. Also download and print the handout "Who? What? When? Where? How? in the Local Diocese" (Document #: TX001476), one for each student, and gather sheets of blank paper, one for each student.

2. Distribute the sheets of blank paper, and offer the following instructions to the students:

   ➤ Before we begin this section on our local church leadership, let's do a quick survey of what we already know about our diocese. Write your answers on your blank sheet of paper:

   *Allow time between each question for the students to write their answers.*

   - Who is the bishop (archbishop) of this diocese (archdiocese)?
   - Does he have any auxiliaries? If so, what are their names?
   - Where does he live (city)?
   - How long has he been the bishop (archbishop) here?
   - How old is this diocese? (When was it formally organized?)
   - What are the boundaries of this diocese? (Or what are the names of the bordering dioceses or archdioceses?)
   - What is the title of three people who work with the bishop or archbishop?
   - Name three religious orders that work in the diocese or archdiocese.

3. After the students have answered these questions for themselves, discuss the answers with the whole class. Ask:

   ➤ Where could you find the answers to these questions?

   *the diocesan directory or Web site*

4. Distribute the handout as well as pages from the local diocesan directory, or provide the students with access to the diocesan Web site to see an online diocesan directory.

5. Instruct the students to try to find answers to all the questions regarding parishes, chancery offices, personnel, and contact information, or have different teams compete to see who can find the information the fastest. Allow 10 to 15 minutes for this research.

6. After the students have located all the information, ask these questions:

    ➤ Why does the Church need all of these offices?

    *to serve the People of God in every area of their lives and to provide an organized way of going about doing so*

    ➤ Are most of these offices managed by laypeople, ordained or consecrated people, or both? Why do you think so?

## Optional Extension

If you have access to it, distribute a copy of the diocesan or archdiocesan's recent budget report (with some explanatory notes about line items on the budget). Ask the students to examine the report and answer the following questions:

➤ Which item is the biggest expense in the budget for this diocese or archdiocese? What service does this office provide?

➤ Which item is the biggest source of income in the budget for this diocese or archdiocese? Why do you think this item generates the most income?

➤ If you could change one budget expense in your diocesan's or archdiocesan's budget, what would it be and why?

➤ If you could change one source of income in the budget for this diocese or archdiocese, what would it be and why?

Articles
47, 48

## Step 8

*Present student book and other material about the role of the vowed religious in the Church's mission of salvation.*

1. Prepare for this learning experience by creating a list of Web sites of religious congregations in your local area (city or diocese). Reserve the computer lab or media center so the students will have access to the Internet. Also download and print the handout "Congregation Information" (Document #: TX001477), one for each student.

2. As background have the students read student book articles 47 and 48, "The Consecrated Life: Religious Orders" and "Other Types of Consecrated Life."

3. Begin by reviewing the content from unit 2 on how we are all called to abundant life. Pose the following questions and share these key points:

   ➤ How is abundant life salvation for oneself? for others?

   ➤ Abundant life is a life lived in relationship, in love.

   ➤ The mission of the Church is achieved by persons who are called to love by living one of a variety of primary lifestyles. Some are called to love as vowed members of religious communities.

   ➤ Persons in religious life live out their baptismal call by responding to God's invitation to love in a specific way.

> **Teacher Note**
>
> As an option, you may wish to prepare for this learning experience by meeting with members of religious congregation(s) who are on your faculty, in your parish or diocese, or in another ministry in your local community. You might also consider inviting a vowed religious to come as a guest to your class to help to put a human face on the text material.

4. Present a brief review of student book material on the role of the vowed religious, whose role in the Church's mission flows from the founding charism of the congregation. Be sure to share the following definition of the word *charism* with the class and emphasize that the charisms of religious congregations are gifts for the Church:

   ➤ **charism:** This word (from the Greek *charis,* meaning "gift") refers to a special gift or grace of the Holy Spirit given to an individual Christian or community, commonly for the benefit and building up of the entire Church.

5. Distribute the handout and share the list of Web sites you identified for religious congregations in the area. Allow about 15 minutes for the students to complete the handout.

6. When the students have completed the handout, invite them to report on the congregations they researched. As a student reports on a particular congregation, list the charisms and works of the congregation on the board.

7. Conclude by reviewing the variety of charisms and works shared by religious congregations in the area. Emphasize the gift that religious congregations are to the Church and to the world. You might also share that in fact all of the resources for this curriculum are a result of the charism and work of a religious congregation, the Christian Brothers.

Articles
45, 46

# Step 9

*Present a learning experience related to the role of the laity in the Church's mission of salvation, using the jigsaw process.*

1. Prepare for this learning experience by locating five current articles from a variety of Catholic resources (e.g., *U.S. Catholic, Origins, America*, your diocesan newspaper, the resources in your school library, etc.) that show the involvement of the laity in the life of the Church. Examples of involvement could be Marriage preparation, ministry to a homebound person, action on behalf of justice, and so on. Make the number of copies of each article equal to the number of students in your class divided by five. (A class of twenty would need four copies of each article; a class of thirty would need six copies of each article.) Also gather sheets of blank paper, two for each student in the class, as well as a highlighter for each student.

2. As background have the students read student book articles 45 and 46, "The Mission of the Laity" and "The Work and Vocation of the Laity." If the students have already read these articles in unit 3, ask them to simply review them.

3. Divide the class into small groups of five (these will be the home groups) and distribute a highlighter and a different article to each member of each group.

4. Direct the students to read their articles and highlight information that demonstrates how the laity is involved in the Church.

5. Regroup the students so that the students who read the same article are in a group together. These new groups are now to work together to identify the main points of their articles and prepare what they will share with their home groups. Distribute a blank sheet of paper to each student for note taking.

6. Have the students return to their home groups and present the information they learned from their individual articles. Each home group should then identify common elements from the articles.

7. Now distribute a clean sheet of paper to each student, and then direct the students to individually write a paragraph addressing the following questions:

   ➤ What will I remember about the role of the laity in the Church? Why is this important?

Article
46

## Step 10

*Introduce the concept of the family as the domestic church and help the students to identify ways their families have the qualities of a domestic church.*

1. Prepare for this learning experience by downloading and printing the handout "Signs of the Domestic Church" (Document #: TX001478), one for each student. Also gather blank sheets of paper, one for each student. Additionally, the PowerPoint "The Domestic Church" (Document #: TX001510) can be used with this step.

2. As background have the students read student book article 46, "The Work and Vocation of the Laity."

3. Begin by posing the following questions to the class:

   ➤ The Church has a variety of ways of carrying out its mission. What role does the family play in carrying out Christ's mission for the world?

   ➤ The Second Vatican Council refers to the family as the domestic church. What does this mean?

4. Continue by sharing the following points regarding the meaning of *domestic church:*

   ➤ "The Christian home is the place where children receive the first proclamation of the faith. For this reason the family home is rightly called 'the domestic church,' a community of grace and prayer, a school of human virtues and of Christian charity" (*Catechism of the Catholic Church [CCC],* 1666).

   ➤ In fact, Pope Benedict has an even more dramatic image for family: the Trinity!

   ➤ "Among the different analogies of the ineffable mystery of the Triune God that believers are able to discern, I would like to cite that of the family. It is called to be a community of love and life where differences must contribute to forming a 'parable of communion'" (Benedict XVI, *Angelus,* June 11, 2006).

5. Continue by sharing:

   ➤ Now, this may not exactly sound like our families, with all the demands placed on our lives. It is also true that everyone's family is different and that there are countless variations of what a family is. Every family,

> **Teacher Note**
>
> This learning experience invites the students to reflect on their families as the domestic church. This requires a sensitivity to the variety of family situations in which the students live. If you are concerned about this surfacing negative feelings for some students, you can make it a more general reflection on the understanding of the family as the domestic church and remove the elements calling for personal reflection on the students' own families.

however, is called to be a domestic church that serves as "a community of grace and prayer, a school of human virtues and of Christian charity" (*CCC,* 1666).

6. Distribute the handout and direct the students to check off the items on the sheet that they recognize in their home.

7. When the students have completed the survey, have them discuss the following questions:

➤ How important are these items in reminding your family to try to live out its identity as "a community of grace and prayer"? Explain.

➤ How would your family be different (if at all) without these symbolic reminders of your identity as a Christian family? Why do you think so?

8. Conclude by distributing blank sheets of paper and inviting the students to answer these questions (write these on the board):

- What are three qualities of the domestic church you would like to see more present in your home, and what would help in bringing out existing qualities? Explain.

- What is one item (or up to three items) from the list you would like to see in your home to help your family remember that it is "a community of love (like the Trinity)" and "a community of grace and prayer"? Why do you think these items would help?

> **Teacher Note**
>
> This topic may provoke some unease among the students, as some families do not use or provide much symbolic evidence of their faith life, while other families struggle to identify themselves as Christian in a strongly denominational sense at all. You should, of course, take care not to create the impression that "more is better" when it comes to Christian symbols or media present in the students' homes.

**Step 11**

Now that the students are closer to the end of the unit, make sure they are all on track with their final performance tasks, if you have assigned them.

If possible, devote 50 to 60 minutes for the students to ask questions about the tasks and to work individually or in their small groups.

1. Remind the students to bring to class any work they have already prepared so that they can work on it during the class period. If necessary, reserve the library or media center so the students can do any book or online research.

2. Provide some class time for the students to work on their performance tasks. This then allows you to work with the students who need additional guidance with the project.

**Reflect**

## Step 12

*Provide the students with a tool to use for reflecting about what they learned in the unit and how they learned.*

This learning experience provides the students with an opportunity to reflect on how their understanding of the Church's missionary mandate to evangelize and share the Good News of Jesus Christ has developed throughout the unit.

1. To prepare for this learning experience, download and print the handout "Learning about Learning" (Document #: TX001159; see Appendix), one for each student.

2. Distribute the handout, and give the students about 15 minutes to answer the questions quietly. Invite them to share any reflections they have about the content they learned as well as their insights into the way they learned.

# Final Performance Task Options for Unit 5

## Important Information for Both Options

The following are the main ideas you are to understand from this unit. They should appear in this final performance task so your teacher can assess whether you learned the most essential content.

- The Church's people share a common mission.

- The hierarchy's unique role in the Church is to teach, govern, and sanctify the Church.

- Vowed religious further the Church's mission through their vows of chastity, poverty, and obedience.

- The laity's unique role in the Church is to proclaim Christ by word and example in the ordinary circumstances of the world.

Reflect on this quotation from Pope Benedict XVI as you begin your research:

> Dear brothers and sisters, in the finest traditions of the Church in this country, may you also be the first friend of the poor, the homeless, the stranger, the sick and all who suffer. Act as beacons of hope, casting the light of Christ upon the world, and encouraging young people to discover the beauty of a life given completely to the Lord and his Church. (From homily given at the Votive Mass for the Universal Church, Saint Patrick's Cathedral, April 19, 2008)

## Option 1: "The Mission Belongs to All of Us"

### Chart and Reflection

You have been asked by your pastor to present information on a variety of Catholic organizations throughout the world that embrace the mission of the Church, as expressed in the quotation from Pope Benedict XVI, so that parishioners can learn more about what is being done and how they can get involved. You are to identify and research a minimum of ten different Catholic organizations throughout the world. Follow these guidelines in researching information on each organization and composing your presentation:

- Identify the organization's mission statement or an explanation of its stated purpose (providing meals for homeless persons, celebrating Sacraments, and so on) and how it relates to the mission of the Church.

- Identify how the organization fulfills it mission, providing concrete examples.

- Provide contact information for the organization and ways someone can get involved with the work it does.

- Create a chart on poster board presenting the organization and the information you discovered.

- Write a personal reflection on the statement by Pope Benedict XVI and on the mission we are all given at Baptism.

# Option 2: Mission Brochure

You have been asked to produce a brochure that shows that all the baptized share in the mission of the church in your home (arch)diocese to be shared at a diocesan ministry fair. The challenge is that you have been asked to include people living the various primary lifestyles (lay, single, married, religious) as well as those who have specific functions or roles in the hierarchy of the Church. You are to research at least six different ways (ministries) the mission of the Church is being carried out in your (arch)diocese. Follow these guidelines in researching for your brochure:

- Provide the church's mission statement or an explanation of its stated purpose (providing meals for homeless persons, celebrating the Sacraments, and so on).

- Identify who is involved.

- Provide the church's contact information.

- Include pictures of people engaged in the work of the ministry. Include representatives from each of the lifestyles (lay, single, married, and religious) as well as the hierarchy.

- Submit, with your brochure, a one-page, typed personal reflection that explains how you think those who see your brochure will respond.

# Rubric for Final Performance Tasks for Unit 5

| Criteria | 4 | 3 | 2 | 1 |
|---|---|---|---|---|
| **Assignment includes all items requested in the directions.** | Assignment not only includes all items requested, but they are completed above expectations. | Assignment includes all items requested. | Assignment includes more than half of the items requested. | Assignment includes less than half of the items requested. |
| **Assignment shows understanding of the concept *the Church's people share a common mission.*** | Assignment shows unusually insightful understanding of this concept. | Assignment shows good understanding of this concept. | Assignment shows adequate understanding of this concept. | Assignment shows little understanding of this concept. |
| **Assignment shows understanding of the concept *the hierarchy's unique role in the Church is to teach, govern, and sanctify the Church.*** | Assignment shows unusually insightful understanding of this concept. | Assignment shows good understanding of this concept. | Assignment shows adequate understanding of this concept. | Assignment shows little understanding of this concept. |
| **Assignment shows understanding of the concept *vowed religious further the Church's mission through their vows of chastity, poverty, and obedience.*** | Assignment shows unusually insightful understanding of this concept. | Assignment shows good understanding of this concept. | Assignment shows adequate understanding of this concept. | Assignment shows little understanding of this concept. |
| **Assignment shows understanding of the concept *the laity's unique role in the Church is to proclaim Christ by word and example in the ordinary circumstances of the world.*** | Assignment shows unusually insightful understanding of this concept. | Assignment shows good understanding of this concept. | Assignment shows adequate understanding of this concept. | Assignment shows little understanding of this concept. |
| **Assignment uses proper grammar and spelling.** | Assignment has no grammar or spelling errors. | Assignment has one grammar or spelling error. | Assignment has two grammar or spelling errors. | Assignment has more than two grammar or spelling errors. |

© 2010 by Saint Mary's Press
Living in Christ Series

Document #: TX001472

# Vocabulary for Unit 5

**bishop:** One who has received the fullness of the Sacrament of Holy Orders and is a successor to the Apostles.

**candidacy:** A formal period of discernment with other men who are considering the priesthood. Also known as pre-theology, this generally lasts for two years.

**college of bishops:** The assembly of bishops, headed by the Pope, that holds the teaching authority and responsibility in the Church.

**collegial:** Characterized by the equal sharing of responsibility and authority among the members of a group who form a college. The bishops of the Church together with the Pope at their head form a college, which has full authority over the Church.

**consecrated life:** A state of life recognized by the Church in which a person publicly professes vows of poverty, chastity, and obedience.

**discernment:** From a Latin word meaning "to separate or to distinguish between," it is the practice of listening for God's call in our lives and distinguishing between good and bad choices.

**domestic:** Relating to household or family.

**domestic church:** Another name for the first and most fundamental community of faith: the family.

**eremitic:** Having to do with hermits.

**hermit:** A person who lives a solitary life in order to commit himself or herself more fully to prayer and in some cases to be completely free for service to others.

**hierarchy:** In general, the line of authority in the Church; more narrowly the Pope and the bishops, as successors of the Apostles, in their authoritative roles as leaders of the Church.

**Holy See:** This term is a translation of the Latin *sancta sedes,* which literally means "holy seat." The word *see* refers to a diocese or seat of a bishop. The Holy See is the seat of the central administration of the whole Church, under the leadership of the Pope, the Bishop of Rome.

**institute:** An organization devoted to a common cause. Religious orders are a type of religious institute.

**Latin Church, Latin Rite:** That part of the Catholic Church that follows the disciplines and teachings of the Diocese of Rome, especially the liturgical traditions. It is called the Latin Church or Latin Rite because Latin has been the official language since the fourth century. The majority of the world's Catholics belong to the Latin Rite.

**ministry:** Based on a word for "service," a way of caring for and serving others and helping the Church fulfill its mission. *Ministry* especially refers to the work of sanctification performed by those in Holy Orders

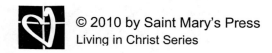

through the preaching of God's Word and the celebration of the Sacraments. The laity helps the Church fulfill its mission through lay ministries, such as that of lector or catechist.

**monk:** Someone who withdraws from ordinary life, and lives alone or in community, in order to devote oneself to prayer and work in total dedication to God.

**presbytery, presbyterate:** The name given to priests as a group, especially in a diocese; based on the Greek work *presbyter*, which means "elder."

**priesthood:** When a transitional deacon is ready, he is ordained by the bishop with Holy Orders to the priesthood.

**province:** A grouping of two or more dioceses with an archbishop as its head.

**(religious) brother:** A lay man in a religious order who has made permanent vows of poverty, chastity, and obedience.

**(religious) sister:** A lay woman in a religious order who has made permanent vows of poverty, chastity, and obedience.

**secular:** Relating to worldly concerns; something that is not overtly religious.

**seminary study:** Sponsored by his diocese, a priest candidate enters seminary for priestly formation and theological studies, generally lasting four years, plus one year of working in a parish in the diocese.

**Transitional Diaconate:** About a year before ordination to the priesthood, a seminarian is ordained to the Transitional Diaconate (different from the Permanent Diaconate), at which time he makes vows of celibacy and obedience to the bishop.

**vicar:** Someone who serves as a substitute or agent for someone else. As the Vicar of Christ, the Pope acts for Christ, his human representative on earth.

**vocation:** A call from God to all members of the Church to embrace a life of holiness. Specifically, it refers to a call to live the holy life as an ordained minister, as a vowed religious (sister or brother), in a Christian marriage, or in single life.

# Catholic Church Role Description

Church Role: _____

Role Description (Write several sentences explaining what this role entails.)

_____

_____

_____

_____

_____

Qualifications

_____

_____

_____

_____

_____

Responsibilities

_____

_____

_____

_____

_____

Document #: TX001474

# "Tools of Evangelization" Word Search

```
I  S  R  E  P  A  P  S  W  E  N  P  W  T  C  T  T  A  L
O  E  P  L  N  N  H  S  P  O  L  U  R  W  O  L  T  S  C
P  I  P  U  S  E  O  I  C  O  R  T  A  U  U  V  E  O  O
T  V  D  I  O  C  T  I  S  B  H  D  R  C  R  S  N  S  U
R  O  R  M  L  R  O  W  S  C  I  S  U  M  S  V  R  C  N
S  M  E  T  A  G  G  N  O  S  S  B  K  A  E  P  E  A  C
S  T  Y  E  I  G  R  H  C  R  U  P  L  R  S  U  T  N  N
S  R  A  L  I  G  A  I  T  E  K  C  S  E  O  Y  N  H  S
K  C  R  E  R  S  P  Z  M  U  R  I  S  G  S  W  I  O  G
C  R  P  V  R  L  H  R  I  A  O  T  N  I  V  T  A  L  L
B  T  O  I  E  T  Y  D  U  N  G  Y  S  G  D  T  U  I  S
P  I  H  S  D  N  E  I  R  F  E  E  R  R  M  T  F  D  O
L  T  H  I  E  C  P  R  D  E  H  S  S  A  O  E  S  A  Y
T  I  I  O  E  L  R  E  U  C  H  A  R  I  S  T  N  Y  Y
P  S  T  N  E  M  E  C  E  D  U  C  A  T  I  O  N  S  G
E  I  N  V  I  T  A  T  I  O  N  S  Y  T  M  R  R  E  I
R  M  A  S  S  I  A  I  S  A  E  L  P  M  A  X  E  L  M
T  R  S  A  P  C  Y  O  L  S  E  H  C  R  U  H  C  N  D
T  G  M  E  E  T  I  N  G  S  G  O  L  B  T  C  S  S  Y
```

| | | |
|---|---|---|
| BIBLE STUDY | EXAMPLE | PHOTOGRAPHY |
| BLOGS | FRIENDSHIP | PILGRIMAGES |
| CATECHESIS | HOLIDAYS | PRAYER |
| CHURCHES | INTERNET | RCIA |
| CLASSES | INVITATION | RETREATS |
| CONCERTS | LIFESTYLE | ROSARY |
| CONVERSION | MAGAZINES | TELEVISION |
| COURSES | MASS | TOURS |
| DIRECTION | MEETINGS | TRAVEL |
| DISCIPLESHIP | MENTOR | WORD |
| DISCUSSION | MOVIES | WORKSHOPS |
| EDUCATION | MUSIC | YOUTH GROUP |
| E-MAIL | NETWORKING | |
| EUCHARIST | NEWSPAPERS | |

Document #: TX001475

# "Tools of Evangelization" Word Search Solution

Document #: TX001502

# Who? What? When? Where? How? in the Local Diocese

Using your diocese's or archdiocese's directory (either a hardcopy or an online version), fill in the following items:

(n/p/e = name, phone number, e-mail address)

| | |
|---|---|
| Find the name of a parish dedicated to Mary, and the Mass times at the parish. | |
| Find the n/p/e of a Catholic chaplain for a hospital. | |
| Find the n/p/e for a Catholic cemetery. | |
| Find the n/p/e for a Catholic community services office. | |
| Find the n/p/e of a ministry that serves immigrants. | |
| Find the n/p/e of Marriage Encounter. | |

Document #: TX001476

Who? What? When? Where? How? in the Local Diocese

Page | 2

| | |
|---|---|
| Find the n/p/e of the diocesan archives. | |
| Find the n/p/e of closest parish to your school. | |
| What deanery is this parish in? | |
| Find the n/p/e of nearest Catholic Newman Center (Catholic ministry for college students). | |
| Find the n/p/e of a Catholic youth organization. | |
| Find the n/p/e of a missions office. | |
| Find the n/p/e of a Marriage Tribunal. | |
| Find the n/p/e of one men's religious order. | |

| | |
|---|---|
| Find the n/p/e of one women's religious order. | |
| Find the n/p/e of the cathedral parish and the n/p/e/ of the pastor there. | |
| Find the n/p/e of oldest parish. | |
| Find the n/p/e of newest parish. | |
| Find the n/p/e of a ministry to prisoners. | |
| Find the n/p/e of the Society of Saint Vincent de Paul. | |
| Find the n/p/e of the vocations director. | |
| Find the n/p/e of the Liturgy / Worship Office. | |

© 2010 by Saint Mary's Press
Living in Christ Series

Document #: TX001476

Who? What? When? Where? How? in the Local Diocese

Page | 4

| | |
|---|---|
| Find the n/p/e of Knights of Columbus. | |
| Find the n/p/e of Military Chaplains. | |
| Find the n/p/e of a Catholic School Office. | |
| Find the n/p/e of a vicar for clergy. | |
| Find the n/p/e of a chancellor to the Archbishop. | |
| Name one special collection that is taken up in this diocese / archdiocese. | |
| How many parishes are in the diocese / archdiocese? | |
| How many Catholics are in the diocese / archdiocese? | |

Document #: TX001476

# Congregation Information

Name of congregation: _____

Web site: _____

Founder: _____

Foundation date: _____

**Charism:**

_____

_____

**Mission statement:**

_____

_____

_____

_____

**Local ministries (e.g., teaching, our school):**

_____

_____

_____

_____

**Other ministries and their locations (e.g., missionary health care, Uganda):**

_____

_____

_____

_____

© 2010 by Saint Mary's Press
Living in Christ Series

Document #: TX001477

# Signs of the Domestic Church

Put an *X* in front of any of the following items you are aware of in your home.

1. _____ a rosary

2. _____ a crucifix

3. _____ a picture of a saint (not Mary, the Mother of God)

4. _____ holy cards

5. _____ a Bible

6. _____ a bulletin from a church

7. _____ a picture of Mary, the Mother of God

8. _____ a poster with a Scripture verse on it

9. _____ a Christian newspaper or magazine

10. _____ a book about Christian spirituality or history

11. _____ a baptismal candle

12. _____ a memorial of First Communion

13. _____ a religious medal (to be worn around the neck)

14. _____ a religious cross (to be worn around the neck)

15. _____ a religious pin

16. _____ a CD of Christian music

17. _____ a CD of religious Christmas music

18. _____ a Nativity scene at Christmas

19. _____ holy water

20. _____ a candle used for prayer

21. _____ a prayer book

22. _____ a liturgical calendar

23. _____ an Advent wreath

24. _____ blessed palms

25. _____ a Saint Christopher medal (in the family car)

© 2010 by Saint Mary's Press
Living in Christ Series

Document #: TX001478

# Unit 5 Test

## Part 1: Multiple Choice

Write your answers in the blank spaces provided at the left.

1. _____ The Church has a missionary mandate to help all people to share in the communion of the Holy Trinity. _____ is the primary way we accomplish this mission.

   **A.** Reading the Bible
   **B.** Evangelization
   **C.** Tithing
   **D.** Receiving the Sacraments

2. _____ Everyone in the Church has a responsibility to share the _____ of Jesus Christ.

   **A.** cup of salvation
   **B.** walk
   **C.** last moments
   **D.** Good News

3. _____ _____ evangelize through the witness of their special love of God as expressed by their dedicated lifestyle.

   **A.** Contemplative orders
   **B.** Sinners
   **C.** Swedish Guards
   **D.** The unforgiven

4. _____ _____ are entrusted with both the pastoral care of a specific community and the evangelization of those who do not yet know Christ.

   **A.** Priests
   **B.** Parents
   **C.** The unbaptized
   **D.** Sacristans

5. _____ The earliest Christian missionaries were successful not because of new techniques of preaching but because of the holiness of the _____.

   **A.** Gentiles
   **B.** ancient Romans
   **C.** preachers
   **D.** Rosetta Stone

6. _____  _____ involves a respectful encounter between the Christian faith and a particular culture.

    **A.** Inculturation
    **B.** Bipartisanship
    **C.** Heresy
    **D.** Lend-lease

7. _____ Like any organization, the Church needs clear and well-defined _____.

    **A.** road maps
    **B.** leadership
    **C.** vaulted ceilings
    **D.** consequences

8. _____  _____, the bishop of Rome, is leader of the whole Church, the successor to Peter.

    **A.** The bishop
    **B.** Cardinal Otero
    **C.** The Pope
    **D.** The Orthodox Patriarch

9. _____ The ordained ministers of the Church, through the grace of _____, use Christ's authority to govern, teach, and sanctify the Church.

    **A.** Sacraments and holy cards
    **B.** Holy Orders
    **C.** the Beloved Disciple
    **D.** greater knowledge and understanding

10. _____ Ordained ministers of the Church make Christ present to us through the _____.

    **A.** foyer of the church
    **B.** dispensations
    **C.** Sacraments
    **D.** use of oil and bread

11. _____ The Church comprises two distinct but interconnected groups: the _____ and the laity.

    **A.** hierarchy
    **B.** powerful
    **C.** sinless
    **D.** baptized

12. _____    All members of the Church are equal in _____ but are called to different roles and ministries.

    **A.** dignity
    **B.** levels of holiness
    **C.** kindness
    **D.** knee-deep water

13. _____    The _____ is composed of the ordained ministers of the Church: bishops (including the Pope), priests, and deacons.

    **A.** elite
    **B.** *Magnificat*
    **C.** sacramental
    **D.** hierarchy

14. _____    The _____ is a bishop with supreme power over the whole Church.

    **A.** archangel
    **B.** *Magisterium*
    **C.** cardinal
    **D.** Pope

15. _____    The Pope's residence is known as the _____.

    **A.** seat of Saint Peter
    **B.** Holy See
    **C.** *Vaticanus*
    **D.** *Apartementati*

# Part 2: Definitions

Define each of the following terms in a complete sentence or two on a separate sheet of paper.

apostolic
monk
secular
vicar
laypeople (laity)
ecclesial
discernment
bishop
grace

# Part 3: Short Answer

Answer the following questions in paragraph form on a separate sheet of paper.

1. What is the role of the Pope, and what are some of his titles?

2. What is the role of bishops in the Church?

3. What is the role of priests in the Church?

Document #: TX001479

# Unit 5 Test Answer Key

## Part 1: Multiple Choice

| | | |
|---|---|---|
| **1.** B. | **6.** A. | **11.** A. |
| **2.** D.. | **7.** B. | **12.** A. |
| **3.** A. | **8.** C. | **13.** D. |
| **4.** A. | **9.** B. | **14.** D. |
| **5.** C. | **10.** C. | **15.** B. |

## Part 2: Definitions

**apostolic:** To be founded on the Twelve Apostles.

**monk:** Someone who withdraws from ordinary life, and lives alone or in community, in order to devote oneself to prayer and work in total dedication to God.

**secular:** Relating to worldly concerns, something that is not overtly religious.

**vicar:** Someone who serves as a substitute or agent for someone else. As the Vicar of Christ, the Pope acts for Christ, his human representative on earth.

**laypeople (laity):** All members of the Church, with the exception of those who are ordained or in consecrated life. The laity shares in Christ's role as priest, prophet, and king, witnessing to God's love and power in the world.

**ecclesial:** Of or relating to church.

**discernment:** From a Latin word meaning "to separate or to distinguish between," it is the practice of listening for God's call in our lives and distinguishing between good and bad choices.

**bishop:** One who has received the fullness of the Sacrament of Holy Orders and is a successor to the Apostles.

**grace:** The free and undeserved gift of God's loving and active presence in the universe and in our lives, empowering us to respond to his call and to live as his adopted sons and daughters. Grace restores our loving communion with the Holy Trinity, lost through sin.

# Part 3: Short Answer

1.   The Pope is first a bishop. That means he has all the rights and authority of a bishop, a successor of the Apostles. But the Pope is not just a bishop; he is the leader of all bishops and leader of the Church. His chief titles help clarify his unique identity and role:

   - Successor to Peter:  Christ established his Apostles as a permanent college with Peter at their head. The Pope is the successor of Peter, just as the bishops are the successors of the Apostles. Christ gave Peter the "power of the keys"—that is, the authority to govern the Church. That authority is passed down to each new pope.

   - Bishop of Rome:  During the lifetime of the first Apostles, the city of Rome was established as the spiritual center of the Church. The Apostles Peter and Paul, two of the great leaders of the early Church, both ended up in Rome and were eventually martyred there.

   - Head of the college of bishops:  All the bishops of the world are united with one another, with the Pope as their head. The Pope has the responsibility of providing leadership to the college of bishops. The college of bishops has no authority unless united with the Pope. As head of the college of bishops, the Pope has the authority to appoint the bishops throughout the world.

   - Vicar of Christ:  The Pope is the Vicar of Christ, meaning that he acts for Christ as Christ's human representative on earth. Just as Christ himself is the single head of his Body, the Church, so too the Pope is the visible and juridical head of the Church. The Pope is the visible sign of Christ's presence on earth. He is a personal sign and guarantee of the Church's unity in its belief, its Sacraments, and its authority that has its origins with Peter and the Apostles.

   - Pastor of the Universal Church:  The Pope has the responsibility to minister to Catholics throughout the world.

2.   The bishops, in communion with the Pope, are given the task of teaching, sanctifying, and governing the Church. When Christ first called his Twelve Apostles, he formed them as a permanent group, or "college," with Peter as their head. As successors to the Apostles, they are entrusted with faithfully passing down the Apostolic Tradition, by authentically teaching the faith, celebrating divine worship, especially the Eucharist, and acting as the pastoral leaders in their own dioceses. Each bishop is the visible head of a particular church, or diocese. Within his diocese, the bishop is the visible source and foundation of unity. In other words, the bishop is a living symbol that his particular church is unified with the universal Church, through Apostolic Succession, through sharing the same truths, and in celebrating the same Sacraments. All bishops are ordained priests before they become bishops. The bishop has final authority and responsibility for all decisions affecting the spiritual and corporal welfare of the diocese. He serves the People of God, promotes their true interests, and helps them to reach the goal of salvation.

3.     The priest's primary role is that of sacramental minister. The Sacrament of Holy Orders confers a sacred power on the priest, which is to be used in service to the faithful. He represents Christ to the community, serving in the name and in the person of Christ within the community. He exercises his service to the People of God through teaching, divine worship, and pastoral leadership. He presides over the celebration of the Eucharist in his parish on Sundays and weekdays. He also offers the faithful the grace of the Sacraments of Baptism, Penance and Reconciliation, Anointing of the Sick, Matrimony, and Confirmation. (Only priests and bishops may celebrate the Eucharist, Penance and Reconciliation, Anointing of the Sick, and Confirmation.) The priest also oversees the religious education in their parish and Catholic school, if there is one. He visits the sick and offers spiritual care to those who need it. He oversees the work of the parish staff and makes sure the parish buildings are in good repair. He also participates in the universal mission of the Apostles, whom Christ sent out "to make disciples of all nations" (Matthew 28:19).

© 2010 by Saint Mary's Press
Living in Christ Series

Document #: TX001480

# Unit 6    The Church Is a Light to All People

## Overview

This unit guides the students in understanding the truth that Jesus Christ is the one true path to salvation and that God has entrusted that truth to the Church. Thus the Church has the obligation to proclaim the truth to the world, an obligation that inspires and gives life to the Church's missionary activity.

### Key Understandings and Questions

Upon completing this unit, the students will have a deeper understanding of the following key concepts:

- The Church is local, national, and global.
- The Church seeks Christian unity through ecumenical dialogue.
- The Church seeks understanding between religious traditions through interreligious dialogue.
- The Church serves and seeks justice for people of all nations and faith traditions.

Upon completing the unit, the students will have answered the following questions:
- Where is the Church?
- How does the Church relate with other Christian denominations?
- How does the Church relate with other religions?
- How does the Church interact in politics or in other non-Church matters?

### Student Book Articles

This unit draws on articles from *The Church: Christ in the World Today* student book and incorporates them into the unit instruction. Whenever the teaching steps for the unit require the students to refer to or read an article from the student book, the following symbol appears in the margin: (📖). The articles covered in the unit are from "Section 2: The Church Is One, Holy, Catholic, and Apostolic" and "Section 3: The Church's Salvation and Mission," and are as follows:

- "Wounds to Unity" (article 18, pp. 70–74)
- "Ecumenism" (article 19, pp. 74–78)
- "The Communion of Saints" (article 22, pp. 87–89)
- "The Saints: Models and Intercessors" (article 23, pp. 89–92)
- "Mary: Perfect Model of Holiness" (article 24, pp. 92–96)
- "Salvation for Those Outside the Church" (article 34, pp. 129–132)

- "Who Needs Organized Religion?" (article 35, pp. 132–135)
- "Engaging the World" (article 36, pp. 138–139)
- "Engaging Modern Culture" (article 37, pp. 140–141)
- "The Church and Evangelization" (article 38, pp. 141–145)

## How Will You Know the Students Understand?

The following resources will help you assess the students' understanding of the key concepts covered in this unit:

- handout "Final Performance Task Options for Unit 6" (Document #: TX001481)
- handout "Rubric for Final Performance Tasks for Unit 6" (Document #: TX001482)
- handout "Unit 6 Test" (Document #: TX001485)

## The Suggested Path to Understanding

This unit in the teacher guide provides you with one learning path to take with the students, to enable them to uncover the ways that the Church is a light for all of God's children. It is not necessary to use all the learning experiences provided in the unit; however, if you substitute other material from this course or your own material for some of the material offered here, be sure that you have covered all relevant facets of understanding and that you have not missed any skills or knowledge required for later units.

 **Step 1:** Preassess student knowledge of the Church's reaching out to all people of the world. How is the Church a beacon of hope for all people?

 **Step 2:** Follow this assessment by presenting to the students the handouts "Final Performance Task Options for Unit 6" (Document #: TX001481) and "Rubric for Final Performance Tasks for Unit 6" (Document #: TX001482).

 **Step 3:** Present material to the students about the Church in its local, national, and global natures.

 **Step 4:** Guide the students in exploring the lives of the saints and what cultural significance they offer to the people. Then have the students create a Web page for a saint.

 **Step 5:** Lead the students in exploring the Church's commitment to ecumenism and in creating a prayer service for unity among the Christian Churches.

**Apply** **Step 6:** Have the students take on the role of an ecumenical council and discuss issues that such a council might undertake.

**Empathize** **Step 7:** Guide the students' study of the Church's participation in interreligious dialogue by having them explore the document *Declaration on the Relation of the Church to Non-Christian Religions* (*Nostra Aetate, 1965*).

**Apply** **Step 8:** Have the students identify and summarize how the global and United States Catholic Church is engaging in interreligious dialogue.

**Perceive** **Step 9:** Share with the students some information about the Church's service (both charity and pursuit of justice) on the domestic and international levels. Emphasize that the Church does not serve Catholics alone but anyone who is in need of help. Then have the students each research a Catholic relief group.

**Apply** **Step 10:** Direct the students in creating posters to learn more about the organizations they researched in step 9.

**Understand** **Step 11:** Now that the students are closer to the end of the unit, make sure they are all on track with their final performance tasks, if you have assigned them.

**Reflect** **Step 12:** Provide the students with a tool to use for reflecting about what they learned in the unit and how they learned.

## Background for Teaching This Unit

Visit *smp.org/LivinginChrist* for additional information about these and other theological concepts taught in this unit:

- "Christian Unity and Ecumenical Dialogue" (Document #: TX00529)
- "Catholicism and World Religions" (Document #: TX001528)

The Web site also includes information on these and other teaching methods used in the unit:

- "The Fishbowl Method" (Document #: TX001530)
- "Using Primary Sources" (Document #: TX001313)

## Scripture Passages

Scripture is an important part of the Living in Christ series and is frequently used in the learning experiences for each unit. The Scripture passages featured in this unit are as follows:

- Colossians 1:15–20 (his person and work)
- 2 Corinthians 5:14–19 (the ministry of reconciliation)
- Ephesians 1:7–11 (fulfillment through Christ)
- John 1:9–10 (the true light)
- John 3:17 (God sent Jesus not to condemn but to save)
- John 5:19–22 (the work of the Son)
- John 12:31–32 (the time of Judgment)
- John 14:6 (the way and the truth and the life)
- Luke 15:4–10 (the Parables of the Lost Sheep and the Lost Coin)
- Mark 9:11–13 (the coming of Elijah)
- Matthew 17:10–11 (the coming of Elijah)
- Matthew 19:25–26 (for God all things are possible)
- Matthew 21:18–22 (the cursing of the fig tree)
- 2 Peter 3:8–9 (the Lord's patience)
- Philippians 4:12–13 (strength through him)
- Romans 5:9–12,19–21 (grace overflows)
- Romans 8:30–32,38–39 (If God is for us, who can be against us?)
- Romans 9:14–16 (Is there injustice on the part of God?)
- Romans 11:32–33 (the triumph of God's mercy)
- 1 Timothy 2:3–6 (God wills everyone to be saved)
- Titus 2:11 (the grace of God)
- Wisdom 11:21–26 (God's mercy for all)

## Vocabulary

The student book and the teacher guide include the following key terms for this unit. To provide the students with a list of these terms and their definitions, download and print the handout "Vocabulary for Unit 6" (Document #: TX001483).

| | |
|---|---|
| Assumption of Mary | schism |
| ecumenism | *sola gratia* |
| excommunication | *sola scriptura* |
| *fiat* | theologian |
| heresy | theology |
| indulgence | *Theotokos* |
| Purgatory | |

# Learning Experiences

## Step 1

Preassess student knowledge of the Church's reaching out to all people of the world. How is the Church a beacon of hope for all people?

Tell the students that you will read a list of statements. For each statement, have the students stand if they think the answer to it is true, or stay seated if they think the answer is false.

Read these statements:

➤ Most of the members of the Catholic Church reside in the United States.

➤ Catholic Relief Services was started by Dorothy Day.

➤ The Church is a beacon of hope for all people.

➤ The Church is present on every continent in the world.

➤ The Church is not apostolic by nature.

➤ It is often said that Pope John Paul II was a beacon of hope for all people.

➤ Maryknoll Fathers and Brothers is a United States–based Catholic mission group serving in all parts of the world.

➤ Caritas International is a Catholic organization that works to help the poor and to bring about peace in two hundred countries.

## Step 2

Follow this assessment by presenting to the students the handouts "Final Performance Task Options for Unit 6" (Document #: TX001481) and "Rubric for Final Performance Tasks for Unit 6" (Document #: TX001482).

This unit provides you with two ways to assess that the students have a deep understanding of the most important concepts in the unit: creating a PowerPoint presentation on ecumenism or summarizing the Church's teachings on ecumenism and interreligious dialogue by researching three Church-supported organizations or efforts under way in these areas. Refer to "Using

Final Performance Tasks to Assess Understanding" (Document #: TX001011) and "Using Rubrics to Assess Work" (Document #: TX001012) at *smp.org/ LivinginChrist.*

1. Prepare for this learning experience by downloading and printing the handouts "Final Performance Task Options for Unit 2" (Document #: TX001481) and "Rubric for Final Performance Tasks for Unit 2" (Document #: TX001482), one for each student.

2. Distribute the handouts. Give the students a choice as to which performance task they choose and add more options if you so choose. Review the directions, expectations, and rubric in class, allowing the students to ask questions. You may want to say something to this effect:

    ➤ You may work with no more than two other people on option 1. If you want to work on your own, you may choose either option 1 or option 2.

    ➤ Near the end of the unit, you will have one full class period to work on your final performance task. Please keep in mind, however, that you should be working on this task throughout the course of the unit. Please do not wait until this class period to begin work on your final performance task.

> **Teacher Note**
>
> You will want to assign due dates for the final performance tasks.
>
> If you have done these performance tasks, or very similar ones, with students before, place examples of this work in the classroom. During this introduction explain how each is a good example of what you are looking for, for different reasons. This allows the students to concretely understand that there is not only one way to succeed.

**Explain**

## Step 3

*Present material to the students about the Church in its local, national, and global natures.*

1. Prepare for this learning experience by gathering three sheets of newsprint and three sets of markers. Also have available a roll of masking tape. If you choose to use the session extension, have the appropriate equipment available.

2. Divide the classroom into three areas and designate one area as "local," one as "national," and one as "global."

3. Now divide the class into three small groups. Assign each small group one of the areas and then have the groups move to their respective areas. Distribute the newsprint and markers.

4. At their assigned areas, the students are to brainstorm on the sheet of newsprint all the ways the Church exists in the world, either locally, nationally, or globally. For example, the students in the "local" group could write the name of their diocese, the names of as many parishes in their diocese

as they can think of, Catholic Charities, and so on. The students in the "national" group could list the Unites States Conference of Catholic Bishops, the United States Campaign for Human Development, and so on. The students in the "global" group could list organizations associated with the Vatican, Catholic Relief Services, Maryknoll Missionaries, and so on.

5. Allow the small groups 7 to 10 minutes for brainstorming. Then have one spokesperson for each small group share the group's ideas with the rest of the class. After each spokesperson shares, ask the rest of the class to add any thoughts or ideas to what the group has already generated.

6. When the sharing has concluded, post the sheets of newsprint on the walls around the room.

## Optional Extension

At this point, you could continue with the session by showing some of the groups mentioned, either by using the PowerPoint "The Church in the World" (Document #: TX001511), or by direct link to organizations' Web sites on the Internet.

7. Conclude by emphasizing that when we talk about the Church, it is important to recognize that the earthly structure of the Church is manifest in a wide range of ways, from the local to the global level.

Articles
22, 23,
24

# Step 4

*Guide the students in exploring the lives of the saints and what cultural significance they offer to the people. Then have the students create a Web page for a saint.*

This learning experience emphasizes that the Church is inclusive of all and that no one in the Catholic Church is "less than" anyone else. The students research several lesser known saints and create a Web page for one of them in an effort to teach others about the unique roles of the saint.

1. Prepare for this learning experience by reviewing the links for researching the saints available at *smp.org/LivinginChrist.* If you plan to assign saints to the students, be sure there is adequate information available for the saints you have chosen. Reserve the computer lab or media center for the students' research and Web page work. Have art supplies available for any students who may choose to create their "Web pages" on paper.

2. As background have the students read student book articles 22–24, "The Communion of Saints," "The Saints: Models and Intercessors," and "Mary, Perfect Model of Holiness."

3. Begin by sharing the following information with the students:

   ➤ The Catholic Church venerates more than ten thousand named saints, many from the early years of the Church but a good many that have been added in the last century.

   ➤ There are both men and women saints for a wide variety of cultures, ethnicities, socioeconomic backgrounds, and ages.

   ➤ The saints are reminders to us that no one in the Catholic faith is "less than." The saints affirm the multicultural and inclusive natures of the Church.

4. Share with the students that they will be researching a particular saint and designing a Web page to share information about that saint. You can either direct the students to identify a saint they would like to research or assign saints to the students. Below is a list of possible saints:

   • Saint Dymphna (patron saint of the mentally ill and epileptic)

   • Saint Francis de Sales (patron saint of the deaf)

   • Saint Lucy (patron saint of the blind)

   • Saint Peregrine (patron saint of those who suffer from cancer)

   • Saint Damien (patron saint of those who suffer from HIV / AIDS)

   • Saint Angela Merici (patron saint of the physically challenged)

   • Saint Jeanne de Lestonnac (patron saint of abuse victims)

   • Blessed Kateri Tekakwitha (Native American) (patron saint of environmentalism)

   • Saint Jerome (Croatia) (patron saint of Bible scholars)

   • Saint Martin de Porres (patron saint of nurses and health care assistants)

   • Saint Rose of Lima (patron saint of Latin America and the Philippines)

   • Saint Alphonsa (first female Catholic saint from India)

> **Teacher Note**
>
> You may want to clarify the misconception that Catholics pray to the saints. Explain that in the Catholic Tradition, we pray *with* the saints, asking them to intercede on our behalf. Just as we might ask a friend or family member to pray for us, we may ask the saints to pray for us as well.

5. Now explain that the students are to research the saint, identifying the following:

   • death and life span of the person

   • significant aspects of the person's life

   • why this person was canonized

   • prayers or writings attributed to the saint

   • images or artworks depicting the saint

   • any other significant information

Allow the students 10 to 15 minutes to research their saints.

6. Once the students have researched the saint, they are to create a Web page, sharing the information they uncovered. They may create a real Web page or a sample Web page on paper or in a PowerPoint presentation. The Web page should include information from their research and images of the saint. Allow the students 25 to 30 minutes to create their Web pages.

7. Invite the students to present their Web pages to class.

Articles
18, 19

## Step 5

*Lead the students in exploring the Church's commitment to ecumenism and in creating a prayer service for unity among the Christian Churches.*

1. Prepare for this learning experience by gathering six pens or pencils and six sheets of blank paper.

2. As background for this learning experience, have the students read student book articles 18 and 19, "Wounds to Unity" and "Ecumenism."

3. Begin by dividing the class into six small groups. Assign each small group one (or two, where given) of the following sections from the two assigned articles to summarize and present to the rest of the class:

   • "Heresy"
   • "Schisms"
   • "The Church of Christ" and "The Protestant Reformation"
   • "Catholics and Other Christians" and "Christian Denominations"
   • "The Ecumenical Movement"
   • "Essential Elements to the Movement Toward Unity"

   Distribute the pens or pencils and the sheets of blank paper. Allow the small groups 5 minutes to read their articles and prepare their summaries.

4. Gather the students back in the large group and have the small groups present their summaries to the class in the order they are listed in part 2.

5. Next lead the class in a discussion of the following questions:

   ➤ What do you understand ecumenism to be?
   ➤ What are issues that hinder the ecumenical movement?
   ➤ What are elements and beliefs common to all Christian churches?
   ➤ What are some misconceptions non-Catholic Christians might have about the Catholic Church?

➤ What are some misconceptions Catholics might have about other Christian Churches?

6. Have the students return to their small groups and then offer the following direction:

➤ One of the elements of the movement toward unity is prayer for unity. As a class we are going to create and pray a prayer service for Christian unity. Each small group will be assigned an element of the prayer service. Your group is to create your assigned part and lead the class in praying that part.

7. Assign the following parts of the prayer service to the small groups:

- opening prayer for Christian unity
- Scripture reading reflecting the call to Christian unity and a three-sentence reflection on the Scripture verse
- three intercessory prayers for Christian unity
- three intercessory prayers for Christian unity
- three questions for quiet reflection on what the students can do to promote Christian unity
- closing prayer for Christian unity

You will want to review the various parts while the small groups are working on them and prior to the prayer service.

8. Once the groups have completed their assigned parts and you have reviewed them for appropriateness, lead the class in praying their prayer for unity.

Articles
36, 37,
38

## Step 6

*Have the students take on the role of an ecumenical council and discuss issues that such a council might undertake.*

If you are new to using this style of learning experience, refer to the article "The Fishbowl Method" (Document #: TX001530) at *smp.org/LivinginChrist*.

1. As background for this learning experience, have the students read student book articles 36–38: "Engaging the World," "Engaging Modern Culture," and "The Church and Evangelization."

2. Begin by asking for five volunteers who are willing to be members of an ecumenical council.

3. Have the students move six chairs or desks into the center of the classroom for the "council." Instruct the volunteers to sit in the "fishbowl." One chair or desk will be empty. Be sure the rest of the students in the class can clearly see the students in the "fishbowl." Rearrange seats as needed.

4. Tell the students in the fishbowl that their assignment is to engage in a thoughtful discussion as members of an ecumenical council. Each of the members must actively engage in the conversation. If audience members would like to join the fishbowl, they can join by sitting in the empty seat, one at a time, and adding their voice to the discussion. When a member from the audience joins the fishbowl, a current member of the fishbowl must leave and join the audience.

5. Assign the "council" one of the following topics for discussion:

   • whether the Church should change its stance on euthanasia
   • how to address the culture of materialism that exists in the United States
   • how to address the issue of global poverty
   • how to get young people involved in their Church
   • how to spread the word about the modern Church in the world today

6. When the fishbowl members have concluded their discussion (20 to 30 minutes), have them comment on how they did as a council. Offer the following questions to spark discussion:

   ➤ Did the council members listen to one another?
   ➤ Did they adequately address the topic? Did they make good points?
   ➤ Were their comments realistic?

7. Ask the audience for constructive feedback, using the same questions you asked the council members in part 5.

8. Conclude by explaining that an ecumenical council gathering is not something that happens very often. When it does it involves discussing the relevant issues, but it also includes intense prayer and discernment. Ecumenical council decisions are not made lightly; they rely on the Scriptures, Tradition, and the guidance of the Holy Spirit.

Articles
34, 35

Empathize

## Step 7

*Guide the students' study of the Church's participation in interreligious dialogue by having them explore the document Declaration on the Relation of the Church to Non-Christian Religions (Nostra Aetate, 1965).*

1. Prepare for this learning experience by downloading and printing the handout "Exploring *Declaration on the Relation of the Church to Non-Christian Religions* (*Nostra Aetate,* 1965)" (Document #: TX001484), one for each student.

2. As background have the students read student book articles 34 and 35, "Salvation for Those Outside the Church" and "Who Needs Organized Religion?"

3. Distribute the handout to the students. Either as homework or as class work, have them read *Relation of the Church to Non-Christian Religions* (a link to this document is available at *smp.org/LivinginChrist*) and answer the questions on the handout.

4. When the students are finished, have them share their responses to the questions on the handout. You may wish to pause after each question to clarify what the document says and to respond to any questions the students might have.

5. After you have gone through the entire handout with the class, lead a discussion on the following questions:

   ➤ What in *Relation of the Church to Non-Christian Religions* do you find surprising or most interesting?

   ➤ What does the document challenge each one of us to do in relation to non-Christian religions?

   ➤ What in the document is most important in relation to current international crises and conflicts?

6. Conclude by emphasizing that interreligious dialogue does not involve "giving up" what we believe and know is true. Instead it means looking for common ground and treating others with respect and dignity.

**Apply**

# Step 8

Have the students identify and summarize how the global and United States Catholic Church is engaging in interreligious dialogue.

1. Prepare for this learning experience by gathering sheets of blank paper, two for each student. Reserve the computer lab or media center, as the students will need access to the Internet.

2. Begin by distributing one sheet of paper to each student and having them each summarize what they learned in the last step when they read *Relation of the Church to Non-Christian Religions.*

3. Next tell the students they will now have the opportunity to identify and research specific ways the Church is living out the commitment to interreligious dialogue. You can choose to have the students work individually or in pairs.

4. Distribute another sheet of paper to each student. Explain that they are to identify and summarize two concrete examples of how the Catholic Church is engaging in interreligious dialogue. One example should be occurring on the international level. (If you wish, you can direct students to the Pontifical Council for Interreligious Dialogue. A link is provided at *smp.org/Livingin Christ*). One example should be occurring in the United States. (If you wish, you can direct students to the United States Conference of Catholic Bishops' Secretariat for Ecumenical and Interreligious Affairs. A link is provided at *smp.org/LivinginChrist*). For each example the students are to identify the following:

   - the non-Christian religion the Church is in dialogue with
   - the topic addressed in the dialogue
   - results or next steps from the dialogue
   - statements or quotations that reflect *Relation of the Church to Non-Christian Religions*

   Allow 10 to 15 minutes for the students to research and write.

5. When the students are done researching and have finished writing their summaries, have them share their research with the class. Then collect the written summaries.

6. Conclude by leading a class discussion on the following questions:
   ➤ What do you believe are the biggest challenges to interreligious dialogue?
   ➤ What do you believe are the benefits of respectful interreligious dialogue?

**Perceive**

# Step 9

Share with the students some information about the Church's service (both charity and pursuit of justice) on the domestic and international levels. Emphasize that the Church does not serve Catholics alone but anyone who is in need of help. Then have the students each research a Catholic relief group.

This learning experience provides a great opportunity to familiarize students with the Catholic Campaign for Human Development, local Catholic community service organizations, Catholic Relief Services, and Caritas International.

1. Prepare for this learning experience by ensuring you will have access to a computer with Internet access and an LCD projector.

2. Begin by sharing that the Church does not serve Catholics alone but responds to need wherever it is found, whoever is in need. Also mention that the Catholic relief groups are often the first who are invited to respond to disasters around the world, even in countries where the primary religion is not Christian.

3. Show the students the Web sites for the following organizations. Links are available at *smp.org/LivinginChrist.* You may choose to also show them the Web sites of local diocesan and parish services. Tell the students that they will be selecting one of the Web sites to explore, so they should note, as you are going through each site, which ones interest them.
   - Catholic Campaign for Human Development
   - Catholic Relief Services
   - Caritas International
   - Maryknoll Office for Global Concerns
   - Pax Christi International
   - Pax Christi USA

4. When you are finished presenting all the Web sites, direct the students to select one of the organizations. Be sure that each organization is selected or assigned to at least two students.

5. As homework, have the students research the organizations, identifying the following information:
   - how the organization started
   - what the organization's mission is
   - the services the organization provides

- locations where the organization serves those in need
- how someone can volunteer or contribute to the organization's work
- needs the organization has for continuing its work
- printed images from the organization of its work (if available)

6. Instruct the students to bring the results of their research to the next class, as it will be used for the next learning experience.

## Step 10

*Direct the students in creating posters to learn more about the organizations they researched in step 9.*

1. Prepare for this learning experience by reminding the students to bring their research to class. Gather six sheets of newsprint, one for each organization researched, art supplies for the students to make posters promoting the organizations, and a pad of small sticky notes. Also post a large map of the world for the small groups to use in their presentations.

2. Begin by reminding the students that the organizations they researched are a part of the mission of the global Church.

3. Have the students form pairs or small groups according to the organizations they researched. Distribute a sheet of newsprint and art supplies to each small group.

4. Direct the small groups to do the following:

   - Create a simple poster that includes the name of the organization, its mission, and pictures.
   - Prepare and give a brief presentation to the class, offering more information about the organization, pointing to location(s) on the world map where the organization is active, and responding to questions from the rest of the class.

   Allow the small groups 15 to 20 minutes to work on their posters and presentations.

5. When the small groups have finished their posters, have them present to the class. Invite the class to ask questions concerning the organization. If you have a map of the world, have the small-group members place sticky notes on locations where their organizations serve the People of God.

## Step 11

Now that the students are closer to the end of the unit, make sure they are all on track with their final performance tasks, if you have assigned them.

If possible, devote 50 to 60 minutes for the students to ask questions about the tasks and to work individually or in their small groups.

1. Remind the students to bring to class any work they have already prepared so that they can work on it during the class period. If necessary, reserve the library or media center so the students can do any book or online research.

2. Provide some class time for the students to work on their performance tasks. This then allows you to work with the students who need additional guidance with the project.

## Step 12

Provide the students with a tool to use for reflecting about what they learned in the unit and how they learned.

This learning experience provides the students with an excellent opportunity to reflect on how their understanding of the Church's mission to proclaim the truth to the world has developed throughout the unit.

1. To prepare for this learning experience, make copies of the handout "Learning about Learning" (Document #: TX001159; see Appendix), one for each student.

2. Distribute the handout, and give the students about 15 minutes to answer the questions quietly. Invite them to share any reflections they have about the content they learned as well as their insights into the way they learned.

# Final Performance Task Options for Unit 6

## Important Information for Both Options

The following are the main ideas you are to understand from this unit. They should appear in this final performance task so your teacher can assess whether you learned the most essential content.

- The Church is local, national, and global.

- The Church seeks Christian unity through ecumenical dialogue.

- The Church seeks understanding between religious traditions through interreligious dialogue.

- The Church serves and seeks justice for people of all nations and faith traditions.

## Option: 1: Ecumenism

You are the new director of the local parish youth ministry team who has friends in other churches. You have invited them to participate with your youth group in dialogue and in work on a local social justice project. You must develop an introduction that begins the process of working together toward a common goal that is grounded in shared faith. You must prepare a twelve- to fifteen-slide PowerPoint presentation on how the participation of the Church encourages and fosters dialogue and understanding among persons of different faith traditions. Your goal is to foster dialogue and understanding among youth of different faith traditions. Follow these guidelines in preparing your presentation:

- Include information from at least three Church documents that address ecumenism.

- Show how your gathering in an effort to understand one another and collaborate in service has its roots in a Church that is local, national, and global.

- Conclude by introducing the social justice project you have identified.

- On your final slide, list the resources you used for quotations, information, and images.

- For this final performance task, you will turn in:

  o an electronic copy of your PowerPoint presentation

  o an outline of talking points addressed on each slide

  o a two- to three-page reflection paper that explains your understanding of ecumenism and the role it plays in the life and mission of the Church

# Option 2: Ecumenical / Interreligious Organizations and Efforts

You have been asked to present to a group of area pastors and religious leaders about the ecumenical and interreligious efforts of the Catholic Church. As a part of your presentation, you have been asked to share about ecumenical and interreligious organizations or efforts the Catholic Church supports. Follow these guidelines in creating a two-page handout for your presentation:

- Summarize your understanding of the Catholic view of ecumenism and interreligious dialogue, quoting at least two Church documents.

- Identify three ecumenical or interreligious organizations or efforts supported by the Church. You must have at least one ecumenical and one interreligious; the third one can be either. For each organization or effort, address the following:

  o  What is the organization or effort called?

  o  Who is the sponsoring organization or effort?

  o  How is the Catholic Church involved?

  o  What steps or actions have been taken or are under way for the organization or effort?

  o  Why is this work important, and what does the organization or effort hope to achieve?

  o  How could someone find out more information about the organization or effort?

# Rubric for Final Performance Tasks for Unit 6

| Criteria | 4 | 3 | 2 | 1 |
|---|---|---|---|---|
| **Assignment includes all items requested in the directions.** | Assignment not only includes all items requested, but they are completed above expectations. | Assignment includes all items requested. | Assignment includes more than half of the items requested. | Assignment includes less than half of the items requested. |
| **Assignment shows understanding of the concept *the Church is local, national, and global.*** | Assignment shows unusually insightful understanding of this concept. | Assignment shows good understanding of this concept. | Assignment shows adequate understanding of this concept. | Assignment shows little understanding of this concept. |
| **Assignment shows understanding of the concept *the Church seeks Christian unity through ecumenical dialogue.*** | Assignment shows unusually insightful understanding of this concept. | Assignment shows good understanding of this concept. | Assignment shows adequate understanding of this concept. | Assignment shows little understanding of this concept. |
| **Assignment shows understanding of the concept *the Church seeks understanding between religious traditions through interreligious dialogue.*** | Assignment shows unusually insightful understanding of this concept. | Assignment shows good understanding of this concept. | Assignment shows adequate understanding of this concept. | Assignment shows little understanding of this concept. |
| **Assignment shows understanding of the concept *the Church serves and seeks justice for people of all nations and faith traditions.*** | Assignment shows unusually insightful understanding of this concept. | Assignment shows good understanding of this concept. | Assignment shows adequate understanding of this concept. | Assignment shows little understanding of this concept. |
| **Assignment uses proper grammar and spelling.** | Assignment has no grammar or spelling errors. | Assignment has one grammar or spelling error. | Assignment has two grammar or spelling errors. | Assignment has more than two grammar or spelling errors. |

© 2010 by Saint Mary's Press
Living in Christ Series

Document #: TX001482

# Vocabulary for Unit 6

**Assumption of Mary:** The dogma that recognizes that the body of the Blessed Virgin Mary was taken directly to Heaven after her life on earth had ended.

**ecumenism:** The movement to restore unity among all Christians.

**excommunication:** A severe penalty that results from grave sin against Church law. The penalty is either imposed by a Church official or happens automatically as a result of the offense. An excommunicated person is not permitted to celebrate or receive the Sacraments.

*fiat:* Latin for "let it be done."

**heresy:** The conscious and deliberate rejection of a dogma of the Church.

**indulgence:** The means by which the Church takes away the punishment that a person would receive in Purgatory.

**Purgatory:** A state of final purification or cleansing, which one may need to enter following death and before entering Heaven.

**schism:** A major break that causes division. A schism in the Church is caused by the refusal to submit to the Pope or to be in communion with the Church's members.

*sola gratia:* Central to the Reformation, this phrase means "grace alone," which means that salvation comes through God's grace alone rather than through any human effort. This sole focus on grace contradicts the truth that while God's grace is ultimately the source of salvation, human beings can cooperate with it through their good works, or deny it.

*sola scriptura:* Central to the Reformation, this phrase means that "Scripture alone," rather than Scripture and Tradition, should be the basis for Church teaching, in contradiction to the truth of Catholic teaching.

**theologian:** A person who studies theology. Theology is "the study of God"; the academic discipline and effort to understand, interpret, and order our experience of God and Christian faith; classically defined as "faith seeking understanding."

**theology:** Literally, the "study of God"; the academic discipline and effort to understand, interpret, and order our experience of God and Christian faith.

*Theotokos:* A Greek title for Mary meaning "God bearer."

## Exploring the *Declaration on the Relation of the Church to Non-Christian Religions* (*Nostra Aetate*, 1965)

While reading *Relation of the Church to Non-Christian Religions,* respond to the following questions:

1.  What does the Church assert that all people have in common that draws us to fellowship?

    •

    •

    •

2.  What are the unsolved riddles of the human condition?

    •

    •

    •

    •

3.  What does the document say the Church has in common with, or should respect about, the following religions?

    •  Hinduism

    •  Buddhism

    •  Islam

    •  Judaism

4.  Summarize section 5.

# Unit 6 Test

## Part 1: True or False

Write *true* or *false* in the space next to each statement.

1. _____ The Church is united by bonds of professed faith, worship, and Apostolic Succession.

2. _____ A heresy occurs when a person consciously and deliberately rejects a dogma of the Church.

3. _____ A Church in schism with the Catholic Church is one that does not recognize the supreme authority of the Pope, or refuses to be in communion with the Church's members.

4. _____ The ancient Roman Empire was divided in half, into north and south.

5. _____ The current schism between Southern Orthodox Christianity and the Catholic Church is often dated to 1054.

6. _____ Only the Catholic Church has kept the structure of leadership that Christ established.

7. _____ Martin Luther King, a German monk, was the most prominent of the Protestant Reformers.

8. _____ The term *sola scriptura* means "Scripture alone."

9. _____ The term *sola gratia* means "grace alone."

10. _____ The term *sola pisces* means "Zodiac alone."

11. _____ Christ uses other Christian denominations as a means of salvation.

12. _____ The Eastern Orthodox Churches, though not in full communion with the Church, are especially close to the Catholic Church, as they have remained within the Apostolic Succession.

13. _____ The Catholic Church recognizes that all those "who believe in Christ and have been properly baptized are put in some, though imperfect, communion with the Catholic Church" (*Catechism of the Catholic Church,* 838).

14. _____ The ecumenical movement is an effort by Christians from different churches and communities to be more open to one another and to work to restore unity among all Christians.

15. _____ Achieving Christian unity is a work of the whole Church but cannot come from human effort alone.

16. _____ When we recite the Apostles' Creed, we profess our belief in the Communion of Saints.

17. _____ Mary is called the New Eve.

Document #: TX001485

**18.** _____ The Church has a unique relationship with the Jewish people and religion; many links bind us together.

**19.** _____ Although Christians are a people of the New Covenant, we should not assume that God has rejected or cursed the Jews and their Covenant with God.

**20.** _____ The liturgical celebration is essentially individual rather than communal.

# Part 2: Definitions

Define each of the following terms in a complete sentence or two on a separate sheet of paper.

bishop
creed
ecumenism
excommunication
heresy

indulgence
Purgatory
schism
*sola gratia*
*sola scriptura*

# Part 3: Short Answer

Answer the following questions in paragraph form on a separate sheet of paper.

**1.** Why is it important to honor God and Jesus Christ within community rather than in private worship only?

**2.** What is the fundamental mission of the Church?

**3.** Why must the Church combat the culture of death in the modern world?

(The quotation in question 13 of part 1 is from the English translation of the *Catechism of the Catholic Church* for use in the United States of America, second edition, number 838. Copyright © 1994 by the United States Catholic Conference, Inc.—Libreria Editrice Vaticana. English translation of the *Catechism of the Catholic Church: Modifications from the Editio Typica* copyright © 1997 by the United States Catholic Conference, Inc.—Libreria Editirice Vaticana.)

# Unit 6 Test Answer Key

## Part 1: True or False

1. True
2. True
3. True
4. False
5. False
6. True
7. False

8. True
9. True
10. False
11. True
12. True
13. True
14. True

15. True
16. False
17. True
18. True
19. True
20. False

## Part 2: Definitions

**bishop:** One who has received the fullness of the Sacrament of Holy Orders and is a successor to the Apostles.

**creed:** A short summary statement or profession of faith. The Nicene and Apostles' Creeds are the Church's most familiar and important creeds.

**ecumenism:** The movement to restore unity among all Christians.

**excommunication:** A severe penalty that results from grave sin against Church law. The penalty is either imposed by a Church official or happens automatically as a result of the offense. An excommunicated person is not permitted to celebrate or receive the Sacraments.

**heresy:** The conscious and deliberate rejection of a dogma of the Church.

**indulgence:** The means by which the Church takes away the punishment that a person would receive in Purgatory.

**Purgatory:** A state of final purification or cleansing, which one may need to enter following death and before entering Heaven.

**schism:** A major break that causes division. A schism in the Church is caused by the refusal to submit to the Pope or to be in communion with the Church's members.

***sola gratia***: Central to the Reformation, this phrase means "grace alone," which means that salvation comes through God's grace alone rather than through any human effort. This sole focus on grace contradicts the truth that though God's grace is ultimately the source of salvation, human beings can cooperate with it through their good works, or deny it.

***sola scriptura***: Central to the Reformation, this phrase means that "Scripture alone," rather than Scripture and Tradition, should be the basis for Church teaching, in contradiction to the truth of Catholic teaching.

 © 2010 by Saint Mary's Press
Living in Christ Series

Document #: TX001486

# Part 3: Short Answer

1. When we participate in the Mass, or the Eucharist, we are part of a community at many different levels. We are part of the liturgical assembly, those gathered with us. We are part of the local church or diocese. And we are part of the People of God throughout the world. The liturgical celebration is the work of the whole Christ, the head in union with the body. The liturgy unites us with not only Christ and the Church on earth but also with the worshippers in Heaven, both angels and those humans who have attained Heaven. It is important to know that as individual human beings, we cannot save ourselves. We depend completely on Christ's free gift of grace. Christ distributes this gift through the community of the Church. It is in community where we encounter Jesus when we hear the Gospel proclaimed. In fact, Christ assured that we encounter him in community when he said, "Where two or three are gathered together in my name, there am I in the midst of them" (Matthew 18:20). The goal is communion with God and unity among all people. Our personal, private worship should both draw us to communal prayer and complement the communal worship of the Church.

2. The Church was entrusted with the task of handing down the Apostolic Tradition, the truths of the Catholic faith transmitted through the Scriptures and in Church teachings. Together, Sacred Tradition and Sacred Scripture are a single deposit of the Word of God where the Church encounters God. Through her teaching, life, and worship, the Church gives to each generation all that she is and all that she believes. The Church shares the Good News of Christ with the world, proclaiming the Gospel message.

3. One of the most pressing issues the Church must work to transform in the world is what Pope John Paul II called the "culture of death." The prevalence of abortion and the growing acceptance of euthanasia are elements of this culture of death. The Church recognizes that from the moment of conception to the time of natural death, all life is sacred and should be treated with care and dignity. For this reason the Church must stand firm in promoting a culture of life, in which all life is seen as sacred, and death is in the hands of God alone. At the heart of this mission is the effort to educate people to have a profound respect for the sacredness of every human life. The Church is also calling for new programs to care for the sick and the elderly, and for political action against unjust laws that do not respect the right to life of innocent persons. When any public group promotes social or political policies that threaten God-given human rights, the Church has a responsibility to speak out publicly.

# Unit 7 The Church Interprets the Signs of the Time in Light of the Gospel

## Overview

This unit helps the students to understand that the Church was entrusted with the task of handing down the Apostolic Tradition, the truths of the Catholic faith transmitted through the Scriptures and in Church teachings, and that it is the Church's responsibility to look at the circumstances of each generation and interpret them in light of the Scriptures and Tradition. It is not enough for the Church to simply proclaim the Gospel message; she must be able to apply that message to the issues facing each successive generation.

### Key Understandings and Questions

Upon completing this unit, the students will have a deeper understanding of the following key concepts:

- The Magisterium interprets how the Scriptures and Tradition relate to the events and challenges of today.
- The Magisterium communicates its teaching in a variety of different ways and at different levels—from the Vatican, national conferences of bishops, bishops' teachings, the preaching of the priests at Mass, teachers and catechists, and the conduct and words of everyday Catholics.
- Church members must learn how to make decisions about applying Church teaching to their individual circumstances.
- The Church makes moral judgments about political and social matters when human dignity or salvation is at risk. The Church's mission is distinct from political authorities, even when it speaks in the political arena.

Upon completing the unit, the students will have answered the following questions:

- How does the Magisterium evaluate the issues of today with the Scriptures and Traditions of yesterday?
- How can I learn what the Church teaches?
- How can I apply what the Church teaches?
- Is it appropriate for the Church to be involved in political issues?

## Student Book Articles

This unit draws on articles from *The Church: Christ in the World Today* student book and incorporates them into the unit instruction. Whenever the teaching steps for the unit require the students to refer to or read an article from the student book, the following symbol appears in the margin: (📖). The articles covered in the unit are from "Section 4: The Lived Mission of the Church," and are as follows:

- "The Magisterium" (article 49, pp. 187–190)
- "Indefectibility and Infallibility" (article 50, pp. 190–193)
- "The Magisterium and Truth" (article 51, pp. 193–196)

## How Will You Know the Students Understand?

The following resources will help you assess the students' understanding of the key concepts covered in this unit:

- handout "Final Performance Task Options for Unit 7" (Document #: TX001487)
- handout "Rubric for Final Performance Tasks for Unit 7" (Document #: TX001488)
- handout "Unit 7 Test" (Document #: TX001493)

## The Suggested Path to Understanding

This unit in the teacher guide provides you with one learning path to take with the students, to enable them to deepen their understanding of the Church's responsibility to interpret the signs of the time in light of the Gospel. It is not necessary to use all the learning experiences provided in the unit; however, if you substitute other material from this course or your own material for some of the material offered here, be sure that you have covered all relevant facets of understanding and that you have not missed any skills or knowledge required for later units.

**Step 1:** Preassess student knowledge of Church teaching, its forms, and its application to personal and political life by using an agree / disagree exercise.

**Step 2:** Follow this assessment by presenting to the students the handouts "Final Performance Task Options for Unit 7" (Document #: TX001487) and "Rubric for Final Performance Tasks for Unit 7" (Document #: TX001488).

**Explain**

**Step 3:** Present material that explains the role of the Magisterium in the Church and how it interprets the signs of the times in relation to the events and challenges of today.

**Interpret**

**Step 4:** Discuss the major changes of the Second Vatican Council and have the students prepare PowerPoint or video presentations or skits to demonstrate their understanding.

**Apply**

**Step 5:** Facilitate a "God moments" exercise to help the students to see the sacred in their everyday lives.

**Apply**

**Step 6:** Have the students work in small groups to investigate, using Church documents, the variety of ways the Magisterium of the Church teaches. Then guide them in creating presentations to demonstrate their understanding.

**Perceive**

**Step 7:** Present material about making decisions by applying Church teaching to individual circumstances.

**Apply**

**Step 8:** Discuss the document *Forming Consciences for Faithful Citizenship: A Call to Political Responsibility from the Catholic Bishops of the United States* and how the Church interacts with moral, social, and political issues.

**Empathize**

**Step 9:** Present material about the Church's interaction with moral, social, and political issues using Catholic-centered documents that discuss hot-button issues facing the world today. How does the Church voice its concerns about human dignity or threats to salvation without violating the boundaries between Church and State?

**Perceive**

**Step 10:** Discuss the separation of Church and State and what this really means. Have the students write an opinion piece supporting the role of Catholics in policy discussions and determination.

**Understand**

**Step 11:** Now that the students are closer to the end of the unit, make sure they are all on track with their final performance tasks, if you have assigned them.

**Reflect**

**Step 12:** Provide the students with a tool to use for reflecting about what they learned in the unit and how they learned.

## Background for Teaching This Unit

Visit *smp.org/LivinginChrist* for additional information about these and other theological concepts taught in this unit:

- "Applying Church Teachings in the Process of Making Moral Decisions" (Document #: TX001531)
- "Discipleship versus Citizenship" (Document #: TX001532)

The Web site also includes information on these and other teaching methods used in the unit:

- "Guidelines for Assigning and Assessing PowerPoint Presentations" (Document #: TX001534)
- "Using Primary Sources" (Document #: TX001313)

## Scripture Passages

Scripture is an important part of the Living in Christ series and is frequently used in the learning experiences for each unit. The Scripture passages featured in this unit are as follows:

- Luke 22:54–62 (Peter denies Jesus)
- Mark 8:31–33 (Jesus foretells his death and Resurrection)
- Mark 10:41–45 (Jesus came to give his life as a ransom for many)
- Matthew 14:28–33 (Peter walks on water)
- Matthew 16:13–20 ("Upon this rock I will build my church.")

## Vocabulary

The student book and the teacher guide include the following key terms for this unit. To provide the students with a list of these terms and their definitions, download and print the handout "Vocabulary for Unit 7" (Document #: TX001489).

| | |
|---|---|
| doctrine | infallibility |
| dogma | Magisterium |
| Ecumenical Council | ministry |
| episcopacy | province |
| episcopal | Sacrament of Holy Orders |
| indefectibility of the Church | |

# Learning Experiences

## Step 1

*Preassess student knowledge of Church teaching, its forms, and its application to personal and political life by using an agree / disagree exercise.*

1. Prepare for this learning experience by downloading and printing a single copy of the handout "Statements for the Agree / Disagree Preassessment Exercise" (Document #: TX001490). You will also need to prepare four posters, one with each of the following categories listed in large print:

   • STRONGLY AGREE
   • AGREE
   • DISAGREE
   • STRONGLY DISAGREE

   Post the posters on a continuum the length of the classroom with STRONGLY AGREE and STRONGLY DISAGREE at opposite ends and AGREE and DISAGREE evenly spaced between them.

2. Begin by presenting this exercise to the class, saying something like this:

   ➤ This is an exercise that asks you to tell the class what you already know about the teaching role of the Church. The exercise is nonverbal. You will decide if you strongly agree, agree, disagree, or strongly disagree with each statement.

3. Have the students stand near you to begin the exercise, and then read the first statement to students. (You may decide to write the statement on the board for the students to refer to as they decide on the response, or you might use the PowerPoint "Preassessment" [Document #: TX001512] to present the statements beforehand.)

4. Allow the students a few moments to reflect on the statement, reminding them that this is a nonverbal exercise and that they do not have to form a verbal response. Tell them to decide if they strongly agree, agree, disagree, or strongly disagree with the statement you read and to then move to the appropriate place in the room, corresponding to their responses. Continue reading statements, having the students move for each response.

**Teacher Note**

It is handy to take brief notes on the groupings, for your edification but also to use when leading a discussion. Remember, this is an assessment for you to gauge how much the students understand about the teaching authority of the Church.

5. If you choose, at the end of the activity, discuss your interpretation of the students' responses and knowledge. This will serve as their introduction to this unit.

## Step 2

Follow this assessment by presenting to the students the handouts "Final Performance Task Options for Unit 7" (Document #: TX001487) and "Rubric for Final Performance Tasks for Unit 7" (Document #: TX001488).

This unit provides you with two ways to assess that the students have a deep understanding of the most important concepts in the unit: creating a presentation on the annual United States Conference of Catholic Bishops (USCCB) General Assembly or writing a series of short articles to publish as a bulletin to explain how the teaching of the Church guides the parish social justice committee in the decision-making process. Refer to "Using Final Performance Tasks to Assess Understanding" (Document #: TX001011) and "Using Rubrics to Assess Work" (Document #: TX001012) at *smp.org/LivinginChrist* for background information.

1. Prepare by downloading and printing the handouts "Final Performance Task Options for Unit 7" (Document #: TX001487) and "Rubric for Final Performance Tasks for Unit 7" (Document #: TX001488), one for each student.

2. Distribute the handouts. Give the students a choice as to which performance task they choose and add more options if you so choose. Review the directions, expectations, and rubric in class, allowing the students to ask questions. You may want to say something to this effect:

   ➤ Near the end of the unit, you will have one full class period to work on your final performance task. Please keep in mind, however, that you should be working on this task throughout the course of the unit. Please do not wait until this class period to begin work on your final performance task.

### Teacher Note

You will want to assign due dates for the final performance tasks.

If you have done these performance tasks, or very similar ones, with students before, place examples of this work in the classroom. During this introduction explain how each is a good example of what you are looking for, for different reasons. This allows the students to concretely understand that there is not only one way to succeed.

Articles
49, 50,
51

# Step 3

*Present material that explains the role of the Magisterium in the Church and how it interprets the signs of the times in relation to the events and challenges of today.*

1. Prepare for this learning experience by gathering sheets of blank paper and pens or pencils, one of each for each student.

2. As background have the students read student book articles 49–51, "The Magisterium," "Indefectibility and Infallibility," and "The Magisterium and Truth."

3. Begin by explaining to the class that for this learning experience, they are going to be the teachers.

4. Have the students form pairs. There are ten statements or concepts for this exercise. If you have more than twenty students, have some of the students work in groups of three.

5. Assign each pair or group one of the following statements or concepts:

   - The Church perpetuates and transmits to all generations all that she is and all that she believes through her doctrine, life, and worship.

   - Sacred Tradition, Sacred Scripture, and the Magisterium are so closely connected that one cannot stand apart from the others.

   - The Magisterium is the name given to the official teaching authority of the Church, whose task is to interpret and preserve the truths of the faith transmitted through Scripture and Tradition.

   - *Catechism of the Catholic Church,* Pillar I: the profession of faith (the Creed)

   - *Catechism of the Catholic Church,* Pillar II: the Sacraments of faith

   - *Catechism of the Catholic Church,* Pillar III: the life of faith (the Commandments)

   - *Catechism of the Catholic Church,* Pillar IV: the prayer of the believer (the Lord's Prayer)

   - The indefectibility of the Church means that the one Church established by Jesus will remain, uncorrupted and faithful to Christ's teachings, until the end of human history.

   - Infallibility is the gift of the Holy Spirit to the whole Church by which the leaders of the Church—the Pope and the bishops in union with him—are protected from fundamental error when formulating a specific teaching on a matter of faith and morals.

- The hierarchy of truths does not mean that some truths are less relevant to our faith, but rather that some truths are more fundamental and illuminate other truths.

- Dogmas are those teachings that are recognized as central to Church teaching, defined by the Magisterium and accorded the fullest weight and authority.

6. Distribute the paper and pens or pencils. Explain that the pairs or small groups will have class time to prepare a 5- to 10-minute lesson about their assigned statement or concept that they will share with the class. As part of the assignment, they will turn in their lesson plans. To prepare, they should do the following:

   - research their statement or concept for the purpose of being better able to explain it

   - identify examples that will help their classmates understand the statement or concept

   - create two or three discussion questions related to the statement or concept

7. Once the pairs or small groups have prepared their lesson plans, have each pair or group "teach" the class. The order for the teaching should follow the order in which the statements or concepts are listed in part 5. You will want to fill in any missing information, clarify any confusing points, and address any misconceptions or inaccuracies that surface.

8. When all the groups have finished presenting, collect the lesson plans.

**Interpret**

## Step 4

Discuss the major changes of the Second Vatican Council and have the students prepare PowerPoint or video presentations or skits to demonstrate their understanding.

Vatican Council II invoked many changes that affected the liturgy and practice of the Catholic Church. This step provides two options to help the students to better understand those changes and how they impacted both the Church and its people.

### Option 1: PowerPoint or Video Presentation

1. Divide the class into small groups of four or five.

2. Assign, or let each group select, one of the following changes instituted by Vatican Council II:

- Laypeople (nonordained) were encouraged to be more involved in the Church and in the liturgy (as lectors, Eucharistic ministers, etc.).
- The Mass was now to be said in the vernacular of the people (English, Spanish, Vietnamese, etc.) instead of in Latin.
- The Church encouraged the study of the Bible by all Catholics.
- The altar was moved to face the people.
- The name of the Sacrament of Extreme Unction was changed to the Sacrament of Anointing of the Sick and the emphasis of the Sacrament was changed from forgiveness to healing.
- The Council invited conversation with all religions and expressed an appreciation for ecumenism.
- Religious orders were asked to return to wearing the dress of the day.
- The Council released a document called *Declaration on the Relation of the Church to Non-Christian Religions* (*Nostra Aetate,* 1965), which stated that the Jews were not responsible for the death of Jesus.

3. Have each small group create and present a PowerPoint presentation of seven to ten slides on their topic or a video with sound and music. The presentation is to fully explain the change instituted by the Second Vatican Council including the reason for the change and the implications the change had/has for the Church. The PowerPoint presentation or video must also contain citations for works consulted.

## Option 2: Skits

1. Divide the class into small groups of four or five.
2. Assign, or let each group select, one of the changes instituted by Vatican Council II as listed in option 1.
3. Have each group create a before-and-after skit to demonstrate the change that was instituted. Each skit must be at least 3 minutes in length and must present accurate information.
4. Have each group submit a one-page paper about the change and how it impacted the Church, citing all works consulted.

## Step 5

*Facilitate a "God moments" exercise to help the students to see the sacred in their everyday lives.*

This learning experience helps the students to be more aware of the presence of God in their daily lives and is also an excellent faith-sharing exercise.

1. Prepare for this learning experience by having available a pad of sticky notes and by writing on the board or on a large sheet of posted newsprint the phrase "God Moments."

2. Distribute a sticky note to each student.

3. Ask the students to quietly reflect on the following questions:
   ➤ What has happened in your life in the past twenty-four hours?
   ➤ What is one way you saw or experienced God in the past twenty-four hours? Has someone acted toward you in a way that showed God's love? Have you been blessed with a special event or surprise that shows God's generosity? Have you witnessed something in nature that displayed God's glory?

   Have the students write their responses on their sticky notes.

4. Now invite the students to come up one at a time and place the sticky note(s) around where you have written "God Moments" and share what they have written. Ask the class to be reverent and respectful as each student shares.

5. When the last student has finished sharing, lead the class in a brief prayer:
   ➤ Loving God, thank you for the many ways you reveal yourself to us in the everyday moments of our lives. We give you praise and thanksgiving for the many blessings you have given us, and we pray that we will always be aware of your loving presence and grace in our lives. In Jesus' name we pray. Amen.

6. Conclude by sharing the following with the class:
   ➤ God is always present and working in our lives and the world. One way God is present to us is through the Church. Just as God reaches out to us in the moments and realities of our lives, the Church works to share the Good News of Jesus in the circumstances of our ever-changing world.

### Teacher Note

This is a good opportunity to talk about salvation history: God is revealed to us in the past, present, and future as well as in the people, places, and events of our lives.

# Step 6

Have the students work in small groups to investigate, using Church documents, the variety of ways the Magisterium of the Church teaches. Then guide them in creating presentations to demonstrate their understanding.

1. Prepare for this learning experience by gathering copies of the *Catechism of the Catholic Church*, one for each student, and sheets of blank paper, two for each small group of three or four. Also download and print the handout "Where Does the Church Say . . . ?" (Document #: TX001491), one for each student. Reserve the computer lab or media center to ensure that the students will have access to the Internet.

2. Begin by sharing the following:

   ➤ Discovering *why* the Church teaches what she does involves learning *how* she teaches. Since the beginning, the Church has developed a variety of communication means to articulate her message, depending on the audience and the authority of those issuing the teaching document.

3. Distribute the handout and explain that it lists the different types of Church teaching documents, their level of importance in explaining a fuller understanding of our faith, and where one can access these types of documents today. Instruct the students to look at the handout and respond to the following question:

   ➤ What is the difference between the most authoritative and the least authoritative Church teaching documents? Why?

4. Now divide the class into small groups of three or four. Instruct the small groups to each choose (or you may assign) a topic of interest regarding the life or teachings of the Church. Direct them to the index of the *Catechism of the Catholic Church* for possible ideas. Each group should have a different topic. Some possible topics include family, marriage, justice, abortion, citizenship, ecumenism, euthanasia, lying, political authority, violence, sexuality, temptation, and war.

5. When the groups have selected their topics, direct them to use the *Catechism* to find a section that pertains to their topic. They are to read that section, taking note of at least three other Church documents that are cross-referenced in footnotes. Distribute a sheet of paper to each small group for taking notes.

6. Next the small groups are to look up the cross-referenced Church documents online and read the sections of those documents that are footnoted in the *Catechism*.

7. The last part of the small groups' research is to find one or two additional Church documents that relate to their topic. These documents should be different types of Church documents than those cited in the *Catechism* footnotes. Encourage the students to look for documents from the United States Conference of Catholic Bishops or their local bishop. At the end of the research, they should have reviewed a minimum of five Church documents (including the *Catechism*).

8. When the students have completed their research, their final task is to write a paragraph for each of the documents, identifying the type of document it is, who authored it, and whom the audience is, and then summarizing the teaching related to their topic. Distribute another sheet of paper to each small group for this work. Another option is to have the small groups create a PowerPoint presentation that cites all the documents and demonstrates their understanding of the Church teachings.

**Perceive**

## Step 7

*Present material about making decisions by applying Church teaching to individual circumstances.*

Note that this should not come across as relativism but rather as how Catholics apply Gospel values and Church teaching to everyday life situations. This step serves as a starting point for steps 8 and 9, in which the students spend time exploring *Forming Consciences for Faithful Citizenship: A Call to Political Responsibility from the Catholic Bishops of the United States.*

1. Prepare for this learning experience by downloading and printing the handout "Quiz: Are You a Faithful Citizen?" (Document #: TX001492), one for each student.

2. Begin by telling the students they are going to have a pop quiz.

3. Distribute the handout and give the students time to complete the quiz. Tell them the quiz will not be graded. They should answer honestly about themselves and their opinions rather than try to give an answer that they think is the "right" answer in terms of the Church.

4. When the students have completed the quiz, briefly discuss each question with the class. Invite the students to share their answers and opinions.

5. Explain that in the next two learning experiences, the students will be exploring what the United States Conference of Catholic Bishops says about faithful citizenship and the responsibility of the Church in relation to issues of public policy and politics.

Sidebar
p. 142

Apply

# Step 8

*Discuss the document Forming Consciences for Faithful Citizenship: A Call to Political Responsibility from the Catholic Bishops of the United States and how the Church interacts with moral, social, and political issues.*

The students will read a portion of *Forming Consciences for Faithful Citizenship* and debate the pros and cons of Catholics' getting involved in politics and the pros and cons of the creation of civil policy. As background you may want to direct the students to read the sidebar "Faithful Citizenship," on page 142 of the student book.

1. As background for this learning experience, have the students read "Part I: Forming Consciences for Faithful Citizenship: The U.S. Bishops' Reflection on Catholic Teaching" from *Forming Consciences for Faithful Citizenship*. A link to the document is available at *smp.org/LivinginChrist*.

2. Review with the class the main points of the bishops' statement involving the Church's role and the role of the faithful in deciding public policy.

3. Divide the class into two teams and tell them they will be debating the Church's call to responsible citizenship and the moral obligation of all Catholics to participate in the political process. Team 1 will argue in favor of civic engagement viewed through the lens of faith. Team 2 will present reasons why religion and politics shouldn't mix.

4. Allow the teams 10 minutes to prepare for the debate. You will want to share the following rules and guidelines for the debate as the teams prepare so they can assign roles as needed:

    ➤ No one is allowed to speak more than once until everyone on the team has shared.

    ➤ This is a debate about the topic; there will be no personal attacks, no yelling, and no interrupting.

    ➤ Each team can make a 1-minute opening statement.

    ➤ Following the opening statements, team 1 has 30 seconds to respond to team 2's opening statement. Then team 2 has 30 seconds to respond to team 1's opening statement.

---

**Teacher Note**

At *smp.org/LivinginChrist* you will find a collection of links to documents that address the Church's position on a wide range of moral, social, and political issues.

➤ Team 2 can then ask a question directly of team 1, who will have 30 seconds to respond. Then team 1 can ask a question team 2, who will have 30 seconds to respond. Continue this process as long as you like.

➤ Each team will then have 1 minute for a closing statement.

5. Follow the debate with a discussion, using quotations from the *Forming Consciences for Faithful Citizenship* document, particularly paragraphs 5–16.

 **Empathize**

## Step 9

Present material about the Church's interaction with moral, social, and political issues using Catholic-centered documents that discuss hot-button issues facing the world today. How does the Church voice its concerns about human dignity or threats to salvation without violating the boundaries between Church and State?

> **Teacher Note**
>
> At *smp.org/LivinginChrist* you will find a collection of links to documents that address the Church's position on a wide range of moral, social, and political issues.

1. As background for this learning experience, have the students read "Part II: Applying Catholic Teaching to Major Issues: A Summary of Policy Positions of the United States Conference of Catholic Bishops" from *Forming Consciences for Faithful Citizenship: A Call to Political Responsibility from the Catholic Bishops of the United States.* A link is available at *smp.org/ LivinginChrist.*

2. Begin by explaining that the Church has the responsibility to speak out on issues with significant moral dimensions. In *Forming Consciences for Faithful Citizenship,* the U.S. Bishops identified four areas of special concern: human life, family life, social justice, and global solidarity. For this learning experience, the students will look at a specific topic that falls under one of these four areas of concern.

3. Divide the class into four small groups. Assign the groups topics as follows:

   • Group 1: Human Life

   • Group 2: Family Life

   • Group 3: Social Justice

   • Group 4: Global Solidarity

4. Direct the small groups to reread the section of part II of *Forming Consciences for Faithful Citizenship* that addresses their topic.

5. The students should then choose one of the topics in bold in their assigned topic area. Each student in a group should have a different topic. For example, the Family Life group can choose from marriage, wages, parents' right to choose the education best suited to the needs of their children, or media.

6. Each student is then to do the following, either as homework or in class:

   - Write a letter to your U.S. senator or congressperson explaining the Church teaching, and encourage the senator or congressperson to work to support legislation that is in line with the Church teaching.

   - Identify two ways you could address the topic locally through service or education.

7. Conclude by emphasizing that being a faithful citizen and a faithful Catholic are not in opposition to each other. We have a responsibility to have our faith inform and influence our political action. Additionally, being a faithful citizen and a faithful Catholic doesn't mean we are politically active by voting only; we have a responsibility to work for change through service, education, and advocacy.

## Step 10

*Discuss the separation of Church and State and what this really means. Have the students write an opinion piece supporting the role of Catholics in policy discussions and determination.*

In this learning experience, the students will examine resources regarding the Catholic point of view on certain hot-button topics and will make a presentation on the Catholic view of each topic. Students will need access to the Internet or you will need to provide copies of documents from the United States Conference of Catholic Bishops. A link is provided at *smp.org/LivinginChrist*.

1. Begin by having the students identify some of the hot-button issues facing Catholics and society today. You will want to list the topics on the board. Rather than have the students generate a list, another option is to provide a list of topics. A few topics are capital punishment, cloning, war, euthanasia, abortion, same-sex marriage, and immigration.

2. Lead a discussion with the class about what the controversy or conflict is concerning these issues and the teachings of the Church.

3. Have the students form pairs, and let each pair select a topic from the list. If you have more pairs of students than topics, you can have the students form groups of three.

4. Direct each pair or group to research the Church's position on their topic using the links provided, the *Catechism,* and other reliable sources. Each pair or group is to write a two-page, double-spaced opinion article in which they present both sides of the topic and finish with a definitive statement of the Catholic perspective and action responsibility. The article should clearly explain the reasoning for the Church's position, citing relevant sources. Additionally, each pair or group should write a one-paragraph summary of the Church's position.

5. Conclude by having the pairs or groups share their summary paragraph with the rest of the class.

## Step 11

Now that the students are closer to the end of the unit, make sure they are all on track with their final performance tasks, if you have assigned them.

If possible, devote 50 to 60 minutes for the students to ask questions about the tasks and to work individually or in their small groups.

1. Remind the students to bring to class any work they have already prepared so that they can work on it during the class period. If necessary, reserve the library or media center so the students can do any book or online research.

2. Provide some class time for the students to work on their performance tasks. This then allows you to work with the students who need additional guidance with the project.

# Step 12

*Provide the students with a tool to use for reflecting about what they learned in the unit and how they learned.*

This learning experience provides the students with an excellent opportunity to reflect on how their understanding of the Church's role in interpreting the signs of the time in light of the Gospel has developed throughout the unit.

1. To prepare for this learning experience, make copies of the handout "Learning about Learning" (Document #: TX001159; see Appendix), one for each student.

2. Distribute the handout, and give the students about 15 minutes to answer the questions quietly. Invite them to share any reflections they have about the content they learned as well as their insights into the way they learned.

# Final Performance Task Options for Unit 7

## Important Information for Both Options

The following are the main ideas you are to understand from this unit. They should appear in this final performance task so your teacher can assess whether you learned the most essential content.

- The Magisterium interprets how the Scriptures and Tradition relate to the events and challenges of today.

- The Magisterium communicates its teaching in a variety of different ways and at different levels—from the Vatican, national conferences of bishops, bishops' teachings, the preaching of the priests at Mass, teachers and catechists, and the conduct and words of everyday Catholics.

- Church members must learn how to make decisions about applying Church teaching to their individual circumstances.

- The Church makes moral judgment about political and social matters when human dignity or salvation is at risk. The Church's mission is distinct from political authorities, even when it speaks in the political arena.

## Option 1: The United States Conference of Catholic Bishops General Assembly Meeting

You have been asked to research and create a 15- to 20-minute presentation on the most recent meeting of the United States Conference of Catholic Bishops (USCCB) General Assembly meeting (held the previous November) for an RCIA (Rite of Christian Initiation of Adults) session at your parish. The purpose of the presentation is to help new members of the Church to understand the role of the Magisterium and topics the Magisterium is addressing in the United States. Your presentation is to explain what the general assembly is, what the agenda was for the most recent meeting, and the key topics addressed by the assembly. Follow these guidelines in creating your presentation:

- Include a brief description of what the USCCB General Assembly is, who comes to it, and what its role is.

- Summarize the agenda for the most recent meeting, including the length of the assembly gathering and the role of prayer over the days of the assembly.

- Describe three of the topics discussed.

- Identify three Church documents or teachings that are relevant to each of the topics discussed and cite a specific part of these that is relevant to the debate.

- Summarize the actions taken or decisions made by the USCCB General Assembly in relation to the three topics you identified.

Additionally, you are to write a two-page reflection on the role of the bishops' conference, concluding with a summary of your impressions of the bishops' conference and a response to this question: How will the decisions made at the most recent general assembly meeting impact your daily life, the lives of other Catholics, and your parish over the next three years? Provide specific examples.

As part of this final performance task, you may choose to contact the bishop's office of your local diocese and ask to speak with the bishop or his representative about this project. Before contacting your local bishop, review with your teacher questions you would like to ask and receive approval to proceed. Here are some questions you might consider asking:

- What are the procedural processes for the USCCB General Assembly? How does a topic get placed on the agenda, and what goes into addressing that topic before the assembly?

- What do you believe are the benefits and challenges of the USCCB General Assembly process?

- What topics addressed by the general assembly do you have particularly strong feelings about? Why?

# Option 2: Bulletin Article Series

You are on the parish council. The social justice committee has expressed the need to educate the parish about the connection between the Gospel and action on behalf of justice. The council wants to educate the parish members about how the teaching of the Church can serve as a guide in making decisions that influence their lives and the lives of others. Your task is to write five one- to two-page articles to publish as bulletin inserts for Sunday liturgy. Follow these guidelines in writing your articles:

- The first article is to explain the role of the Magisterium for the faith community today.

- The second, third, and fourth articles are to address specific justice issues relevant in the United States.

- The fifth article is to identify a local justice issue, cite the Gospels and Church documents that address the issue, and challenge the parish community to take action.

- Incorporate basic definitions as well as quotations from the Scriptures and Church documents that summarize the teaching role of the Church.

- For each article write one reflection question that challenges parish members to consider their own individual response to the issue presented. Include your personal reflection on each of the questions.

# Rubric for Final Performance Tasks for Unit 7

| Criteria | 4 | 3 | 2 | 1 |
|---|---|---|---|---|
| **Assignment includes all items requested in the directions.** | Assignment not only includes all items requested, but they are completed above expectations. | Assignment includes all items requested. | Assignment includes more than half of the items requested. | Assignment includes less than half of the items requested. |
| **Assignment shows understanding of the concept *the Magisterium interprets how the Scriptures and Tradition relate to the events and challenges of today.*** | Assignment shows unusually insightful understanding of this concept. | Assignment shows good understanding of this concept. | Assignment shows adequate understanding of this concept. | Assignment shows little understanding of this concept. |
| **Assignment shows understanding of the concept *the Magisterium communicates its teaching in a variety of different ways and at different levels—from the Vatican, national conferences of bishops, bishops' teaching, the preaching of the priest at Mass, teachers and catechists, and the conduct and words of everyday Catholics.*** | Assignment shows unusually insightful understanding of this concept. | Assignment shows good understanding of this concept. | Assignment shows adequate understanding of this concept. | Assignment shows little understanding of this concept. |
| **Assignment shows understanding of the concept *Church members must learn how to make decisions about applying Church teaching to individual circumstances.*** | Assignment shows unusually insightful understanding of this concept. | Assignment shows good understanding of this concept. | Assignment shows adequate understanding of this concept. | Assignment shows little understanding of this concept. |
| **Assignment shows understanding of the concept *the Church makes moral judgment about political and social matters when human dignity or salvation is at risk. The Church's mission is distinct from political authorities even when it speaks in the political arena.*** | Assignment shows unusually insightful understanding of this concept. | Assignment shows good understanding of this concept. | Assignment shows adequate understanding of this concept. | Assignment shows little understanding of this concept. |
| **Assignment uses proper grammar and spelling.** | Assignment has no grammar or spelling errors. | Assignment has one grammar or spelling error. | Assignment has two grammar or spelling errors. | Assignment has more than two grammar or spelling errors. |

# Vocabulary for Unit 7

**doctrine:** An official, authoritative teaching of the Church based on the Revelation of God.

**dogma:** Teachings recognized as central to Church teaching, defined by the Magisterium and accorded the fullest weight and authority.

**Ecumenical Council:** A gathering of the Church's bishops from around the world convened by the Pope or approved by him to address pressing issues in the Church.

**episcopacy:** A term for the bishop's governance of his Church.

**episcopal:** Of or relating to a bishop.

**indefectibility of the Church:** The Church's remaining uncorrupted and faithful to Christ's teachings, until the end of human history.

**infallibility:** The gift given by the Holy Spirit to the Pope and the bishops in union with him to teach on matters of faith and morals without error.

**Magisterium:** The Church's living teaching office, which consists of all bishops, in communion with the Pope.

**ministry:** Based on a word for "service," a way of caring for and serving others and helping the Church fulfill its mission. *Ministry* especially refers to the work of sanctification performed by those in Holy Orders through the preaching of God's Word and the celebration of the Sacraments. The laity helps the Church fulfill its mission through lay ministries, such as that of lector or catechist.

**province:** A grouping of two or more dioceses with an archbishop as its head.

**Sacrament of Holy Orders:** The Sacrament by which members of the Church are ordained for permanent ministry in the Church as bishops, priests, or deacons.

# Statements for the Agree / Disagree Preassessment Exercise

I know what the Magisterium is.

The Church has a major role in teaching people how to live.

The Church must change with the times, adjusting to society's needs.

People can make moral and ethical decisions on their own.

The Pope is the successor of Peter.

The Pope and bishops are the official teachers of the Church.

The Magisterium is a secret society within the Church.

Infallibility means the Church never makes a mistake.

The Church says that people are responsible for defining their own morals and ethics.

The faith of the Church is protected by the Magisterium.

The Church teaches us what we need to know to make good decisions.

Any time the Pope speaks, he speaks infallibly.

Every Church dogma is voted on annually.

Bishop (*name your bishop)* has an important teaching role in our diocese.

The Church's understanding of doctrine does not change.

Each Pope decides which rules to follow during his papacy.

The experience of its members is important in official Church teaching.

The Church teaches in different ways.

An encyclical is an official letter from the Pope to the global Church.

Doctrine is an official Church teaching expressed by the Magisterium.

The Church is right to speak out on issues of justice.

The Church cannot speak about politics and civil laws.

Document #: TX001490

# Where Does the Church Say?

| Type of Document | Author | Audience | What's in It? / Examples |
|---|---|---|---|
| **Sacred Scriptures** | various writers inspired by the Holy Spirit | all people | the Word of God in the words of humans |
| **Dogmatic Constitution** | the Pope and Ecumenical Council fathers (example: Vatican Council II) | all the people of God | a solemn, formal decree that expresses the dogma or doctrinal understanding of the Church in a particular era (example: *Dogmatic Constitution on the Church* [*Lumen Gentium,* 1964] from Vatican Council II) |
| **Apostolic Constitution** | the Pope in his own name | usually all the faithful, but see greeting for specific group being addressed | solemn, formal document on matters of highest consequence concerning doctrine or disciplinary matters that are published as either universal or particular law of the Church (example: *Catechism of the Catholic Church*) |
| **Encyclical (*encyclica epistola:* literally "circular letter")** | the Pope in his own name | usually addressed to the bishops, clergy, and faithful of the entire Church, but also to "all people of good will" | a pastoral letter that attempts to refine our understanding of some doctrine or part of the human condition through the Pope's ordinary teaching office (example *Caritas in Veritate,* by Pope Benedict XVI) |
| **Apostolic Letter** | the Pope in his own name or a Vatican congregation | addressed to particular audience in greeting | a formal papal teaching document, not used for dogmatic definitions of doctrine but to give counsel to the Church on points of doctrine that require deeper explanation in the light of particular circumstances or situations in various parts of the world (example: *Rosarium Virginis Mariae,* by Pope John Paul II) |
| **Apostolic Exhortation** | the Pope in his own name | addressed to bishops, clergy, and all the faithful of the entire Catholic Church | a reflection on a particular topic that does not contain dogmatic definitions or policy directives; not a legislative document (example: *Familiaris Consortio,* by Pope John Paul II) |
| ***Motu Proprio* (literally "by one's own initiative")** | the Pope in his own name | addressed to bishops, clergy, and all the faithful of the entire Catholic Church | a legislative document or decree issued by the Pope on his own initiative, not in response to a request (example: *"Summorum Pontificum,"* by Pope Benedict XVI) |

Document #: TX001491

| | | | |
|---|---|---|---|
| **Declaration and Decree** | specific Vatican congregations or specific bishop groups | addressed to specific group in greeting of the document | a statement involving Church law, precepts or judicial decisions on a specific matter; an ordinance given by one having the power of jurisdiction (worldwide or local diocese) (example: *On the Unicity and Salvific Universality of Jesus Christ and the Church [Dominus Iesus]* from Congregation for the Doctrine of Faith) |
| **Instruction** | specific Vatican congregations | addressed to specific group in greeting of the document | explains or amplifies a document that has legislative force, such as apostolic constitutions, and states how its precepts are to be applied (example: *General Instruction on the Roman Missal*) |
| **Pastoral Letter** | national bishops' conferences or local bishop | the faithful within the country or the local diocese | an explanation of how Church teaching applies to or is to be put into effect within a given country or diocese (example: *Economic Justice for All*, by the United States Conference of Catholic Bishops) |

Document #: TX001491

# Quiz: Are You a Faithful Citizen?

1.  How many times a week do you read or watch the news?

    a.  every day
    b.  most days
    c.  only sometimes
    d.  hardly at all or never

2.  Which of the following best describes you around election times?

    a.  Even if I can't vote yet, I read about the candidates and watch the debates to try to find out candidates' positions on issues I care about.
    b.  I usually pick up some things about the candidates and have some basis to form an opinion, but if I could vote, I might not feel totally informed to make a decision.
    c.  I don't really pay that much attention, so my opinion of the candidates, if I have one, might be based on what I hear from others.
    d.  I'm so sick of politics. I try to tune it out or watch or read something else.

3.  How many of the seven themes of Catholic social teaching can you name?

    a.  life and _____ of the human person
    b.  call to family, _____, and participation
    c.  rights and _____
    d.  option for the _____ and vulnerable
    e.  the dignity of work and the _____ _____ _____
    f.  _____ (one word)
    g.  care for God's _____

4.  Which of the following opinions about faith and politics do you agree with most?

    a.  Faith is a moral guidepost for the decisions we make, including how we vote. Faith should definitely be brought into the political realm.
    b.  Faith can be helpful in encouraging us to make good decisions, but sometimes it can get in the way of what would really be the best way to do things.
    c.  People shouldn't bring their religion into politics. The Constitution says they should be separate.

5.  If someone asked you to explain why your religion holds a certain perspective on a moral issue, like abortion or poverty, what would your response be?

    a.  "I know all about that." (Then you launch into a detailed explanation.)
    b.  "I think I can explain that." (Then you have a couple of things to say.)
    c.  "Umm . . . I'm not really sure. You should ask someone else."

© 2010 by Saint Mary's Press
Living in Christ Series

6. How many times a year do you participate in activities such as writing letters, calling, or e-mailing your local or national leaders; walking in marches or participating in demonstrations; educating others about important issues affecting human life and dignity; or participating in other advocacy efforts to protect the poor and vulnerable?

   a. twelve times a year (about once a month)
   b. six times a year (about every other month)
   c. a couple of times a year
   d. rarely or never

7. How many hours of community service do you do each month?

   a. 10 or more
   b. 6 to 9
   c. 3 to 5
   d. 0 to 2

8. Which best describes the way you decide which positions to hold about the issues being debated?

   a. I usually don't take sides; I like to remain neutral.
   b. I tend to go along with what others around me think. If everyone believes something, they are probably right.
   c. I usually just have a gut feeling that I listen to.
   d. I take my responsibility to form my conscience seriously, so I make an effort to learn about teachings of the Church and the Scriptures, I examine the facts, and I prayerfully reflect on the issues so I can make the best decision possible.

9. Whose role is it to make the world a better place?

   a. All of us have an equally pressing responsibility to make positive change in both our local communities and in the world.
   b. Everyone should be concerned about it, but we also have our own lives to worry about. We should all devote some time to helping others, but realistically, there is not a whole lot we can do.
   c. Adults have more education and training, so it is their responsibility. There isn't much I can do.

# Unit 7 Test

## Part 1: Multiple Choice

Write your answers in the blank spaces at the left.

1. _____    The first Pope was _____.

   A. elected by majority vote
   B. called "the Rock"
   C. living in Avignon, France
   D. the most well educated of the Apostles

2. _____    _____ helps all members of the Church as they grow in their understanding of the Church's heritage of faith contained in the Scriptures and Tradition.

   A. Reader's Digest
   B. Fasting on Fridays
   C. The Holy Spirit
   D. Mary, Mother of God,

3. _____    The _____ is the name given to the official teaching authority of the Church.

   A. Magisterium
   B. Colloquium
   C. Mysterium
   D. Tritium

4. _____    Sacred Tradition, _____, and the Magisterium are so closely connected that one cannot stand apart from the other.

   A. the Pope
   B. the college of bishops
   C. the Sacred Scriptures
   D. the Sacraments

5. _____    The _____ is one tool the Church uses to present the faith.

   A. *Catechism of the Catholic Church*
   B. dogmatic congress
   C. Book of Mormon
   D. Talmud

Document #: TX001493

6. _____   Because God created us with a longing for him, we have the obligation to _____.

   A. pay one-tenth of our income in tithing
   B. love others until that longing is fulfilled
   C. ignore mankind and seek only him
   D. search for the truth about God and his Church

7. _____   For centuries the Church taught the faithful to _____ in order to commemorate Jesus' suffering and death.

   A. wear sandals without socks
   B. cover their heads in church
   C. name their children with saints' names
   D. abstain from eating meat on Fridays

8. _____   The Church is both indefectible and _____.

   A. unadorned
   B. infallible
   C. inconsumable
   D. inconsolate

9. _____   The First Vatican Council declared that under the leadership of Peter and his successors as popes, the Church will remain _____.

   A. a merely human institution
   B. indestructible until the end of time
   C. in Rome until the second coming
   D. a haven for tax collectors

10. _____   If the Church is without defect, it must also be without _____.

   A. mistake
   B. sinners
   C. opposition
   D. hope

                                   Document #: TX001493

# Part 2: Matching

Match each statement in column 1 with a term from column 2. Write the letter that corresponds to your choice in the space provided. (*Note:* There are two extra items in column 2.)

## Column 1

**1.** _____ This is a gathering of the Church's bishops from around the world convened by the Pope or approved by him to address pressing issues in the Church.

**2.** _____ The Church is without mistake in her teachings.

**3.** _____ This is the name given to the official teaching authority of the Church, whose task it is to interpret and preserve the truths of faith transmitted through the Scriptures and Tradition.

**4.** _____ An official, authoritative teaching of the Church, based on the Revelation of God.

**5.** _____ The Church's remaining uncorrupted and faithful to Christ's teachings, until the end of human history.

**6.** _____ These are teachings that are recognized as central to Church teaching, defined by the Magisterium and accorded the fullest weight and authority.

**7.** _____ A grouping of two or more dioceses with an archbishop as its head.

**8.** _____ This is based on a word for "service." In a general sense, it is any service offered to help the Church fulfill its mission.

**9.** _____ This means "of or relating to bishops."

**10.** _____ This is the Sacrament by which members of the Church are ordained for permanent ministry in the Church as bishops, priests, or deacons.

## Column 2

**A.** episcopal

**B.** Sacrament of Holy Orders

**C.** Ecumenical Council

**D.** doctrine

**E.** ideology

**F.** Magisterium

**G.** infallible

**H.** ministry

**I.** censorship

**J.** dogmas

**K.** province

**L.** indefectibility of the Church

Document #: TX001493

# Part 3: Short Answer

Answer each of the following questions in paragraph form on a separate sheet of paper:

1. What does it mean for the Church to be indefectible?

2. What does it mean for the Church to be infallible?

3. What is the role of truth in faith?

Document #: TX001493

# Unit 7 Test Answer Key

## Part 1: Multiple Choice

1. B
2. C
3. A
4. C

5. A
6. D
7. D
8. B

9. B
10. A

## Part 2: Matching

1. C
2. G
3. F
4. D

5. L
6. J
7. K
8. H

9. A
10. B

## Part 3: Short Answer

1. The indefectibility of the Church means that the one Church established by Jesus will remain, uncorrupted and faithful to Christ's teachings, until the end of human history. Jesus gave this promise of indefectibility to Peter and the Church when he said, "You are Peter, and upon this rock I will build my church, and the gates of the netherworld shall not prevail against it" (Matthew 16:18). Jesus promised that not even the powers of death would be able to overcome the Church, and the First Vatican Council declared that under the leadership of Peter and his successors as popes, the Church will remain "indestructible until the end of time." The Second Vatican Council taught that by "the power of the Holy Spirit, the Church is the faithful spouse of the Lord and will never fail to be a sign of salvation to the world." Even during the time of the final tribulation, the Church will remain firm.

2. Despite the sins of its members, the Church proclaims the authentic Gospel without error. There is a direct relationship between indefectibility and infallibility. If the Church is without defect, she must also be without mistake, or not fallible, in her teachings. Infallibility is the gift of the Holy Spirit to the whole Church by which leaders of the Church—the Pope and the bishops in union with him—are protected from fundamental error when formulating a specific teaching on a matter of faith and morals. The infallibility of the Magisterium is an expression of the infallibility of the entire Church. The Pope may proclaim infallible teaching on his own authority. When he makes such a definitive teaching, it is known as being *ex cathedra*, Latin for "from the chair." The Pope's gift of infallibility applies only in very specific circumstances, and not every time he speaks. The first *ex cathedra* use of the gift of infallibility occurred when Pope Pius XII proclaimed the Assumption of Mary to be a dogma of faith. A second example of the use of the gift of infallibility occurred with the teaching of the Council of Chalcedon (AD 452), when the Council stated that the two natures of Christ (human

and divine) exist "without confusion, change, division, or separation," using the teaching of Pope Leo I as one of its guidelines.

3.  The Church's teachings can seem overwhelming to someone approaching them for the first time. Luckily, the Church has a hierarchy, or order, of truths, making it possible to identify the most fundamental truths and see how other truths are connected to them. The Trinity, for example, is a central mystery of the Catholic faith and "the source of all the other mysteries of faith, the light that enlightens them" (*Catechism of the Catholic Church [CCC]*, 234). It is important for the believer to see that all the Church teachings are interconnected and that it would be impossible to isolate one teaching and disregard it without also disregarding other truths of faith associated with it. Dogmas are those doctrines that are recognized as central to Church teaching, defined by the Magisterium and accorded the fullest weight and authority. Dogmas express the truths that we need to know for our salvation. It can be tempting to look at a Church teaching as one viewpoint among many. This way of thinking is called *relativism*. One indicator that relativism cannot be an accurate philosophy is that it is built on the premise that there is no absolute truth. Yet the philosophy of relativism depends on the absolute truth that there is no absolute truth. Therefore relativism inherently contradicts itself. "God is Truth itself, whose words cannot deceive. This is why one can abandon oneself in full trust to the truth and faithfulness of his word in all things" (*CCC,* 215).

# Unit 8

# God Calls Us to Live as Disciples in the Church

## Overview

In this unit the students explore how we each have been called to the Church and to Christ and how our relationship with Christ will grow if we respond and come to him. Additionally, this unit focuses on discipleship as a response to being called.

### Key Understandings and Questions

Upon completing this unit, the students will have a deeper understanding of the following key concepts:

- God saves us in community with others rather than by ourselves.
- Discipleship is not just about following rules; rather, the Church shapes disciples into the image of Jesus Christ.
- Discipleship means being "salt and light" for the world by contributing our gifts to the Church and to the human community.
- Christ enriches us in the Church through the Sacraments, prayer, the Eucharist, charity, service, and justice.

Upon completing the unit, the students will have answered the following questions:

- Why can't I just have a personal relationship with Jesus? Isn't that enough?
- Why does the Church focus so much on rules?
- What do I have to offer to the Church anyway?
- What does the Church have to offer to me?

### Student Book Articles

This unit draws on articles from *The Church: Christ in the World Today* student book and incorporates them into the unit instruction. Whenever the teaching steps for the unit require the students to refer to or read an article from the student book, the following symbol appears in the margin: (📖). The articles covered in the unit are from "Section 5: The Church and Young People," and are as follows:

- "Called by God to Belong to the Church" (article 52, pp. 199–202)
- "Christ Enriches Us through Participation in the Life of the Church" (article 53, pp. 202–206)
- "Called to Community" (article 54, pp. 206–210)
- "Sent as a Disciple" (article 55, pp. 212–215)

- "Discipleship in Daily Life" (article 56, pp. 215–219)
- "Empowered by the Holy Spirit" (article 57, pp. 219–222)

## How Will You Know the Students Understand?

The following resources will help you assess the students' understanding of the key concepts covered in this unit:

- handout "Final Performance Task Options for Unit 8" (Document #: TX001495)
- handout "Rubric for Final Performance Tasks for Unit 8" (Document #: TX001496)
- handout "Unit 8 Test" (Document #: TX001500)

## The Suggested Path to Understanding

This unit in the teacher guide provides you with one learning path to take with the students, to enable them to deepen their understanding of how we are all called to live as disciples of Christ in the Church. It is not necessary to use all the learning experiences provided in the unit; however, if you substitute other material from this course or your own material for some of the material offered here, be sure that you have covered all relevant facets of understanding and that you have not missed any skills or knowledge required for later units.

 **Step 1:** Preassess student knowledge of discipleship using the "I Am More Like" exercise.

 **Step 2:** Follow this assessment by presenting to the students the handouts "Final Performance Task Options for Unit 8" (Document #: TX001495) and "Rubric for Final Performance Tasks for Unit 8" (Document #: TX001496).

 **Step 3:** Using a slideshow, present material about God's saving us in community with others rather than by ourselves.

 **Step 4:** Conduct a reflective exercise through which the students individually personalize and then express what they have learned about their own experience of how God saves.

 **Step 5:** Guide the students in brainstorming and performing skits to identify ways people are called by God to belong to the Church.

**Step 6:** Lead the students in researching and reflecting to explore the ways Christ enriches us through participation in the life of the Church.

**Step 7:** Present material about how discipleship means being "salt and light" for the world by contributing our gifts to the Church and to the human community.

 **Step 8:** Introduce the students to a real-life example of a person who has been salt and light for the world through a life of discipleship.

 **Step 9:** Direct the students in exploring the ways the Church shapes disciples into the image of Christ for the world.

 **Step 10:** Help the students to discover the call of ordinary discipleship in light of Matthew 25:31–41.

 **Step 11:** Now that the students are closer to the end of the unit, make sure they are all on track with their final performance tasks, if you have assigned them.

 **Step 12:** Provide the students with a tool to use for reflecting about what they learned in the unit and how they learned.

## Background for Teaching This Unit

Visit *smp.org/LivinginChrist* for additional information about these and other theological concepts taught in this unit:

- "What Is Discipleship?" (Document #: TX001536)
- "Community in the Catholic Church" (Document #: TX001535)

The Web site also includes information on these and other teaching methods used in the unit:

- "Using Final Performance Tasks to Assess Understanding" (Document #: TX001011)
- "Using Rubrics to Assess Work" (Document #: TX001012)

## Scripture Passages

Scripture is an important part of the Living in Christ series and is frequently used in the learning experiences for each unit. The Scripture passages featured in this unit are as follows:

- Acts of the Apostles 2:43–47 (life among the believers)
- Ephesians 6:18 (pray in the Spirit)
- Genesis 2:18 (we are not to be alone)
- Matthew 5:13–16 (salt and light)
- Matthew 7:11 (ask, search, knock)
- Matthew 7:12 (the Golden Rule)
- 1 Thessalonians 5:16–17 (pray without ceasing)

---

## Vocabulary

The student book and the teacher guide include the following key terms for this unit. To provide the students with a list of these terms and their definitions, download and print the handout "Vocabulary for Unit 8" (Document #: TX001497).

| | |
|---|---|
| age of reason | ministry |
| aspiration | Sacred Chrism |
| Body of Christ | |

# Learning Experiences

**Explain**

## Step 1

*Preassess student knowledge of discipleship, using the "I Am More Like" exercise.*

This forced-choice exercise helps the students to articulate and share some of their personal characteristics and to develop an appreciation for differences among people.

1. Gather the students in the center of the room. Tell them that you will start by saying, "Are you more like," and then give them two options, designating one side of the room for each option. They are to move to the side of the room that corresponds to the answer that most fits them. No one is allowed to stay in the middle. Tell the students not to discuss their choices with anyone until after they move. Make it clear that you are asking about what they *are most like*, not what they *like*. You may need to give an example.

2. Read as many of the following pairs as you like, pointing to one side of the room for each option. After reading each pair, pause while the students make their choices, and then ask a few volunteers from each side to state the reasons for their choices.

   ➤ Are you more like . . .

   - a lightbulb or a candle?
   - a spark plug or a battery?
   - a library or an amusement park?
   - a picture or a puzzle?
   - a hotel or a hospital?
   - a murmuring stream or a buzzing chainsaw?
   - a bridge or a tower?
   - an ant or a hawk?
   - a dog or a fox?
   - a rowboat or an ocean liner?
   - a paperclip or a stapler?
   - a television or a book?
   - a fireplace or a furnace?
   - a car or an airplane?
   - a beach or a glacier?

- a golf ball or a Nerf ball?
- a hermit or a rock star?
- a thinker or a doer?

3. Close the exercise by commenting on the uniqueness of people's reasons, the differences in how they are "formed by God," the fascinating works of the human mind, and the wonder of God, who calls each of us, individually, to discipleship.

4. Direct the students to return to their seats and then continue the discussion by talking about how each Christian is called by God and is given the task of discipleship. Then ask what discipleship means and what their responsibility is as disciples of Christ. Talk about community and responsibility in light of discipleship and faithfulness to Christ's request of us.

## Step 2

Follow this assessment by presenting to the students the handouts "Final Performance Task Options for Unit 8" (Document #: TX001495) and "Rubric for Final Performance Tasks for Unit 8" (Document #: TX001496).

This unit provides you with two ways to assess that the students have a deep understanding of the most important concepts in the unit: creating a display for an art gallery that demonstrates the richness of life and experience in the local Church, speaks to the local population, and serves as an introduction to visitors who are not Catholic; or designing a one-day retreat for middle school students that addresses the Church as a saving community for us. Refer to "Using Final Performance Tasks to Assess Understanding" (Document #: TX001011) and "Using Rubrics to Assess Work" (Document #: TX001012) at *smp. org/LivinginChrist* for background information.

1. Prepare for this learning experience by downloading and printing the handouts "Final Performance Task Options for Unit 8" (Document #: TX001495) and "Rubric for Final Performance Tasks for Unit 8" (Document #: TX001496), one of each for each student.

2. Distribute the handouts. Give the students a choice as to which performance task they select and add more options if you so choose. Review the directions, expectations, and rubric in class, allowing the students to ask questions. You may want to say something to this effect:

> **Teacher Note**
>
> You will want to assign due dates for the final performance tasks.
>
> If you have done these performance tasks, or very similar ones, with students before, place examples of this work in the classroom. During this introduction explain how each is a good example of what you are looking for, for different reasons. This allows the students to concretely understand that there is not only one way to succeed.

> ➤ You may work with no more than two other people on option 1. If you want to work on your own, you may choose either option 1 or option 2.

> ➤ Near the end of the unit, you will have one full class period to work on your final performance task. Please keep in mind, however, that you should be working on this task throughout the course of the unit. Please do not wait until this class period to begin work on your final performance task.

Articles 52, 53, 54

## Step 3

*Using a slideshow, present material about God's saving us in community with others rather than by ourselves.*

1. As background for this learning experience, have the students review student book articles 52–54, "Called by God to Belong to the Church," "Christ Enriches Us through Participation in the Life of the Church," and "Called to Community" from the student book, which were assigned in unit 1.

2. Present the PowerPoint "Discipleship" (Document #: TX001513), found at *smp.org/LivinginChrist*, which highlights the key ideas, connects them with the lives of the students, and sparks discussion (small-group discussion leading to class summary discussion, or whole class discussion). The slides have a key concept and a question with a related image. Give the students a few moments for reflection with each slide, and then lead a discussion before moving on to the next slide.

3. Conclude by having the students respond to the following questions, either in a class discussion, as a journal reflection, or as written homework:

> ➤ What does it mean to say that humans are made to live in community?

> ➤ How is the Church similar to and different from other communities you belong to?

## Step 4

*Conduct a reflective exercise through which the students individually personalize and then express what they have learned about their own experience of how God saves.*

1. Prepare for this learning experience by gathering the materials needed for the creative project. Materials should include a variety of art supplies such as paint, markers, glue, clay, and scissors. Also have available a CD of instrumental music and the appropriate player if you choose to play soft music during this learning experience, as well as pens or pencils, one for each student.

2. Begin by distributing the pens or pencils and having the students respond to this journal prompt (write this on the board):

   What in your life assures you of God's saving presence?

3. Next ask the students to think about what some symbols are for them of God's saving presence in their lives. Ask a few volunteers to share.

4. Give the students the following directions:

   ➤ You are now going to have the opportunity to create something that reminds you of God's saving presence in your life. You are to work alone on your project. You can create a drawing, a collage, a poem, a sculpture, or anything else that is a symbol to you of God's saving presence. Be as creative as possible.

   Distribute the art supplies.

5. Allow the students as much time as you like for this step. It is suggested to give them at least 20 minutes. If you choose, play soft instrumental music in the background as the students work.

6. Invite volunteers to share their projects with the class once everyone is finished.

Article
52

## Step 5

*Guide the students in brainstorming and performing skits to identify ways people are called by God to belong to the Church.*

1. Prepare for this learning experience by gathering blank sheets of paper, one for each student.

2. As background have the students read student book article 52, "Called by God to Belong to the Church."

3. Begin by having the students brainstorm ways someone is called by God to belong to the Church. Encourage them to identify both dramatic and subtle ways God calls people. Write the students' responses on the board.

4. Once the students have brainstormed numerous ways God calls people, divide the class into small groups of three or four and assign one of the ways to each group.

5. Direct the small groups to create a 30-second to 1-minute skit illustrating the way God calls someone. Be sure all group members are included in the skit.

6. Have the small groups perform their skits for the class.

7. Distribute a sheet of paper to each student. As a homework assignment or an in-class exercise, have the students individually write a two- to three-paragraph reflection on how God has called them to the Church or how they have seen God call someone they know.

Article
53

## Step 6

Lead the students in researching and reflecting to explore the ways Christ enriches us through participation in the life of the Church.

1. Prepare for this learning experience by gathering several sheets of blank paper for each student. If you choose to do the optional extension at the end of this learning experience, also gather sheets of newsprint and markers, one of each for each student, as well as a roll of masking tape.

2. As background have the students read student book article 53, "Christ Enriches Us through Participation in the Life of the Church."

3. Begin by writing the words *Scriptures, Sacraments,* and *Prayer* on the board.

4. Explain that Christ continually enriches the Church and the life of the People of God. Three specific ways he enriches the Church is through the Scriptures, the Sacraments, and prayer.

5. Invite the students to each select one of the three topics listed on the board. Encourage them to select a topic they feel a special connection with. Try to ensure that all three topics are selected relatively equally.

6. Direct the students to do the following:

➤ Provide three quotations from the *Catechism of the Catholic Church* that express the importance of the topic in the life of the Church. Then explain the quotations.

➤ Describe how the topic is both a communal and a personal experience for the members of the Church.

➤ Provide two examples of the importance of their topic in the life of a saint.

➤ List three concrete examples of how the topic enriches the life of the individual in the Church.

➤ Reflect on your own experience of the assigned topic, identifying how it might have enriched your life in the past and how it can enrich your life in the future.

➤ Complete your research and turn it in with all points clearly identified and fully addressed.

## Optional Extension

As an optional extension for this learning experience, invite the students to write their own aspiration prayers. Have them write out their prayers in large print on a sheet of newsprint and then post them around the room for the remainder of the unit.

Article
55

## Step 7

*Present material about how discipleship means being "salt and light" for the world by contributing our gifts to the Church and to the human community.*

This learning experience leads the students in exploring the meaning of a Catholic Christian's call to be "salt and light" for the world today, how important salt and light were in ancient times, and how important they continue to be today. Both are basic to happiness and health, and both are easily attained.

1. Prepare for this learning experience by downloading and printing the handout "Finding Salt and Light for the World: An Inventory of Discipleship Gifts and Skills" (Document #: TX001498), one for each student. Remind the students to bring their Bibles to class. Also gather sheets of blank paper, one for each student.

2. As background have the students read student book article 55, "Sent as a Disciple."

3. Begin by explaining that each one of us has been blessed with gifts by God and that we are each called to use those gifts for others. Using a "spiritual gifts inventory," the students will be able to recognize the way Christian ministries are "salt and light" for others. At the end of the learning experience, the inventory will also serve as a reflection exercise to help the students recognize their own spiritual gifts for service.

4. Have a student read aloud Matthew 5:13–16. You may wish to have the student read it twice, the second time pausing for a few seconds after each verse.

5. Use the following questions to discuss with the class why Jesus chose the images of salt and light in relation to discipleship:

   ➤ What do we use salt for?

   *for seasoning and preserving food*

   ➤ How is a disciple of Jesus to be "salt for the earth"?

   *Just as salt adds to or brings out the flavor of food, a disciple is meant to add the "flavor" of Christianity to the world and bring out the goodness or "tastiness" of the world.*

   ➤ What is light used for?

   *to bring to vision what is in the dark, to help one see*

   ➤ How is a disciple of Jesus to be "light for the world"?

   *A disciple is meant to bring into view new ways of seeing and living life under the guidance of the Holy Spirit. Like light, the new life energy of Jesus is meant to be made available to all, not kept to oneself, hidden, as it were, under a bushel basket.*

6. Conclude the discussion with the following comments:

   ➤ The call to be a disciple of Jesus is thus twofold: first, like salt we are to bring out or revive or amplify the goodness that God has already planted in the world. Second, like light we are to illumine or discover new ways of living in the world with the life of Christ for and with others. But what are salt-like and light-like qualities disciples possess that allows them to "spice up" or "illuminate" the world with Christ? Let's look at some disciple qualities or disciple gifts that people could possess and then see which of them are active in the lives of several ministries that serve God's People in the world.

7. Distribute a copy of the handout to each student and have the students complete the handout individually. Allow about 10 minutes for this.

8. When the students have completed the handout, have them form small groups of four. Each small group is to compare their individual responses and create a common list of discipleship skills and gifts they agree are necessary for the various ministries. For each ministry they should also explain why these are necessary skills and gifts.

9. After the groups have discussed the required disciple gifts and skills for each ministry, tabulate the results from each group and create a class summary of the important gifts and skills to be "salt and light" for the modern world.

10. Direct the students to hold on to the handouts, as they will use them again in the next step.

11. Conclude the discussion by distributing a sheet of blank paper to each student and then having the students write a reflection on the following question (write this on the board):

   • Imagine you are a member of one of these ministries. What makes being a disciple difficult in this situation and why? What would help you most in using your "salt and light" gifts? Why?

Articles 55, 56, 57

## Step 8

*Introduce the students to a real-life example of a person who has been salt and light for the world through a life of discipleship.*

1. Prepare for this learning experience by obtaining and previewing one of the following videos. Links for ordering copies of these videos are available at *smp.org/LivinginChrist.* Have available a TV and the appropriate player for showing the video in class. Also be sure the students have their copies of the handout "Finding Salt and Light for the World: An Inventory of Discipleship Gifts and Skills" (Document #: TX001498) from step 7.

   • *Don't Call Me a Saint* (2006, 57 minutes, not rated) (Dorothy Day)
   • *Sisters of Selma: Bearing Witness for Change* (2007, 57 minutes, not rated) (PBS, religious women who marched with Martin Luther King Jr.)
   • *The Narrow Path* (2007, 108 minutes, not rated) (John Dear, SJ)
   • *Soul Searching: The Journey of Thomas Merton* (2006, 68 minutes, not rated) (Thomas Merton)
   • *They Killed Sister Dorothy* (2008, 94 minutes, not rated) (threatened authorities with work for justice, killed)
   • *Roses in December* (1982, 56 minutes, not rated) (Jean Donovan and three sisters martyred in El Salvador)

2. As background have the students read student book articles 55–57, "Sent as a Disciple," "Discipleship in Daily Life," and "Empowered by the Holy Spirit."

3. Direct the students to look again at the gifts and skills needed to be a disciple of Christ listed on their handouts and to circle the four gifts or skills they think are most important for discipleship.

4. Now invite some volunteers to share the gifts or skills they feel are most important for discipleship and to explain why.

5. Tell the students they are going to be watching a video that presents the life of a contemporary Catholic who is an example of what it means to be a disciple of Christ. As they watch the movie, they are to circle gifts and skills from the list that they see displayed in the life of the person highlighted in the video.

6. Show all or a portion of the video you selected.

7. Following the video have the students respond to these questions:

   ➤ How was the person in the video salt and light for the world?

   ➤ What did it mean to be a disciple to the person in the video?

   ➤ What gifts and skills from the list did you see displayed in the person's life?

8. Close by directing the students to write, as homework, a one-page reflection paper addressing how the person in the video was a model of discipleship.

## Step 9

Direct the students in exploring the ways the Church shapes disciples into the image of Christ for the world.

1. Prepare for this learning experience by gathering copies of bulletins from local Catholic parishes and blank sheets of paper, one of each for each small group of three or four. Also be sure the students have their copies of the handout "Finding Salt and Light for the World: An Inventory of Discipleship Gifts and Skills" (Document #: TX001498) from step 7.

2. Begin by sharing the following story:

   ➤ One chilly autumn evening, a college student who had become involved in his college's campus ministry decided to pay a visit to the campus priest chaplain regarding his question of the need to attend Mass regularly, as he seemed to be doing just fine spiritually with his pattern of occasional attendance. The priest welcomed the young man and invited him to sit in the living room near the fireplace where a cheery fire crackled. As they both took a chair near the fire and began their evening conversation, the young man expressed his question about the supposed benefit of attending Mass weekly when he seemed to get so little out of it. The priest turned quiet and thoughtful as he looked into the fire and then, without saying a word, reached for the fire tongs and leaned out of his chair to pull a burning coal out of the fire. He set it on the stone hearth and soundlessly sat back in his chair to watch what would happen to the sizzling coal. The college student's eyes followed the gesture intently. As the coal flickered and then died out, the priest said, "I think we are like that coal; when we are in the midst of the community, we can stay aflame and bright, but if we start taking ourselves out of the community, I think our faith slowly dies as well as our contribution to the faith-life of others."

3. Ask the following discussion questions:

> As disciples of Christ, we get our "fire," or our identity, from Christ and his People, but how?

> What does the Church do that shapes us to have the "fire," or the life of Christ, working through our lives for others?

4. Instruct the students to retrieve their copies of the handout they used in step 7. Remind them of the variety of spiritual gifts and skills they have seen at work in the ministries previously discussed. Tell them this time they will look a little closer to home to see what offerings a parish has to help people to discover or to use their spiritual gifts or skills in the parish.

5. Divide the large group into smaller groups of three or four and distribute a copy of a local parish bulletin and a blank sheet of paper to each group.

6. Give the groups the following directions:

> First, on a separate sheet of paper, list the variety of faith opportunities listed in this bulletin. Be as broad as you can be in listing the types of ministries, services, community events, and liturgical or sacramental experiences available at this parish.

> Second, for each ministry, list the spiritual gift(s) or skill(s) that could be developed from that experience and how those discipleship gift(s) or skills(s) could be developed in this ministry.

> Third, describe what gifts or skills of discipleship are most apt to be fostered in our parishes and why? Which gifts or skills are we most in need of fostering if we are to be more Christlike? Explain.

7. Conclude by having the students reflect on this question in their journals:

> What is one way you have been shaped by the Church (be it a parish, a school, a family, or another faith-based community) to be more Christlike? Explain.

## Step 10

*Help the students to discover the call of ordinary discipleship in light of Matthew 25:31–41.*

1. Prepare for this learning experience by downloading and printing the handout "Ordinary Discipleship and Matthew, Chapter 25" (Document #: TX001499), one for each student.

2. Then share the following with the class:

   ➤ As we have seen, discipleship means being led by Christ to share our gifts and talents under the guidance of the Holy Spirit so as to be salt and light for the world. It means that by being with Christ for others we are most fully alive ourselves. So, what are our gifts and talents, and how does Christ use them in our own ordinary lives, like Thérèse of Lisieux, for others?

3. Distribute the handout to the students and read Matthew 25:31–41 aloud to the class.

4. Share the following with the class:

   ➤ This call to discipleship can sound pretty challenging, yet we have opportunities to live out these specific directives to feed, welcome, clothe, and care for those struggling right here at school or within our own families and circles of friends as well. We all have been given spiritual gifts and talents that Christ wants to use to touch the lives of many we come in contact with.

5. Now direct the students to look at the handout and to follow the instructions at the top of the page.

6. When the students have completed the handout, invite them to share their responses.

7. Conclude by emphasizing that discipleship is about not only the "big" things we do but also the little, daily ways we live and share our faith with our families, friends, and communities.

## Step 11

*Now that the students are closer to the end of the unit, make sure they are all on track with their final performance tasks, if you have assigned them.*

If possible, devote 50 to 60 minutes for the students to ask questions about the tasks and to work individually or in their small groups.

1. Remind the students to bring to class any work they have already prepared so that they can work on it during the class period. If necessary, reserve the library or media center so the students can do any book or online research.

2. Provide some class time for the students to work on their performance tasks. This then allows you to work with the students who need additional guidance with the project.

## Step 12

*Provide the students with a tool to use for reflecting about what they learned in the unit and how they learned.*

This learning experience provides the students with an excellent opportunity to reflect on how their understanding of how God calls us to live as disciples in the Church has developed throughout the unit.

1. To prepare for this learning experience, download and print the handout "Learning about Learning" (Document #: TX001159; see Appendix), one for each student.

2. Distribute the handout, and give the students about 15 minutes to answer the questions quietly. Invite them to share any reflections they have about the content they learned as well as their insights into the way they learned.

# Final Performance Task Options for Unit 8

## Important Information for Both Options

The following are the main ideas you are to understand from this unit. They should appear in this final performance task so your teacher can assess whether you learned the most essential content.

- God saves us in community with others rather than by ourselves.

- Discipleship is not just about following rules; rather, the Church shapes disciples into the image of Jesus Christ.

- Discipleship means being "salt and light" for the world by contributing our gifts to the Church and to the human community.

- Christ enriches us in the Church through the Sacraments, prayer, the Eucharist, charity, service, and justice.

## Option 1: We Tell Our Story

A small local art gallery has invited your campus ministry program to provide a display titled "Life in Our Community" as part of their spring exhibit. You have been asked to chair the committee that will design and create the display. It will be in an area that has two tables, standing display panels, and access to power and a computer. Your challenge is to create a display that demonstrates the richness of life and experience in the local church, that speaks to the local population, and that serves as an introduction to visitors who are not Catholic. Follow these guidelines in creating your display:

- Address the following topics:

    1. God saves us in community with others rather than by ourselves.

    2. Discipleship is not just about following rules; rather, the Church shapes disciples into the image of Jesus Christ.

    3. Discipleship means being "salt and light" for the world by contributing our gifts to the Church and to the human community.

    4. Christ enriches us in the Church through the Sacraments, prayer, the Eucharist, charity, service, and justice.

- Create a plan for a display that portrays the life of the church in your local community.

- Use three-dimensional objects as well as pictures in your display.

- Access to power and a computer makes it possible for you to include a looping PowerPoint, a computer-based interactive question-and-answer activity, or music.

- Create a viewer's guide that explains the various elements of the display.

- Present your design in a folder (portfolio) that includes your plan (including any sketches or storyboard), playlist (if you are using music), and viewer's guide.

# Option 2: Middle School Retreat

The coordinator of the parish middle school religious education program has asked your religious studies class to develop a one-day retreat for the middle school. The students in the parish program are focusing on the Church. Your task is to design a retreat that addresses the Church as a saving community for us. The middle school teacher is hoping the retreat day will give her eighteen students an experience to reinforce what they are studying about what it means to belong to the community that is the Church. The retreat should offer a variety of activities. The teacher has told you that the students will do best with activities that are no longer than 30 minutes. The retreat begins at 9:30 a.m. and ends at 2:00 p.m. Follow these guidelines in creating the retreat:

- Create a schedule for a one-day retreat that engages the students in learning about the Church as a saving community, that each person has unique gifts that are meant to be shared, and that there are many ways the Church will help us to grow as followers of Jesus.

- Include activities that appeal to the students and actively involve them in different kinds of activities: prayer, input, large- and small-group activities, quiet time for reflection, recreation. The retreat day includes lunch, so this would be a good place to have a focus on salt and light.

- Type and submit the following in a single folder (portfolio):

    1. your introduction to the retreat

    2. the schedule for the day

    3. an explanation for each activity that tells what the activity is and why you chose it

    4. copies of any handouts you may use

    5. a list of any materials needed for the activities

    6. a playlist of music that includes how you will use each song and why you chose each song

    7. sketches of any posters or diagrams you will use in explaining or leading an activity

    8. a one-page personal reflection on how designing the retreat for middle school students helped you to deepen your own understanding of the Church as a saving community

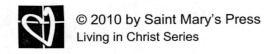
© 2010 by Saint Mary's Press
Living in Christ Series

Document #: TX001495

# Rubric for Final Performance Tasks for Unit 8

| Criteria | 4 | 3 | 2 | 1 |
|---|---|---|---|---|
| **Assignment includes all items requested in the instructions.** | Assignment not only includes all items requested, but they are completed above expectations. | Assignment includes all items requested. | Assignment includes over half of the items requested. | Assignment includes less than half of the items requested. |
| **Assignment shows understanding of the concept *God saves us in community with others rather than by ourselves.*** | Assignment shows unusually insightful understanding of this concept. | Assignment shows good understanding of this concept. | Assignment shows adequate understanding of this concept. | Assignment shows little understanding of this concept. |
| **Assignment shows understanding of the concept *discipleship is not just about following rules; rather, the Church shapes disciples into the image of Jesus Christ.*** | Assignment shows unusually insightful understanding of this concept. | Assignment shows good understanding of this concept. | Assignment shows adequate understanding of this concept. | Assignment shows little understanding of this concept. |
| **Assignment shows understanding of the concept *discipleship means being "salt and light" for the world by contributing our gifts to the Church and the human community.*** | Assignment shows unusually insightful understanding of this concept. | Assignment shows good understanding of this concept. | Assignment shows adequate understanding of this concept. | Assignment shows little understanding of this concept. |
| **Assignment shows understanding of the concept *Christ enriches us in the Church through the Sacraments, prayer, the Eucharist, charity, service, and justice.*** | Assignment shows unusually insightful understanding of this concept. | Assignment shows good understanding of this concept. | Assignment shows adequate understanding of this concept. | Assignment shows little understanding of this concept. |

© 2010 by Saint Mary's Press
Living in Christ Series

Document #: TX001496

| | | | | |
|---|---|---|---|---|
| **Assignment uses proper grammar, spelling, and diction.** | Assignment has no errors in grammar, spelling, or diction. | Assignment has one error in grammar, spelling, or diction. | Assignment has two errors in grammar, spelling, or diction. | Assignment has more than two errors in grammar, spelling, or diction. |
| **Assignment uses its assigned or chosen media effectively.** | Assignment uses its assigned or chosen media in a way that greatly enhances it. | Assignment uses its assigned or chosen media effectively. | Assignment uses its assigned or chosen media somewhat effectively. | Assignment uses its assigned or chosen media ineffectively. |
| **Assignment is neatly done.** | Assignment is not only neat but is exceptionally creative. | Assignment is neatly done. | Assignment is neat for the most part. | Assignment is not neat. |

Document #: TX001496

# Vocabulary for Unit 8

**age of reason:**  The age at which a person can be morally responsible. This is generally regarded to be the age of seven.

**aspiration:**  A short prayer meant to be memorized and repeated throughout the day. The word comes from the Latin *aspirare*, "to breathe upon." In this way we can heed Saint Paul's injunction to pray without ceasing and continually turn our thoughts toward God.

**Body of Christ:** A term that when capitalized designates Jesus' Body in the Eucharist, or the entire Church, which is also referred to as the Mystical Body of Christ.

**ministry:**  Based on a word for "service," a way of caring for and serving others and helping the Church fulfill its mission. *Ministry* especially refers to the work of sanctification performed by those in Holy Orders through the preaching of God's Word and the celebration of the Sacraments. The laity helps the Church fulfill its mission through lay ministries, such as that of lector or catechist.

**Sacred Chrism:** Perfumed olive oil that has been consecrated. It is used for anointing in the Sacraments of Baptism, Confirmation, and Holy Orders.

© 2010 by Saint Mary's Press
Living in Christ Series

Document #: TX001497

# Finding Salt and Light for the World: An Inventory of Discipleship Gifts and Skills

Following is a list of gifts and skills needed to be a disciple of Christ in the world. Below the list is a description of several types of Christian ministries at work in the world. For each ministry, list the gifts or skills you think one would need in order to be "salt for the earth and light for the world." You will use this handout for several learning experiences in this unit, so put it somewhere safe when you are finished.

## Gifts and Skills

1. loving / charitable
2. joyful
3. kind
4. generous
5. loyal
6. hopeful
7. detail-oriented
8. organizes others
9. helps others to work together
10. works behind the scenes
11. good with finances
12. likes to work with hands
13. leads / handles responsibility
14. good listener
15. sensitive to unspoken needs of others
16. handles conflict well
17. comforts sick people
18. seeker of justice for the weak / seeks truth despite resistance
19. merciful
20. prays for others persistently

21. encourages others, lifts people's spirits
22. good sense of humor
23. dedicated and determined in work
24. healer (spiritually, emotionally, or physically)
25. hospitable to strangers
26. curious about new people and cultures
27. musician
28. writer
29. public relations and public speaking
30. humility
31. teacher
32. courageous
33. reverent for God's People and nature
34. insightful about people's behavior
35. grateful
36. passionate
37. compassionate
38. self-control and integrity
39. serves others freely
40. resilient

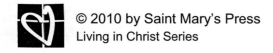

Living in Christ Series

Document #: TX001498

# Ministries

***Catholic Relief Services:*** "Our mission is to assist impoverished and disadvantaged people overseas, working in the spirit of Catholic Social Teaching to promote the sacredness of human life and the dignity of the human person." (CRS Web site)

***L'Arche***: "L'Arche communities, family-like homes where people with and without disabilities share their lives together, give witness to the reality that persons with disabilities possess inherent qualities of welcome, wonderment, spirituality, and friendship." (L'Arche Web site)

***Intercommunity Housing Association***: "The Mission of Intercommunity Housing Association is to provide an environment (especially through housing) which empowers families to determine their own future, and to do so on a foundation of personal dignity, security, and growth." (Intercommunity Housing Association Web site)

***Houston Catholic Worker Casa Juan Diego***: "Casa Juan Diego was founded in 1980, following the Catholic Worker model of Dorothy Day and Peter Maurin, to serve immigrants and refugees and the poor. From one small house it has grown to ten houses. Casa Juan Diego publishes a newspaper, the *Houston Catholic Worker*, six times a year to share the values of the Catholic Worker movement and the stories of the immigrants and refugees uprooted by the realities of the global economy." (Casa Juan Diego Web site)

***Society for the Propagation of the Faith***: "Today the General Fund of the Propagation of the Faith, which gathers gifts from Catholics all over the world, is the basic means of support for the Catholic Church's worldwide missions." (One Family in Mission Web site)

# Ordinary Discipleship and Matthew, Chapter 25

After hearing a reading of Matthew 25:31–41, reflect on how you have carried out these actions within your family, within your circle of friends, at school, at work, and so on, in your own ordinary way. Review the handout "Finding Salt and Light for the World: An Inventory of Discipleship Gifts and Skills" (Document #: TX001498) and, in the right-hand column, list the spiritual gifts or skills you see yourself possessing that help you to carry out these actions.

| Matthew, Chapter 25 | Discipleship Gifts and Skills Needed |
| --- | --- |
| **"For I was hungry and you gave me food."** <br><br> **(verse 35)** | |
| **"I was thirsty and you gave me drink."** <br><br> **(verse 35)** | |
| **"[I was] a stranger and you welcomed me."** <br><br> **(verse 35)** | |

| | |
|---|---|
| **"[I was] naked and you clothed me."**<br><br>**(verse 36)** | |
| **"[I was] ill and you cared for me."**<br><br>**(verse 36)** | |
| **"[I was] in prison and you visited me."**<br><br>**(verse 36)** | |

© 2010 by Saint Mary's Press
Living in Christ Series

Document #: TX001499

# Unit 8 Test

## Part 1: True or False

Write *true* or *false* in the space next to each statement.

1. _____ You have been called to the Church, to Christ.

2. _____ Saint Paul was a tax collector when Jesus called him.

3. _____ The Scriptures, along with Tradition, help us to understand God's Revelation.

4. _____ God has little or no desire to be in relationship with us.

5. _____ God created the world, and all of humanity, out of love.

6. _____ At the Baptism of infants, parents promise to help their children come to know God and to participate fully in the Church.

7. _____ Through the Sacrament of Baptism, you were incorporated into the Church.

8. _____ The age of reason is about sixteen.

9. _____ The Eucharist is the Sacrament at the center of our faith.

10. _____ The Eucharist nourishes our spiritual lives, protects us from sin, and unites us more fully with the Body of Christ.

11. _____ The Scriptures, the Sacraments, and abstaining from fish in December are three important ways Christ offers us an opportunity to get to know him and to receive his grace.

12. _____ Jesus is the Word of God.

13. _____ In reading and praying with the Scriptures, we encounter Jesus himself.

14. _____ Rosary beads are an essential element of our lives as Christians.

15. _____ The Sacraments are gifts from Christ that bring us face-to-face with God.

16. _____ All Christians must adhere to a "one size fits all" way of praying.

17. _____ In the Book of Genesis, we read "It is good for man to be alone" (2:18).

18. _____ As members of the Body of Christ, we are never alone.

19. _____ Christ sends each of us into the world as disciples.

20. _____ Discipleship takes place in daily life and sometimes means acting in a way that is counter to the values of the culture.

© 2010 by Saint Mary's Press
Living in Christ Series

Document #: TX001500

# Part 2: Matching

Match each statement in column 1 with a term from column 2. Write the letter that corresponds to your choice in the space provided. (*Note:* There are two extra items in column 2.)

## Column 1

1. _____ A short prayer meant to be memorized and repeated throughout the day.

2. _____ The age at which a person can be morally responsible. This is generally regarded to be the age of seven.

3. _____ The state or condition of those who have chosen or taken vows to remain unmarried in order to devote themselves entirely to the service of the Church and the Kingdom of God.

4. _____ A special gift or grace of the Holy Spirit given to an individual Christian or community, commonly for the benefit and building up of the entire Church.

5. _____ A change of heart that turns us away from sin and toward God.

6. _____ A group of religious organizations uniting under a single legal and administrative body and subscribing to the same creed and moral code.

7. _____ Relating to household or family.

8. _____ Having to do with hermits.

9. _____ The free and underserved gift of God's loving presence in our lives.

10. _____ A person who suffers death because of his or her beliefs.

## Column 2

A. charism

B. denomination

C. grace

D. aspiration

E. celibacy

F. domestic

G. age of reason

H. conversion

I. unification

J. eremitic

K. platitude

L. martyr

# Part 3: Fill-in-the-Blank

Use the word bank to fill in the blanks in the following sentences. (*Note:* There are two extra terms in the word bank.)

**WORD BANK**

| | | |
|---|---|---|
| disciple | salt | bake |
| deed | Book of Job | light |
| Holy Spirit | gifts | pray |
| mind | missionaries | Acts of the Apostles |

1. _____ Being a _____ means being part of Jesus' mission.

2. _____ Jesus said to his disciples, "You are the _____ of the earth" (Matthew 5:13).

3. _____ Christ also told his disciples, "You are the _____ of the world" (Matthew 5:14).

4. _____ The Apostle John wrote to the earliest Christian disciples, "Children, let us love not in word or speech but in _____ and truth" (1 John 3:18).

5. _____ Jesus told us that we each have talents and _____ to share with others.

6. _____ Take time each day to _____ .

7. _____ On the day of Pentecost, Jesus Christ poured the _____ onto the Church.

8. _____ The Holy Spirit inspires the _____ as well as the heart.

9. _____ The _____ is sometimes called the Book of the Holy Spirit.

10. _____ After Pentecost, the frightened Apostles turned into bold _____ .

# Part 4: Short Answer

Answer the following question in paragraph form on a separate sheet of paper.

1. How does living as a Catholic mean being countercultural?

# Unit 8 Test Answer Key

## Part 1: True or False

| | | |
|---|---|---|
| 1. True | 8. False | 15. True |
| 2. False | 9. True | 16. False |
| 3. True | 10. True | 17. False |
| 4. False | 11. False | 18. True |
| 5. True | 12. True | 19. True |
| 6. True | 13. True | 20. True |
| 7. True | 14. False | |

## Part 2: Matching

| | | |
|---|---|---|
| 1. D | 5. H | 9. C |
| 2. G | 6. B | 10. L |
| 3. E | 7. F | |
| 4. A | 8. J | |

## Part 3: Fill-in-the-Blank

| | |
|---|---|
| 1. disciple | 6. pray |
| 2. salt | 7. Holy Spirit |
| 3. light | 8. mind |
| 4. deed | 9. Acts of the Apostles |
| 5. gifts | 10. missionaries |

## Part 4: Short Answer

1.  Discipleship is countercultural. Our culture so often says, "Me first!" but in the Church we serve one another. Our culture often says, "You are on your own," but in the Church we are one in Jesus Christ, we are a community that supports one another. Our culture so often has many little rules: "Be this! Do this! Wear this! Act like this!" In the Church we adhere to the Gospel, where Jesus gives us the rule: "Do to others whatever you would have them do to you" (Matthew 7:12). Our lives are encompassed by the Ten Commandments, rules that guide us in a proper, upright, trouble-free life. The life of a disciple involves regular participation in the celebration of the Sacraments, most importantly the Eucharist on Sundays. Our culture tends to focus on Sunday as a day of rest, but that does not include going to Church. Catholics should attend Mass every Sunday. Our culture tells us that a woman should have the right to choose where her sexual life is concerned, and that includes premarital or extramarital sex as well as contraception and abortion. Our Church tells us that conceiving a child is a blessing, one that is most blessed within the bonds of marriage. Our Church further tells us that all life is sacred and that the vulnerable especially must be protected; that

Document #: TX001501

includes the unborn and the elderly. Our culture is focused on the here and now; our Church focuses on the blessing of salvation and the promise of Heaven. Our culture focuses on material success and power; our Church focuses on aiding others and protecting the vulnerable. In all things, being a member of the Church means looking out for the well-being of the less capable, the vulnerable, the marginalized. The Church's measure of success is not in dollars earned but in blessings passed on.

# Appendix

## Additional Resources

"Learning about Learning" (Document #: TX001159)

# Learning about Learning

We can understand ourselves better by taking the time to review the process of learning the material in a unit.

Respond by using the scale below. Put a mark where you think your understanding falls. Then write your answers to the other questions below.

Unit Number and Name _____

| |
|---|
| **Knew none of this material before**            **Knew everything already** |

What was your favorite learning experience in this unit and why? Do you usually enjoy this type of learning experience?

What was your least favorite learning experience and why? Do you usually find this type of learning experience challenging?

How did your understanding of the unit's subject matter change throughout the unit?

Was anything you learned particularly interesting? Why?

Write any other observations you have.

Document #: TX001159

# Appendix 2

## Student Book/Teacher Guide Correlation

## Section 1: The Church: Christ's Continued Presence and Work in the World

## Part 4: Images of the Church

# Section 2: The Church Is One, Holy, Catholic, and Apostolic

## Part 1: The Church Is One

## Part 2: The Church Is Holy

# Section 4: The Lived Mission of the Church

## Part 1: The Leadership Structure of the Church

## Part 2: Many Vocations to Holiness

## Part 3: The Magisterium: The Teaching Office of the Church

# Section 5: The Church and Young People

## Part 1: You Have Been Called

## Part 2: Sent with the Holy Spirit

# Acknowledgments

The scriptural quotations in this book are from the *New American Bible with Revised New Testament and Revised Psalms.* Copyright © 1991, 1986, and 1970 by the Confraternity of Christian Doctrine, Washington, D.C. Used by the permission of the copyright owner. All Rights Reserved. No part of the *New American Bible* may be reproduced in any form without permission in writing from the copyright owner.

The list of what makes up a mature understanding on pages 12–13 is from *Understanding by Design,* expanded 2nd edition, by Grant Wiggins and Jay McTighe (Upper Saddle River, NJ: Pearson Education, 2006), page 84. Copyright © 2005 by ASCD. Used with permission of ASCD.

The chart on the handout "Models of the Church Chart" (Document #: TX001441) is adapted from notes provided by Dr. Philip Verhalen, which are based on *Models of the Church,* by Avery Dulles (Garden City, NY: Doubleday, 1974).

The excerpt "From the *Catechism of the Catholic Church*" on the handout "The Mission of the Church" (Document #: TX001458) and the first quotation on page 163 are from the English translation of the *Catechism of the Catholic Church* for use in the United States of America, second edition, numbers 737, 738, and 1666, respectively. Copyright © 1994 by the United States Catholic Conference, Inc.—Libreria Editrice Vaticana (LEV). English translation of the *Catechism of the Catholic Church: Modifications from the Editio Typica* copyright © 1997 by the United States Catholic Conference, Inc.—LEV.

The excerpt "From the *Pastoral Constitution on the Church in the Modern World (Gaudium et Spes)*" on the handout "The Mission of the Church" (Document #: TX001458) is from *Pastoral Constitution on the Church in the Modern World (Gaudium et Spes,* 1965), numbers 45, 89, 92, and 93, respectively, at *www.vatican.va/archive/hist_councils/ii_vatican_council/documents/vat-ii_const_19651207_gaudium-et-spes_en.html.* Copyright © LEV. Used with permission of LEV.

The excerpt "From the *Decree on the Missionary Activity of the Church (Ad Gentes)*" on the handout "The Mission of the Church" (Document #: TX001458) is from *Decree on the Missionary Activity of the Church (Ad Gentes),* numbers 1 and 10, at *www.vatican.va/archive/hist_councils/ii_vatican_council/documents/vat-ii_decree_19651207_ad-gentes_en.html.* Copyright © LEV. Used with permission of LEV.

The excerpt "From 'Message of His Holiness Benedict XVI for the 83rd World Mission Sunday 2009'" on the handout "The Mission of the Church" (Document #: TX001458) is from "Message of His Holiness Benedict XVI for the 83rd World Mission Sunday 2009," at *www.vatican.va/holy_father/benedict_xvi/messages/missions/documents/hf_ben-xvi_mes_20090629_world-mission-day-2009_en.html.* Copyright © 2009 LEV. Used with permission of LEV.

The excerpt "From *On the Vocation and the Mission of the Lay Faithful in the Church and in the World (Christifideles Laici)*" on the handout "The Mission of the Church" (Document #: TX001458) is from *On the Vocation and the Mission of the Lay Faithful in the Church and in the World (Christifideles Laici)*, number 36, at *www.vatican.va/holy_father/john_paul_ii/apost_exhortations/documents/hf_jp-ii_exh_30121988_christifideles-laici_en.html*. Copyright © LEV. Used with permission of LEV.

The second quotation on page 163 is from "Angelus: Solemnity of the Most Holy Trinity, June 11, 2006," at www.vatican.va/holy_father/benedict_xvi/angelus/2006/documents/hf_ben-xvi_ang_20060611_en.html. Copyright © 2006 LEV.

To view copyright terms and conditions for Internet materials cited here, log on to the home pages for the referenced Web sites.

During this book's preparation, all citations, facts, figures, names, addresses, telephone numbers, Internet URLs, and other pieces of information cited within were verified for accuracy. The authors and Saint Mary's Press staff have made every attempt to reference current and valid sources, but we cannot guarantee the content of any source, and we are not responsible for any changes that may have occurred since our verification. If you find an error in, or have a question or concern about, any of the information or sources listed within, please contact Saint Mary's Press.

### Endnote Cited in a Quotation from the *Catechism of the Catholic Church, Second Edition*

**Unit 3**

1. *John* 15:8,16.